Dying, Bereavement and the Healing Arts

Edited by Gillie Bolton

Foreword by Baroness Professor Ilora Finlay of Llandaff

Jessica Kingsley Publishers
London and Philadelphia

'Kindersterben' by Kathe Kollwitz (p.52), copyright © 2006 Artists Rights Society (ARS), New York/VG Bild-Kunst, Bonn. Reproduced with permission.

Excerpt (p.150) from 'Another Reason I Don't Keep A Gun in the House' from *The Apple that Astonished Paris* by Billy Collins, copyright © Billy Collins. Reprinted with the permission of the University of Arkansas Press, www.uapress.com.

Excerpt (p.150) from 'Parkinson's Disease' from *Imperfect Thirst* by Galway Kinnell, copyright © 1994 Galway Kinnell, reprinted by permission of Houghton Mifflin Company. All rights reserved.

'Death row?', 'Charnel house?' and 'Preconceptions, misconceptions' (pp.159–60) by Mitzi Blennerhassett, reproduced with permission of Radcliffe Press.

First published in 2008
by Jessica Kingsley Publishers
116 Pentonville Road
London N1 9JB, UK
and
400 Market Street, Suite 400
Philadelphia, PA 19106, USA

www.jkp.com

Copyright © Jessica Kingsley Publishers 2008
Foreword copyright © Baroness Professor Ilora Finlay of Llandaff 2008
The right of Mark Cobb to be identified as author of Chapter 18 has been asserted by him in accordance with the Copyright, Designs and Patents Act 1988.

Library of Congress Cataloging in Publication Data
A CIP catalog record for this book is available from the Library of Congress

British Library Cataloguing in Publication Data
A CIP catalogue record for this book is available from the British Library

ISBN 978 1 84310 516 9

Printed and bound in Great Britain by
Athenaeum Press, Gateshead, Tyne and Wear

Dying, Bereavement and the Healing Arts

by the same author

Writing Works
A Resource Handbook for Therapeutic Writing Workshops and Activities
Edited by Gillie Bolton, Victoria Field and Kate Thompson
Foreword by Blake Morrison
ISBN 978 1 84310 468 1

The Therapeutic Potential of Creative Writing
Writing Myself
Gillie Bolton
Foreword by Sir Kenneth Calman
ISBN 978 1 85302 599 0

of related interest

The Expressive Arts Activity Book
A Resource for Professionals
Suzanne Darley and Wende Heath
Photography by Mark Darley
Foreword by Gene D. Cohen MD PhD
ISBN 978 1 84310 861 0

Music Therapy in Palliative Care
New Voices
Edited by David Aldridge
ISBN 978 1 85302 739 0

Music Therapy in Children's Hospices
Jessie's Fund in Action
Edited by Mercédès Pavlicevic
Foreword by Victoria Wood
ISBN 978 1 84310 254 0

Attending to the Fact – Staying with Dying
Hilary Elfick and David Head
Edited by Cynthia Fuller
Foreword by Andrew Hoy
ISBN 978 1 84310 247 2

Palliative Care, Social Work and Service Users
Making Life Possible
Peter Beresford, Lesley Adshead and Suzy Croft
Foreword by Dorothy Rowe
ISBN 978 1 84310 465 0

Creative Writing in Health and Social Care
Edited by Fiona Sampson
Foreword by Christina Patterson
ISBN 978 1 84310 136 9

Writing My Way Through Cancer
Myra Schneider
ISBN 978 1 84310 113 0

Dying, Bereavement and the Healing Arts *is dedicated to Julia Darling, Michele Angelo Petrone and Jessica George, who brought the healing of art to others*

Acknowledgements

Dying, Bereavement and the Healing Arts is a picture embroidered by many hands over a long time. I started researching the vital role of therapeutic writing and the arts in palliative care 20 years ago. Many, many people generously contributed jewel-coloured silk to the needlepoint of understandings which underpin this book. I thank all those patients, medical and healthcare professionals, and spiritual leaders. I am very grateful to the book's contributors, patients, survivors, artists and professionals: they have given the light and life of their experience and expertise. Some of the pieces rewritten for *Dying, Bereavement and the Healing Arts* were first published in *The Healer's Art* section of the international medical and healthcare journal *Progress in Palliative Care*, which I edited for many years. We are grateful to Caitlin Meadows, managing editor of the journal, for her support of the section and permission to publish the amended pieces. In addition my grateful thanks go to Sam Ahmedzai who helped start me on this particular embroidery, Bill Noble, Kate Billingham, Rosie Field, Ilora Finlay, Deborah Padfield. The work would not exist however without canvas, needles, embroidery frame, and the love and inspiration needed for artistic endeavour: I thank Dan Rowland, Alice Rowland and Stephen Rowland.

Contents

Foreword

Dying, Bereavement and the Healing Arts is a comforting book. It brings us in contact with the side of our own humanity that we often try to suppress in dealing with the tragedies and the stresses of healthcare. It has been said that stress results from not being in control. This book allows us to recognise the intrinsic and innate differences between human beings and all other creatures with whom we share the planet. We are reminded of the uniqueness of human creativity through art, poetry, music and other artistic expressions that allow the innermost feelings and interpretations of the world around us to be expressed.

Some certainly may argue that art, in its broader sense, cannot and should not be used therapeutically. Yet this would impose an arrogance of artists that would deny the intrinsic human expression from all those who write, compose, draw, paint or tell their story in a different way. Each person's story is full of a complex intermingling of hopes and reality, of past experiences being interpreted and of future fears becoming expressed. As human beings we share so much together and nowhere more than in healthcare are the layers stripped away to leave the clinician facing the vulnerable patient, and in so doing facing his or her own vulnerability.

We talk about a need for people to escape from unrelenting pressure, to debrief after major trauma and to establish a work life balance. It is through artistic expression that these can happen, both for healthcare professionals and for patients and their carers. For we are all on one journey through life together, and we all need to feel confident that our expressions are valid and respected. The picture or the poem written therapeutically may not win a high price in an auction, but it is beyond value in terms of representing the life of a person. Each person's life needs to be cherished, nurtured, sustained and supported with care and respect.

This book will comfort those who haven't yet been able to express the multiple grief experiences they have had as they have cared for patients. So many of us have experienced dreams or nightmares constructed out of the distress that we have witnessed over the years. And so many patients have hesitated to express their fears, fearing that any such discussion would be outside the professional boundaries. This book is a tribute to those from all walks of life, who have faced all situations and had the courage and generosity to express their experience and wish to share it; for it is the humanities that truly express the humane.

Baroness Professor Ilora Finlay of Llandaff

Preface Poem

Nest

Feathering my nest
with books and yet more books

Brooding on the sofa,
incubating thoughts and more thoughts,
more memories,

retreating into my shell,
tortoise-fashion,

I let the walls of our house hold me
and truly house me

You have no house now,
you've rejoined air, earth, fire, water –

So I'm rebuilding this house
from the inside,
brick by invisible brick,

as birds make their nest,
giving harbour to myself
after the storms and the torrents.

Penelope Shuttle

1. Introduction: Dying, Bereavement and the Healing Arts

Gillie Bolton

Dying, Bereavement and the Healing Arts is a celebration of the immense power of art. Dance, song, drumming and cave painting probably gained this power as people developed non-animal forms of communication. Being in genuine contact with others, and with the complexities of oneself, is to be fully alive, and to create is to be fully human. Dying, bereavement and pain are, along with birth, the only certainties of life. So art has always focused on them – helping us to understand and live them to the full, rather than merely to endure. Art helps in our struggling attempt to understand ourselves and our role in the world. We see through a glass darkly: the arts bring illumination.

An artist is a kind of shaman – adventuring boldly into other worlds for wisdom and powerfully enabling images. Returning, they can transport us earthbound mortals, giving of their insight, and enabling us to venture into some part of the fabulous lands. The very process of creating art can be deeply personally illuminative and healing. The products, such as pictures or writings, will also remain behind us for our loved ones. 'Art is the closest you can get to immortality' (Hirst 2006, p.46).

Dying, Bereavement and the Healing Arts seeks to facilitate communication between artist-shaman, medical and healthcare clinicians and related practitioners such as chaplains, and patients. The more the interaction, the more understanding, healing and support can be deepened, and the greater the possibilities for insight, joy and increase in self-confidence. It is illustrative, ranging widely over a broad, developing new field. It aims to invite a broad range of specialists and non-specialists into the artistic realm, rather than provide guidelines or training advice. My hope is that you, our reader, will come closer to understanding the wide range of people who can gain from arts, as well as the artists who offer it, and what, how, when, where and why they can be so supportive, educational, reflective, therapeutic, epiphanic even, at times.

Authors include artists (painters, writers, movement artists, musicians), professionals (medical and healthcare practitioners, therapists, arts therapists, social workers, chaplains), patients and relatives. Many authors tell of personal experiences with arts: how painting helped them come to terms with cancer and life problems for example. Others graphically explain how patients or clients benefited from artistic work they did with them. In a long chapter about the art of care, clinicians discuss attitudes to their practice as an art. Two chaplains discuss spiritual dimensions.

Some arts are significantly more represented than others. Many visual artists and art therapists didn't or couldn't write for *Dying, Bereavement and the Healing Arts*, despite superb practical work: their forte is non-verbal. I interviewed some non-verbal artists and we worked on transcripts together, but there wasn't time for many. The artistic experiences represented here are:

1. a sharing of arts with no overt therapeutic aim

2. directly therapeutic, to enable insight or healing in people

3. to support practitioners professionally as a form of reflective practice.

The artist Damien Hirst (2006), who focuses on death in his work and collecting, said 'We try to avoid death but, if you accept it, there's less of a dark cloud' (p.47).

How to make soup from a stone

Once upon a time a shrewd villager was standing by the front door, enjoying the last of the day's sun. Along came a tired traveller just as the kettle began to whistle inside.

'Hello there', the traveller called. 'You've got a nice garden.'

'Hmm yes, the result of hard work.'

'Is that your kettle I can hear? I'd love to join you in a cup of tea.'

The villager scowled: 'I'm not sure about that. Tea doesn't grow on trees.'

'Well if not tea; how about a nice bowl of soup!' the cheeky traveller responded, only receiving a deeper scowl in reply.

'Do you have such a thing as a nice smooth stone in your garden? I can tell you how to make soup from a stone.'

The scowl immediately lifted, and a gleam came into the villager's eye. 'Can you indeed: here's a stone. And now what?'

'Well you need to wash it well, put it in water in a *big* pan on the stove and perhaps shake in a little pepper and salt.'

This done, the traveller stood beside the stove gazing around the kitchen, and through the window to the vegetable garden with a speculative eye, while pretending to think hard.

'And now?' prompted the villager.

'Weeell. I don't suppose you have such a thing as an onion do you?'

You can guess the rest: the onion wasn't the last ingredient the villager 'happened' to have, and put in the pot. They sat down later together to a magnificent mixed vegetable and meat soup, which by then rather resembled a rich hotpot stew.

Both were very pleased with themselves.

(A story nearly as old as the stone, retold by Gillie Bolton)

Healing art is like magic soup. In the beginning there can seem to be nothing but the heaviness and unproductiveness of a stone. Giving ingredients can seem tiresome, ridiculous, dangerous: because a suggestion to make art is outside many people's normal way of being. An artist-facilitator or arts therapist can make it seem straightforward and enjoyable to dip a paintbrush in colour, feel the clay, make a hand gesture, touch the chime-bar, offer an image, 'my father was like a brick'. These are the onion, gradually peeling open to reveal its layers. Then experienced and loving hands can help the creation of a warm, nourishing, illuminating, utterly satisfying picture, dance, poem, statue, song.

No art gives answers. It does however present fascinating questions, the answering of which is an endless quest. More questions are thrown up, the fundamental ones of life: 'what happens when I die?'; 'what might my bereaved relatives feel?'; 'what is wonderful in this world I am about to leave?'; 'in which way was my life meaningful?' These questions – this life quest – looks inward, and takes the palliative patient-, bereaved relative- or practitioner-artist no further than their bed or chair. It accords with the words of the ancient sage:

> Without going outside, you may know the whole world.
> Without looking through the window, you may see the ways of heaven.
> The further you go the less you know. (Lao Tzu 1973, Chapter 47)

And wisdom adapted from a saying (about travel) by the poet G.K. Chesterton, which stated that the whole object of writing is not to set foot on foreign land; it is at last to set foot on one's own self as a foreign land.

Illness, disability and bereavement can disrupt a person's understanding of their life; the knowledge they are going to die reasonably soon is even more disruptive. Everyone tells themselves a narrative about their life: where they come from and where they are going, what they want to do, and how they think they will live. Even the dying have to have a sense of the trajectory of their life, even if it is much shortened. And if they can come to have a satisfying life story, then their dying will be gentler for them, and enhance the lives of their loved ones, and those who care for them professionally.

Not only can illness, dying and bereavement bring pain, disfigurement, disorientation, lack of mobility or sense impairment, but people also have to readjust their notion of who they are, what their primary relationships are, where and how they might live, what – if at all – their work might be, what their hobbies are, and what their hopes and fears are for their lives. Their sense of the story of their lives has been disrupted; they have to work hard to develop a new, appropriate, yet satisfying story, instead of just dwelling in a depressing sense of destruction. If they can't do this, then their healing journey towards death, coming to terms with bereavement, will be significantly impaired. This re-creation can be as much to deal with as the medical problem itself.

The arts can support professionals and practitioners, and informal carers such as parents and partners as well. The arts can help them to understand those they care for, engender insight into emotions and events, and support with feelings of stress and burnout. The causes of stress and burnout in dying and bereavement care are various and often not obvious (McWilliams 2004).

Involvement in artistic processes can offer primary support in the rewriting of a hopeful, helpful life-towards-death narrative. The practice of an art offers reflective processes upon memories, hopes, fears, anxieties, fears, and angers, without tackling these emotional states head on. Image such as metaphor is used, as is characterisation and plot. The process of writing a story or poem, painting a picture or creating music is enjoyable, life-affirming and confidence enhancing. People do deep emotional, spiritual, and psychological work when they create art products, especially when they are supported by an experienced arts therapist or arts in health practitioner. The editor of the *British Medical Journal* recommended that a percentage of the NHS budget should be spent on the arts (Smith 2002).

Art – the use of the imagination – that magical quality which marks us out as different from all other living beings, can help: achieve increased communication, self-understanding and well-being (Calman 2000; D'Lima 2004; Graham-Pole 2000; Haldane and Loppert 1999; NHS Estates 2002; Staricoff 2004; White 2004); alleviate stress and anxiety (Bolton 1999; Carey 2006; Seftel 2006; Staricoff 2004); dramatically support positive self image (Tasker 2005) and can have significant therapeutic effects (Help the Hospices 2005). This power of the imagination and art has been known about and harnessed for thousands of years. Aristotle, for example, speaks of watching a tragedy on the stage 'producing through the pity and fear caused, a catharsis of those emotions' (1996, p.10 [49b27]).

Due to trends towards more holistic modes of practice (Department of Health 1999), art is used increasingly in healthcare and community settings (Everitt and Hamilton 2003; Haldane and Loppert 1999; Philipp 2002; NHS Estates 2002; White 2004). Help the Hospices' guidelines to arts and arts therapies in palliative care (2005) is invaluable. Palliative care, care of the dying, concerns patients' and families' psychological, physical, spiritual and social needs (Brown 2007); this includes bereavement care.

Practising an art can help patients and practitioners reflect effectively upon experiences, express damaging memories, thoughts and emotions, and facilitate helpful feelings and states of mind, to bring about a greater state of well-being (Everitt and Hamilton 2003; Kirklin and Richardson 2003). I say well-being rather than health, as the latter is often considered to be a purely physical state, like a smoothly running car. Well-being is a state of acceptance with what is – in mind, body and spirit. One can be ill, yet in a state of well-being. The World Health Organization has defined health as: 'a state of complete physical, mental, and social well-being and not merely the absence of disease'. An active involvement in the arts would seem to assist in the development of mental and social well-being, and therefore of health.

Art can enable the expression of the otherwise inexpressible, and the experience of cognitive, emotional and spiritual areas to which people otherwise have no access. Some of these issues are not easy to deal with; art can make the unacceptable possible to face (Bolton 1999; Petrone 1999, 2003; Wolton 2002). This is true of visual artwork (McNiff 1994; Petrone 1999, 2003; Seftel 2006), writing (Bolton 1999; Killick and Allan 2000; Macduff 2002; Petrone 1999, 2003; Robinson

2004; Schneider and Killick 1997; Wolton 2002), music (Aldridge 2000; Austin 2006; Pavlicevic 2005; Robertson, 1996), dance (Cook, Ledger and Scott 2003), drama (Snow, Damico and Tanguay 2003), performing arts (Glass 2006; Sands 2002), play (Carey 2006), and fashion (Tasker 2005). The arts can also be soothing and calming, and offer gentle physical activity distracting from pain and anxiety (Graham-Pole, 2000). The very act of creativity also tends to increase self-confidence, feelings of self-worth, motivation for life (Calman 2000; D'Lima 2004). Art can also be an unparalleled form of communication (Charon 2000a).

Staricoff (2004) has outlined evidence on the value of the arts and humanities in:

- inducing positive psychological and physical changes in clinical outcomes

- reducing drug consumption

- shortening length of stay in hospital

- increasing job satisfaction

- promoting better doctor-patient relationships

- developing health practitioners' empathy across gender and cultural diversity.

T.S. Eliot reminds us of 'The sharp compassion of the healer's art' (1974, p.201). It's not only the steel (or the chemicals) that heal, it's also the art of the healer. The increase in arts activities in palliative care is part of a broader involvement of arts and humanities in medicine and healthcare (see Association of Medical Humanities (www.amh.ac.uk); Centre for Arts and Humanities in Healthcare and Medicine (www.dur.ac.uk/cahhm)).

The arts work in a therapeutic, self-revelatory or soothing way, partly because they are non-directional and non-functional, and will not work for us if coerced to offer definite goals. Alice learned a great deal about life and herself in her adventures in Wonderland, by taking this attitude (and the reader learns alongside her):

'Would you tell me, please, which way I ought to go from here?'
'That depends a good deal on where you want to get to,' said the Cheshire Cat.
'I don't much care where –' said Alice.
'Then it doesn't matter which way you go,' said the Cat.
'So long as I get somewhere,' Alice added as an explanation.
'Oh, you're sure to do that,' said the Cat, 'if you only walk long enough.' (Lewis Carroll 1954, p.54)

The arts can help us walk long enough with each other.

Arts in health has been described as 'creative activities that aim to improve individual/community health and healthcare delivery using arts based approaches, and that seek to enhance the healthcare environment through provision of artworks or performances' (White 2002, p.11). It is therefore a broad umbrella covering active participation in creative activities (such as dancing), and more passive audience or viewer activities (such as paintings hung on hospital walls). Considering process-based and product-based forms of arts provision in more detail will be helpful.

Process based – doing it

Dying, Bereavement and the Healing Arts concerns being involved in creating art, rather than observing it. It primarily concerns arts in health. Though there are several contributions by trained arts therapists (music, art, drama therapy have in-depth postgraduate training and are recognised by the UK Health Professions Council), *Dying, Bereavement and the Healing Arts* concerns the practice of an art rather than a craft. Craftwork is introduced into many hospice dayrooms as a satisfying diversionary activity. People gain great enjoyment and satisfaction from icing cakes, painting glass, needlework and so on. Such activities are relatively easy to provide and are essentially non-threatening; being absorbing activities they are soothing and helpful.

The arts, on the other hand, are capable of disturbing. Neither powerful arts products nor therapeutic benefit are gained solely with ease and enjoyment. The film director Guillermo Del Toro, who experienced horrific events in his native Mexico, said: 'Pain should not be sought, but should never be avoided, because there is a lesson in facing adversity' (Kermode 2006). A session with writing, painting, clay and so on can lead to deep tears and possibly intense emotions such as anger or hurt. This is because arts practice takes us beyond our habitual boundaries and enables us to come face to face with our own deep existential questions. It can break our normal everyday rules for being. Yet, as the sculptor Bernini is reputed to have said, 'Those who never dare to break the rules, never surpass them.'

Artist-facilitators need to hold a safe space for the people with whom they are working. Emotions can be channelled towards constructive benefit by expression and exploration *through the artform* rather than personally. The *images* are damaged or damaging, *not the patient-artist*. A wildly turbulent stream with dead leaves flung by the autumn wind might be depicted: the stream, wind and leaves (the artistic images) are turbulent, rather than the marriage, or personal experience of cancer. Such is the power of art. But such also has to be the experience and skill of artists working with vulnerable people. A complementary medicine cancer centre chief said: 'when I started here someone was thinking of just writing some poems with the patients in workshops: I soon put a stop to that!' Any art, including poetry writing, leads to the creation of powerful images, thence to expression and examination of the significance of the images. Such work needs to be undertaken with experienced care.

> Maybe all poetry, insofar as it moves us and connects with us, is a revealing of something that the writer doesn't actually want to say, but desperately needs to communicate, to be delivered of. Perhaps it's the need to keep it hidden that makes it poetic – makes it poetry. The writer daren't actually put it into words, so it leaks out obliquely, smuggled through analogies [images]. We think we're writing something to amuse, but we're actually saying something we desperately need to share. (Hughes 1995, p.75)

Arts can have greater therapeutic benefit if practised alone, without an associated word-based therapy (Maclagan 1989; Matarasso 1997). Matarasso (1997) reported nearly half of participants in his survey feeling better or healthier having been involved in an arts activity with no word-based therapy. White (2004) reports a structured purely creative arts activity, which resulted in fewer readmissions to psychiatric hospitals than for a control group.

A commonly perceived benefit of arts activities is that they are non-medicalised, non-judgemental and person-centred (White 2004). In medicine and healthcare 'people become patients' (Smith 2002); in arts in health projects people become artists. Participants make their own choices, and remain in control of their activity and level of psychological and social involvement. Practice in the arts can encourage self-motivation and self-care. They encourage community collaborative work – the work is more like a 'conversation' (Everit and Hamilton 2003), and people only participate because they want to.

The arts are, perhaps most importantly, enjoyable and fun. Playfulness can create social and psychological bonds between people. Due to its unthreatening and naturally easy-seeming nature, playfulness can moreover enable healing exploration and expression of deeper levels of experience, knowledge, memories and ideas.

Many artists deplore art being offered therapeutically, considering art is only art if practised for its own sake. We live in a world where people suffer more than they need, and enjoy fewer of life's experiences. Most people would consider art is reserved for special people: artists, denying others a vital panoply of experience. The more unhelpful boundaries that can be dissolved the better. Artistic expression is one of the most naturally powerful activities with which ordinary humans can readily engage. It is, therefore, unlikely to be damaged by any practice.

Arts therapy (art, music, drama, dance) is practised by qualified therapists skilled in their particular art form. Arts therapists are primarily therapists who use an art. Help the Hospices' excellent guidelines (2005) offer clear and helpful statements on the use of arts and arts therapies.

Dying, Bereavement and the Healing Arts primarily concerns Arts in Health, in which practitioners are primarily artists; they are not therapists, and do not consider they offer therapy. Arts therapists have sometimes felt that artists without therapy skills should not work with patients. Artists with therapeutic training or experience make ideal artists-in-residence.

Product based – experiencing it

Concerts, literature, artworks can be experienced (listened to, read, looked at) for healthful benefit. Artistic products have helped people understand and perceive better, probably as long as people have been able to think and feel in the way we think of as human.

Art products can take an audience away from painful, depressing, grieving or humdrum concerns, actions and feelings, and can enable reflexive thinking about the self and personal and social situations (Duncan 2003; Kenyon 2003; Staricoff and Loppert 2003). Uplifting environments can have positive effects on patient and staff morale (NHS Estates 2002). To be art, a piece of music, sculpture, poetry has to be of a quality to transport the audience, perhaps from a state of anxiety, by encouraging deep, often critical, engagement. We all know what it is to curl up with a brilliant book, become immersed in music, film, play, or lost in an art gallery.

Music is rhythmical like the heartbeat, soothing, exhilarating, or a mode of communication (Pavlicevik 2005; Schatzberger 2001); fiction and drama have the power of narrative, plot and characterisation enabling readers to inhabit the fictional world, to empathise with the characters, and roam in unfamiliar landscapes (Bolton 1999; Harris 2003; Sampson 2004). Poetry takes readers sharply to the heart of something vital, and can therefore have great emotional or insightful impact (Bolton 1999; Fox 1997, 2003; Harris 2003; Mazza 2003). A painting can tell things about the personal or everyday world which might never otherwise be perceived, or simply be restful and calming (Higgs 2003; Kenyon 2003; Padfield 2003).

Art is also intensely educational. Literature and visual art are full of detail about the way people live in unfamiliar cultures, about suffering, healing, medical practices: every aspect of life (Charon 2000b; Evans 2003; Salinsky 2002). Art can inform about how emotions work on people, how people think and communicate, how they relate to others, and about the impact of social structures on people and populations. Much of this learning can also be therapeutic. The line between therapy and education can narrow to non-existence.

How is art different from other communication?

A great musician-composer was asked to explain the wonderful piece of music he'd just played. He thought a moment or two, opened and closed his mouth, then turned back to the keyboard and played it again. Trying to describe a poem, painting, dance, play, sculpture, sonata, instead of presenting the piece of art, will have no power. Each word, note, movement, brushstroke only works just where the artist put it; and it only works in collaboration with the viewer, audience or reader. Michelangelo sought to release *David* and the *Pieta* from the marble. The results are electrifying. Copies of the *David* are lifeless. Rodin felt 'a figure was already enclosed [in the stone] and my work consisted of breaking off all the rough stone that hid it from me.' He also believed in sculpture as 'incantation by which the soul is brought down into the stone' (quoted in Gormley 2006, p12).

Art can express the otherwise inexpressible. It can seem to say what we cannot express otherwise about our own experience, and help us to understand it better. And this isn't just our huge experiences of life and death, but commonplaces of everyday, the touch of a hand on skin perhaps, the every-night epiphany of Orion hanging guardian in the sky.

Arts can be redemptive because it can put us back in contact with powerful existential truths. Arts can be a witness to what happens in life: tragic, beautiful, radiant, horrifying, but all essential elements of life itself. Arts can connect people suffering grief, agony, fear because artists can be brave enough to go close enough to these huge areas to express them: with art people no longer feel alone in their experience and emotion. This is true of all arts, despite John Carey's assertion that only literature can offer a rigorous enough critique to be useful (2005).

Ours is an age of anxiety, tension, hyperactivity (multi-tasking, hot-desking, hitting the ground running), an era of inflated public emotion (a sea of flowers for a dead princess, road rage, televised devastated war-torn victims). There is little reflective, reflexive or simply mentally absent space allowed. People go for walks or to the gym nodding in time to an MP3 player, watching a video, gabbling on a mobile phone or to a party of co-walkers. Art cannot completely redress the balance, but it can go some way to providing missing images, reflective observations presented simply and tellingly.

Creative involvement can have sustained and positive impacts on mental and social well-being. A practical involvement in the arts can offer a wide range of benefits to vulnerable or sick people. This is true of both arts therapies and arts in health, as defined above. Arts as facilitated by artists themselves, with no overt therapeutic input, can be powerfully healing.

> If I was God I'd encourage people to be involved in the creating process more rather than just witnessing it. It seems the best way to give the world a bit of sanity. (Tim Jeeves, teenage cancer patient (see Chapter 16))

With very little money, people and communities can be supported towards not just a greater measure of sanity, but also increased health and well-being and the shamanic joy of creation. Art can put people in touch.

Note on confidentiality

Written permission is held by chapter authors for all material quoted. Names and identities of individuals discussed in the text have been disguised or omitted throughout to preserve anonymity: permission has been gained from all.

2. A Death Photographed: Michael Willson's Story

Paul Schatzberger and Gillie Bolton

Michael Willson managed his death in his own way. Having photographs taken was an important part of this management, and the images were pinned up on the walls all around him in his house. Visual appearances were very important to him; he learned a great deal from being able to communicate with his own image. He hoped other people might also gain after his death. Michael's own reflections on the project, as well as those of the photographer, Paul Schatzberger, are included below.

The only certainty in life is death, and yet in our society it is rarely spoken of, and even more rarely photographed, except in war and disaster photojournalism. Designed to protect the ill and their loved ones, this taboo perhaps does only the opposite, making death more mysterious and threatening. Paul Schatzberger's photographs of Michael Willson suggest an alternative approach. The images show the everyday facts of terminal illness in pragmatic but sensitive detail. In showing death in this way, they celebrate life.

Michael Willson was born in 1947 and died of carcinoma of the gastro-oesophageal junction in 1996. A self-employed psychologist engaged in consultancy with the probation service, he was a well-respected charismatic free spirit with a gift for friendship. He rode his horse bareback, and was often seen walking out in top hat and morning suit.

Determined to enjoy the last years of his life, he travelled and took on more work. Untrammelled by such things as urban parking restrictions, he once stopped his Dormobile on double yellow lines, commenting: 'I won't be around to pay the fine will I?' Having built his own coffin, he took pleasure in showing the specialist palliative care nurse how well he fitted into it. Having declined palliative chemo-therapy he died at home according to his desire, cared for by his wife and six close friends (some of whom had medical training).

Michael managed his death in his own way. Encouraging Paul Schatzberger, a GP/photographer acquaintance, to photograph him was part of this, as was living with the images on the walls all around him in his house. He wrote: 'These pictures are not for the album and later reminiscence; they are for now.' He wished to relate himself to the changing images of his dying. He also wanted them used after his death to help those of us left behind to understand dying better.

This documentary project was Michael's wish, following Paul's suggestion, allowing for the dying process and his relationship with the pictures to be recorded. In its realism and honesty we are confronted with the transience of a moment and the long lasting existence of the photograph after the subject has gone. We see a very literal demonstration of the durability of the photograph and its use as a legacy. What is offered is not blind panic, or sudden and unexplained detachment but a conscious process of very personal documentation over a period of diminishing time. What is left seems calm, familiar, dignified absence.

Michael wrote:

As you steam past 40 you start to ask yourself 'Who have I become?', rather than 'What am I going to be?' until, in the last days of your dying, you find an answer. If you have time, you can also use the last months to compose the last movement of your sonata in which the previous themes are not just repeated but are combined into a further final theme. But this is an activity that requires attention, which in turn requires objects, thoughts and images to carry it.

Sitting for and then studying these photographs has been very valuable in this respect. The photographs provide many different images and perspectives, whereas staring into the mirror provides only one. And the photographs provide me with sequences of images, some linked by the three-second gap between each exposure and others through their documenting how I change each week as my body leaves my mind.

The face, the place, the body and the context become objects to be placed against each other and understood together and then, so it seems, to be separated again from myself. These pictures are not for the album and later reminiscence; they are for now.

Paul Schatzberger wrote:

Michael encouraged me to photograph his experience, to help us both. His attitude to dying provides an alternative to the traditional stereotypes. It is possible to die well. Photography helped Michael define his identity and to deal with his terminal illness. I believe that he derived benefit from a creative process that also challenges society's taboo concerning the depiction of mortality.

One sequence of portraits, seen on the wall behind Michael's coffin in the photograph, showed three expressions in as many seconds: posing for the camera, seeing his image reflected in the lens, and confronting the reality of dying. We agreed that the project should include photographs taken after his death. In his death announcement, which he wrote himself, Michael asked mourners to contribute by allowing the work to continue. He gave written consent for the posthumous use of the images.

This text is a composite from material by Michael; Simon O'Connor *et al.* (2003); Nina Othen (2006); Paul Schatzberger; Sheila Payne; and my own memories of Michael.

Gillie Bolton

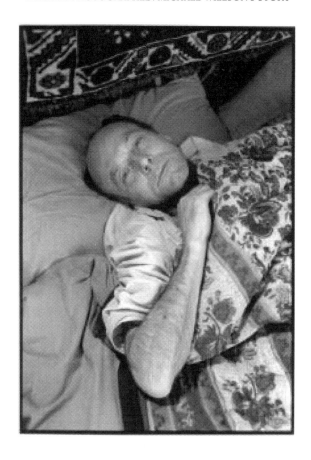

3. Arts, Electronic Media, Movement: Rosetta Life

Filipa Pereira-Stubbs and Chris Rawlence

You're not trying to fix what's broken in me, you're working with what's whole in me.

John

Rosetta Life and movement art   *Filipa Pereira-Stubbs*

Rosetta Life works with people living with a life-threatening illness in a creative capacity, facilitating and encouraging their sense of their potential as creative individuals, as individuals in control of aspects of their lives, as individuals who have a meaningful personal narrative to relate. An artist-led charity, Rosetta Life aims to deliver artwork of a consistently high quality to as wide an audience as possible.

These personal narratives can be developed in a wide range of media forms for a range of audiences. So, a mother might write a story specifically for her son, or a woman might tell the story of her pain through digital film that will be shown to her friends, family and medical team. Somebody else might have a cherished walk they feel they can share with others through photography, or they might want to record themselves reading their favourite poems.

The process of being heard and related to as another human being, and not simply as a patient, allows people to find out what it is they want and need to do creatively, and to give it shape and form. There is also the matter of finding the right audience; initially there is an audience of one: themselves. But the sense of one's audience can change. There is no prescriptive formula that caters to all; developing work involves collaboration between the patient and the artist; the journey undertaken is unique to each relationship. The process of shaping and making work can also necessitate that the audience changes – possibly to become more far-reaching and public, or to become more private.

Whilst the main focus is on the making of the work, the effect the work has on those around the individual can grow to become as important. Often the creative process unexpectedly opens doors of communication or of understanding: allowing the work to become deeply cathartic at times. The work can become a communicating channel between a patient and a relative or indeed with the wider world. As the initial audience of one grows and widens, so does the sense of place the patient has of himself or herself. People's sense of their role in their life, and in the life of their family and friends, changes.

One lady we worked with had fought a terrible battle of bitterness fuelled by her anger at her children's seemingly uncaring attitude towards her. When we started working together, it became possible to identify her anger as revolving around her sadness that she no longer felt herself to be their main line of support. She had been replaced. However she felt she had so much to say, and, in clarifying what it was she wanted to say, hoped that her words would be of relevance to her grandchildren. She wrote a series of questions and answers, using sparse but eloquent language. One outcome was that her grandchildren's parents read her words, and were moved sufficiently to tell her how meaningful it was for them to have been given the opportunity to hear her while she was still alive: to re-enter into conversation with their mother.

There is often a great yearning in all of us to find ourselves, express ourselves. The inclination to do so is usually thwarted by the pressures of daily living. However, with the palliative population, people find themselves with their worlds turned upside down, their usual daily anchors of work, lifestyle, etc. diminished, if not altogether changed. Time often becomes the one factor that is available. The Rosetta Life work helps individuals re-engage with a sense of themselves and, in doing so, to find new ways of expressing themselves. It can uncover new directions, new leases of life.

The Rosetta Life artist is there to support the many possible directions this journey of re-engagement might take. People often don't know how to do this on their own; it's too big a task. It can be frightening, overwhelming. Where does one begin? Given that every individual is unique, the journey they will take will have to be unique to them as well.

The artistic work

Rosetta Life artists come with strong art practices – filmmakers, writers, poets, dancers, photographers, painters. Because the work is the result of a collaboration between two individuals, both working first and foremost on an equal basis of humanness, it is important that the artists work as artists, and not as art educators or arts therapists.

However the traditional role of the artist-in-residence who develops their own work in response to their environment is also not applicable. The Rosetta Life artist helps people find the ability to author their own work, to become an artist in their own right. The artist is there to find ways of realising what might have up to now have been a dream or an unrealised ambition – it is paradoxically often about new beginnings. The ethos of Rosetta Life supports entirely the belief that every individual, as long as they carry the breath of life in them, carries the potential for creative exploration, and that this very potential of creativity is a vital aspect of a deeper sense of well-being. Even in the face of one's mortality it is possible to exude well-being.

People work to very different levels. Some will do something short, quick and personally satisfying. Others will work at more complicated projects, involving more time. The level of work does not negate in any way the level of creativity – often people find themselves with very little time, and yet work very deeply with necessary clarity. What is important is that everyone makes something that really matters to them. It is the artist's job to help people become more aware of what matters to them, and to be able to find the strength and creative power to be able to achieve creating something which is their own. The artist supports people into an awareness of their far wider sphere. People tend to live with too narrow a notion of who they are.

Once people relax into their creative space they begin to perceive what they would like to make. Artists help them to make and shape the work to as high a standard as possible. This is very different from craftwork which, whilst important, is largely designed to while away time creatively and enjoyably. Craftwork is a fairly straightforward means to an end; Rosetta Life embraces journeys of discovery.

Two examples of films

Gone Fishing (A Sense of Reflection) (2003, www.rosettalife.org/content/gallery/projects/6.html) is a video by Jon Butler and artist-in-residence Heidi Morstang. In this video Jon explains why fishing is important to him, and his reflections on living with a terminal illness. Heidi says:

> I always try to find what is unique about each person I work with and start finding ideas of creative stories that I suggest to the person. The work is highly collaborative, and as time is often crucial, the time we spend together is intense, inspiring, challenging and giving. Working with people who are in a difficult life situation has a special intensity that is highly creative. It is important to encourage that force and the people often discover their own voice. The work is very much about being.

City within a City (A Sense of Space) (Marshall, Hyde and Barnett 2003) is a video by artists-in-residence Helen Marshall and Simon Hyde, and Londoner Clive Barnett, who says: 'Once you're a Londoner you are there to stay, it's about being at the centre of things.' Clive juxtaposes this with the clinical and emotional experiences of being on the wards through voice, film and photography and brings us a vision that is truly from the front line.

Special projects

Rosetta Requiem is a cycle of songs and films made by people living with life-threatening illness and established film-makers, songwriters and composers. It enables people to express themselves through art at a time when words are not enough. For example, Maxine Edgington, who died of breast cancer in September 2006, wrote a song called *We Laughed* for her daughter Jessica, with singer-songwriter Billy Bragg. It reached number 11 in the charts in November 2005. Beverley Ashill, who has lung cancer, became aware of the miracle of breath on a recent trip to Kefalonia. She wrote about it in *That Very Breath*. British composer David Matthews set her extraordinary lines about breathing to music, creating a remarkable performance. (See www.rosettarequiem.org/songs/beverley_davidmatthewsperforms.html.)

The Senses

> Dennis Potter spoke passionately about his sensory experience of life in the final interview he gave to Channel Four before he died in June 1994. He saw from his window in May the 'blossomiest of blossoms'. I remember … seeing blossom through his eyes, the fragile delicacy of the apple blossom and the fullness of the cherry blossom, watching the way the boughs bend under the weight of the petals. This sensorial awareness was the inspiration for this site. It grows from a hunger for life, a thirst for sensory experience that is known by those who are facing the end of their lives. *The Senses* is an artwork that consists of twenty short films from fifteen hospices and hospitals that explore our senses. (Lucinda Jarrett, Rosetta Life artistic director)

The wisdom of the body: Reflections on working with movement

Movement and dance had been the means to unlocking people's essential selves when I was working as a movement therapist. Movement as a tool to revealing a sense of life, of belonging, a sense of place and identity has continued to be a vital part of the Rosetta Life work.

The kind of movement we use draws on natural body impulses, the most essential being breath. Non-prescriptive movement draws upon the natural body movements, working with the systems of the body. We are drawing upon the wisdom of the body, its ability to reflect and to reveal our authentic selves. Through moving with a patient we are able to witness and support the aspects of themselves that emerge to tell their story.

To begin with, we simply *be* together, sitting in a comfortable position. We take the time to listen to our breath, to notice how the body is, to attune ourselves to our bodies. We do this together, both of us taking the time to listen to ourselves, and as we do so our awareness shifts into a deeper level of perception, of kinaesthetic awareness, and our horizon of attention widens to encapsulate the other person or persons, and we allow ourselves to attune to them as well.

Simply listening to another's breathing – watching their nascent movements begin to flesh out an image, an emotion, a thought – is the beginning of the journey.

When you sit with someone in a safe confidential space, and focus on breathing together, a bond immediately forms between two human beings. Two people each take the time to get into their own personal space – nothing special, and yet crucial. A sense of trust and intimacy develops – a shared strength – a shared acknowledgment that they are about to embark on a journey without knowing where they are going to end up. This openness is essential in enabling people to access creativity. It's about being present, waiting for the right time for that person to find what they need to say.

Concentrating on the body and the breath allows one to stop trying to steer the creative process, to relax into becoming aware of what presents itself. One does not know what will emerge, and so the role of the artist now is to witness this beginning stage of expression, to acknowledge the presence of expressions, and to reassure that expression will happen in this way.

Miranda Tufnell writes:

> Creating is a way of listening and of trying to speak more personally from within the various worlds we inhabit. It is a way of discovering our own stories, refreshing and reawakening our language and giving form to the way we feel things… In letting go of my own desires and needs, and simply remaining open to whatever comes, parts or aspects of the world around me (or of my body) suddenly to seem to come alive and sing out in their own particularity. (Tufnell and Crickmay 2004, p.32)

There are images in the body, which are waiting to be called into attention.

Being given the diagnosis of a life-threatening illness initially feels as if everything is falling apart. A source of inspiration and guidance has been the wisdom and understanding Buddhism brings. Pema Chodron writes:

> Things falling apart is a kind of testing and also a kind of healing. We think that the point is to pass the test or to overcome the problem, but the truth is that things don't really get solved. They come together and fall apart again. It's just like that. The healing comes from letting there be room for all this to happen: room for grief, for relief, for misery, for joy. Letting there be room for not knowing is the most important thing of all. (Chodron 2000, p.36)

But as one patient said 'You feel you are in the abyss, and you are going to fall, but you are caught.' She talks about being held by the love of her friends, and her family, but it is also the innermost core creative self that can catch one. Even in the face of the awfulness of facing one's own mortality, one can be held and nourished.

Rosetta Life artists' individual art practices have informed us that falling apart creatively can lead to wonderful things. We pass this information on. Patiently. At the right time.

Mosaic tiles and pixels: Some reflections on computers and palliative care   *Chris Rawlence*

It's a Wednesday morning at this hospice day centre. I'm watching Stephen, who runs the craft department, place half a dozen identical mounted mirrors round a table. Quite soon a handful of men and women, in varying stages of terminal illness, will be enhancing the mirrors' bare borders with mosaic tiles. Colour (blue, green, red) will be the only element of choice, for each tile has its strict place in the mosaic grid pattern that will frame each identical mirror. A production line of mirrors, with no clue to the identity of their makers: to supply the hospice shop with gifts for granddaughters and carers.

Mosaic mirrors? For years I had harboured doubts about such formulaic activities that seemed to restrict the creative imagination. Too many people, particularly those with the low self-esteem that comes with terminal illness, think of themselves as lacking in imagination and creative fire.

I had had such negative feelings because my work with Rosetta Life seemed to espouse such different values. Songwriting, storytelling, photography, movement, writing poetry or filmmaking, often mediated by digital technologies, set out to help awaken imaginations that have been stifled by illness. The aim is to help people identify and reach what currently most matters to them: to express it creatively through the art form of their choice and, even, share it with a hospice audience or via a website. And what, I might have found find myself wondering a year or so ago, does the making of a mosaic mirror do for the imagination or the creative instinct?

As I watch today's takers roll in I realise my attitude has mellowed these days. Each makes eagerly for their place at the mirror-mosaic table. There's Frank, the ex-cabbie with a brain tumour; Pete, lung cancer and heart; Diane, breast; Martin, MND, hands so far spared but in a wheelchair; and two others who I don't yet know. A warm banter immediately sets in round the table as each starts on last week's mirror: Fulham holding Chelsea to a draw, Blair's holidays, the price of gas.

'How was the op?' someone asks Pete, who hasn't been seen for some weeks.

'I nearly died', he says. 'In fact I think I did die.'

'That's how I'd like to go,' says Martin. 'In my sleep.'

'I saw the light,' says Pete.

'What light?'

'You know. The Light.'

No one takes Pete up on this and I make a mental note to talk to him about it later: his story might just complete a series of short films about near death experience I'm putting together. Instead, the chat stays in the here and now.

'I can't even see two feet in front of me,' Frank quips. 'Someone help me out here please.'

Frank, brain tumour, is groping towards the tile-filled yoghurt pots beyond his mirror template. Stephen, now at his side, guides his hand gently by the wrist.

'What colour, Frank?'

'I'm colour blind.'

'Can you remember one? One that you'd like? I bet we've got it.'

'Umm.' He falters. 'Umm. Letters. Post.' He looks up and laughs. 'Help me out here, guys, please.'

The others look up from their mirrors, wanting to help but not quite knowing how.

'He wants to name a colour,' Stephen says. 'What colour, Frank?'

'I'm sorry, guys.' Frank looks up, his eyes unfocused and virtually unseeing, as if he'll find the elusive word dancing in front of him. 'Umm. Post a letter.'

A couple of times in my life I've come close to the agonising frustration Frank must be feeling now. Once after a particularly intense migraine I tried to dial home from a New York hotel but couldn't remember the number. A frightening blankness seemed to have smudged out my numeracy. Things only changed when I placed my fingers on the push buttons of the phone and then, strangely, my fingers moved without my urging to the right numbers in the correct order, my home phone rang and I was connected. Some other neural circuitry – like touch – had come to the fore or, maybe, it had been there all along without my knowing.

The second time was more serious. I woke up one morning and could not recall the Christian names of my partner, children or closest friends. For several hours, and in rising panic, I trembled on the brink of naming without being able to do so until, by mid-morning, the correct familiar names came flooding back to me. I don't know what had happened – a mini-stroke, a temporary close-down – but it frightened me.

Witnessing Frank search for the word red brings all this back to me but, unlike me, Frank's situation is permanent. His brain tumour – a particularly aggressive one – has devastated the speech centres of his brain.

'Someone help me', he jokes. 'Post a letter. Pills. Pill box. Pillar box.'

'Red!' shouts Pete.

'Red! That's it!' Frank greets the word as if it were a long-lost brother. 'I want my mirror to be red.'

Stephen guides Frank's hand to the correct yoghurt pot. Frank picks up a red mosaic and holds it two inches from his eyes.

'It's red', he smiles. 'Thanks guys.' The chat turns to diagnosis.

'My doctor just blurted it right out', Pete says. '"You've got three months", he said. "Six if you're lucky." My wife was furious. She nearly strangled him. She thought I wouldn't want to know.'

Frank, bent over the table, his eyes just inches from his mirror as he places, then glues, each pixel-like tile painstakingly in its place, turns his head to one side.

'They got mine wrong at f-first. Told me it was… What's the word? Good, good, a good'un? Come on guys…'

'Benign.'

'Benign', Frank echoes and turns back to his mirror, palpably relieved.

A terminal diagnosis wreaks havoc in the familiar order of a life. Well-laid retirement plans are ruined. A person's identity, as husband, wife, is threatened. Spouses become carers. Security, often striven for over decades, is suddenly no longer there. Self-esteem plummets. Where there was once a semblance of order there is now disorder, fragmentation, a lack of sense and meaning. After the shock of diagnosis come the questions. 'Why me?' 'What now?' Next starts the journey of dependency, of the condition's unfolding, of tests, of hopes, disappointments and, perhaps, increasing pain. And accompanying all this baggage, there is a deepening loss of control, a progressive – and depressive – isolation from the network of relationships that once defined you.

Each of these mirror-makers will have experienced something like this; but being here today suggests they have done something about it. Because the first thing that strikes me about this group is their vivaciousness. It's the prospect of engagement with each other as much as the craft that brings them here. And there's the open way they're talking about what each knows to be a terminal condition: there's a buzz of acceptance, that denial has somewhere been challenged and the reality of dying is out here in the open. Their very 'groupness', defined by the shared activity in front of them, works against possible isolation at home. Their wit, sometimes gallows humour, defies depression.

What is it about this regimented and almost childish activity that holds them? It's certainly the company and the conversation. Beyond this, perhaps, in the diminished world of terminal illness they inhabit, a world that order and sense have deserted, the placing of small tiles becomes a small place where control is possible. Frank, bent over his mirror, can bring order to this tiny part of his once much wider world.

For Frank (brain), the disorder of terminal illness is probably more traumatic than it is for Pete (lung) or Martin (prostate). Pete and Martin may not have the physical ability to mow the lawn or clean out the attic, but they can name things that matter, fill in a diary, plan a will. They still have the faculty of language, evolved in each of them to describe the world out here and retrieve its analogue from whatever constitutes the miracle of memory. The precious and complex neural networks in Frank's temporal lobes, by means of which he learnt to classify, name and, with the help of syntax, describe the world he once encountered, have been devastated. He can, literally, no longer make much sense of the world out here, still less bring order to it.

Now I can see why Frank likes making his mosaic tile mirror. He's in control. It's a tiny world, but he's bringing order to it. Watching them at work, I wonder how they'd get on with computers and digital art. They'd need practical assistance, of course, but there's something about the systematic and persistent way they're going at their tiles that reminds me of pixels and digital bits: a Photoshop picture, zoomed in on, that reveals the deep grid pattern of the digital photograph.

Windows, Mac OSX, and the range of software applications they enable, are ways of organising and classifying information: a means of ordering the world. A file for this, a folder for that, text here, photos there, bills somewhere else, each file usefully named, subdivided and sub-subdivided into further nuances and levels of differentiation, extending both outwards and downwards to whatever level of classification and complexity you choose. Order can be conferred on the chaos of events, memories stored through digital photographs or video; blogging, reflecting can even make sense of life. Such external ways of storing human history and experience seem indispensable.

After simple storage (last summer's holiday photos in that folder), computers offer means of manipulating what is stored. Through simple photo and video editing applications – Photoshop, iMovie – we can toss out the dross, heighten the essential, bring words and images together that tell a story: our own story. In the past these processes would have taken a long time and have been beyond the pocket and the technical ability of most people. Today's computer technology enables us all to order, run and document our lives. Where once the skilled storyteller held sole sway, and we were the captive audience, now – for better or worse – we are all potential storytellers. At the press of a few keys we can seek the whole world as our audience. And how we have leapt at the opportunity: as the millions who use YouTube or MySpace or any of the other proliferating social networking websites demonstrate, the desire for such sharing is colossal.

The appetite for stories, as both listener and storyteller, is universal to human culture. Stories address the big questions we first ask when we become conscious of time and mortality. Most great religions purport to answer these big questions as well through the stories of their founders and prophets: Buddha, Christ, Moses, Mohammed, or other imagined ancestors and Gods. Wherever you look in human history you find stories. When we're done for a while with the holiness and 'high art' of the big stories, we pass the time with soaps, serials and pop songs, the ephemeral nature of most YouTube videos.

The human need for stories goes hand in hand with a desire for order. Stories confer order on chaos; they offer closure or lack of it; they may supply meaning and help us make sense of events.

People facing a terminal diagnosis often speak of their world 'falling apart'. For a while nothing makes sense as they realise the fragility of everything they had taken for granted. Bringing a semblance of order to a shattered life, and making sense of apparent randomness and meaninglessness, is a major aspect of acceptance and the need to live what remains of life differently. Palliative care is as much about this spiritual side of existence as it is about pain relief and the attention to physical suffering.

Watching Frank bring a smidgeon of order to his world by making a mosaic tile mirror, I realise that our use of digital technologies in palliative care is not as far removed from this activity as I had once assumed, for both are about organisation and order.

I think of Keith (lung, diabetes, heart), once a patient, now a volunteer 'in remission' at a hospice where I work. Having once been a school caretaker, the desire for tidiness and order is part of who he is. Computers now enable him to organise a life turned upside down by cancer. Simple photo-editing software lets him store and order the images of his life: a selection process enabling him to chart the history, and make more sense of his life. In spite of quite severe intermittent hand tremor Keith has also become adept at the use of a digital camera and now documents life at the hospice day centre. Patients love his pictures because he has learned how to show them at their best and he can print out the results quickly and easily on the printer in the corner of the room.

The lower cost and immediacy of digital photographs outweighs the excitement of picking up photos from Boots, of discovering what came out well and what didn't.

Computers also enable instant communication. Sometimes the hubbub and jollity of a hospice day centre, where up to 20 elderly people with terminal illness gather for a day a week, can mask the isolation and loneliness many endure. Computers can offer contact and communication for the remaining six days. This may be through email, with guidance and support, through personalised web pages or blogs: people can speak with each other, share feelings about illness, write poetry and so on.

A woman in her forties with small cell lung cancer had once approached David Bowie after a gig. Her personalised web page included a photograph of them together, and a text reliving the smoky sweaty joys of the mosh pit: the area of excess just in front of a rock concert stage. Almost as an afterthought she mentioned her small cell lung cancer. An email came within hours from a young man who'd seen the page and also had small cell lung cancer. He was overjoyed at finding someone else with his condition, who would understand his experience. An email exchange followed, giving each strength from being part of an online community that could defy isolation and make their voices heard.

Obstacles to access and use of computers can be easily overcome if the empowering nature of what digital technologies offer is understood, and there is the will and the resources to make it work. Laptops, a wireless network, a digital camera, a video camera and related software applications are all that is required to make a start. Well, almost all, because central to all this is a person with the energy and skills to drive things forward. I'm not talking about 'the IT man' here but someone who fully grasps the potential of computers and the internet and has the skills to help fashion an online community: in this case a community of the life-threatened.

It also helps if this digital someone is something of an artist, with the skills to identify what interests or most matters to a person. They can help them fashion their concerns through an art form – writing, dancing, photography – which may be expressed digitally to others. Bear with me and I'll show you how this can work…

The mosaic-mirror session is drawing to a close. I want to catch Pete before they go to lunch and probe him a little more about 'seeing the light'. At times like this it's important to act fast. I have a camera – battery fully charged – tape and tripod with me, and I have a hunch that Pete has something important to say about a near death experience and that this is something others will benefit from hearing about. Pete clearly wants to speak about it and now is the time. Tomorrow the mood will have changed. It will be too late.

We head to a corner of the room where I gauge the light quickly and set up, with Pete sitting on a sofa in front of me. I can hear the babble of the mosaic-mirror session in the background through my headphones but with the microphone facing away from them this won't be too intrusive.

'So tell me about this incredible light?'

Pete wades right in.

> I collapsed at home. I didn't know nothing about it until I woke up in hospital. I'd had two heart attacks but all I remember is I was floating on air into the unknown, into this very bright white light. It was so peaceful and quiet. Tranquil really – I've never seen a light as bright. I'm not a religious man, but it was as if something had left my body, kind of thing, but then they sent me back and I woke up in hospital. My wife said I had the paddles on and a brain scan. The doctor said my hearts alright but the bad news is you've got a large tumour on your right kidney. But that light…it was so very tranquil. It seemed sort of normal. I wouldn't mind having the experience again. To explain it? I can't, but I haven't worried since.

I was right. Pete really wanted to talk about this and is thrilled I caught it on camera. He's even more pleased when I suggest his experience of 'the light' might be useful for others. I explain that I would like, with his permission, to put this little video on our website, alongside another with a man who saw a bright orange light. Pete's all for this, flattered in fact that his experience could be useful in some way. It won't take long to complete the video: a simple edit, a little text to contextualise, compress, upload and – hey presto – by tomorrow morning the whole world can view it.

Working quickly like this can take full advantage of the instantaneity of the internet. Other projects may take much longer and involve the participants themselves making video diaries at home, or writing a blog, or keeping a photo-journal of the passing year. However long projects last, whatever the division of labour in their realisation, however small or large they may be, they have in common a terminally ill person's desire to express something that matters and to share this something electronically.

They're trooping off to lunch now. One more week will see the mirrors completed. Maybe I'll buy one or, better still, make one with my young daughter. It would be nice to vary the grid a bit, though, to add a few fish or some foliage. I could do with more colour choice as well. We could even design a digital version on the computer.

There are bridges to be built between traditional hospice crafts and the world of the computer and digital arts. I don't yet know what these are. Whatever happens we should be wary of losing what the hands on reality of craft has to offer: good company, the visceral pleasure of sticky fingers, the satisfaction of making order out of chaos, the pride at something practical accomplished, and a mosaic mirror to go home with.

4. Theatre for Professional Development

Ashley Barnes

Dead Earnest Theatre were commissioned by a UK Primary Care Trust (PCT) to create a short interactive piece of theatre – *forum theatre* – for a day conference of palliative cancer care. It was repeated for a similar conference two years later. We called the piece *Close*: close to death, close to one another or a tenseness as we wait for the rain to come.

We want people to understand each other better. We want people to show each other more empathy and respect. We believe that by encouraging people to recognise facets of behaviour and then challenging them about what is helpful or unhelpful we can offer the tools for change – not a complete transformation, but rather steps in the right direction: progress. Many leave our events having experienced private epiphanies. Change is therefore preceded by recognition and challenge.

Background

Theatre is an involvement in a social interaction. Unlike electronic media (TV, radio), performers and audience are together in the same space. No matter how much actors rehearse, their performance is in real time and space; they express those emotions there in front of the audience.

Feedback is therefore immediate. The audience laugh, gasp and clap…or not. A different audience will make a different performance. A very generous audience responding as hoped can make a big difference to a performance.

Performances and reactions are part of the present, so therefore are the themes and issues in the play. Some plays are naturally more relevant than others but even old classics can, in skilled hands, seem entirely part of the Zeitgeist. This is why theatres throughout history have been censored and closed.

The theatre is a natural place to present ideas and to stimulate debate. Many theatre theorists, mostly on the left, have surmised how to harness the power of theatre and the state of mind it is possible to induce in the audience.

Into this tradition came Augusto Boal (1992, 2000), a Brazilian theatre director determined to use his art to tackle poverty and oppression. As a young theatre maker he set off with a troupe of actors to perform hard-hitting political theatre to Brazilian peasants. One such performance ended with the actors waving wooden guns above their heads, exhorting the audience to take up arms and reclaim their rightful land. Much to their surprise a man with a real gun suggested they all – actors and audience – march together against the land owner. The actors embarrassedly had to explain their weapons were not guns but words, and they weren't prepared to shoot anyone.

The approach had to be changed. They decided to perform a problem, asking the audience to propose solutions within the play. Forum theatre was born when Boal asked an audience member to demonstrate what she meant and she got up on stage, replacing the actor.

In pure forum theatre the acting company presents a performance in which there are mistakes or social errors. There is an initial performance in which the audience just observe but, when this is performed a second time, the audience is invited to replace the actors on stage in order to try different solutions. Most of the time there will be a main protagonist that the audience will recognise as similar to them, and they will try to help them. The other characters unite in not giving the audience an easy time in finding solutions. As in life, there are no easy solutions, but rather realistic and workable ones.

This was also called *The theatre of the oppressed*. Boal, however, discovered that the oppressions in Europe were not the same as in Brazil. Our oppressors are the 'cops' inside our heads.

Forum theatre is not only a way of seeking change, but also a way of trying change for size. The audience (or in Boal's parlance 'spect-actors') can literally rehearse strategies for different behaviour. They can try out different ways of communicating, see if it works and, if it does, adopt similar approaches in their everyday lives. Little wonder that Boal's ideas have influenced techniques used in areas such as drama therapy, psychodrama, family therapy.

Creating an anti-model

The first step for us is to write a script. This needs to show an imperfect model or behaviour that can be improved (Boal refers to this as the anti-model). The PCT client had asked us to feature characters that related to the audience and especially a receptionist, a district nurse (DN) and general medical practitioner (GP): each involved in patient care and treatment from first diagnosis to after death. It was to be part of a day on the trust's palliative practice; so there would be limited time to find solutions to all the issues in the forum, but themes could be revisited later in the day in different workshops. After the event we were told that the audience had consisted of 35.5 per cent GPs, 14.5 per cent PNs (practice nurses), 5 per cent practice managers, 22 per cent receptionists, 9 per cent community nurses, 10.5 per cent admin/office workers and 3.5 per cent others.

It was important for us to find the right tone for the piece. If the mistakes are too obvious, the performance becomes comedic and light. In certain circumstances this can be positive, but when dealing with bereavement we needed to avoid any possibility of flippancy.

After much discussion a synopsis was drawn up in which professionals were put into subtly difficult situations. Their minor mistakes would make things more difficult or perhaps more traumatic for the patient and her husband. Many of their mistakes would be made either by a desire to be personable and friendly when perhaps they needed to be more circumspect, or by having to balance speaking the truth whilst maintaining hope.

Synopsis

Scene 1. Husband phones wife and is surprised when she says that she's going to the doctor. We learn that they are not completely open with each other. She reassures him that it is something minor.

GRAHAM: Hello love, it's me. You couldn't do us a favour could you? Can you stop off at Morrisson's on the way home for us?... Why, where are you?... You didn't tell me you were going to the doctor's. What's this for? I thought you said that was nothing to worry about... Well, don't you think I have a right to know?... Who's picking up Toby from school?... And you've asked Sheila about this already?... It's just that, I wish you'd told me, that's all... So, it's nothing to worry about then?... All right... No, don't worry I'll go... All right, love... See you later.

Scene 2. Woman sees GP. The GP suggests that she needs further tests, but also warns her that she will need to talk through the possible implications with her partner.

Scene 3. Woman walks into the reception area to make another appointment. She is understandably distracted and upset. The friendly receptionist talks to her about their children, but when she asks for another appointment the receptionist sticks to the practice rules and is unable to book one. The woman reacts with anger.

Scene 4. Time has moved on. The woman phones her husband from hospital. We discern that she has had a mastectomy. She asks to talk to her son.

Scene 5. The DN visits woman's house. The DN changes the woman's dressing. The DN tries to find some common ground in their conversation by using a very informal style of conversation and touches on a raw nerve. When the woman reacts with anger, the DN deals with the situation by telling the woman that her feelings are quite natural. There is still a miscommunication.

Scene 6. The husband phones a friend. We discover that the woman's condition has deteriorated and that he needs someone to talk to.

GRAHAM: Dave? It's Graham. How are you?... Not too good, really, mate... She had some more results today... No, they say they still haven't got it all. They're not giving up hope, but it's not looking good... Well, you know what she's like, she's a real fighter, my wife. She'll never give in... Listen, mate, Maureen's taken Toby to see her Mum. You don't fancy a pint do you?

Scene 7. The husband visits the GP about a minor, but stress-related ailment (e.g. eczema). Just as he is about to leave, he asks the GP about his wife. The GP maintains patient confidentiality and doesn't give much away. The husband wants, in particular, to know what to say to his son.

Scene 8. The woman has died. The husband goes to the practice to return his wife's drugs. The receptionist finds the situation embarrassing and is unsure how to deal with it. It is awkward.

There is a sense of unease throughout about talking about unpalatable truths. The GP is the most comfortable in this situation but even he/she worries about opening Pandora's box.

A three-stage approach

Dead Earnest uses a three-stage approach to our work: recognise, challenge and change. This also affects the way we facilitate events.

The use of a facilitator or joker is the other important aspect of forum: the link between audience/spect-actors and performers. In popular terms, the facilitator is much like daytime TV presenters such as Trisha, who walks amongst the audience with a microphone to elicit thoughts or advice for the people on stage. Similarly our facilitators wander amongst the audience to coax responses.

Generally facilitators have three tasks. They start by warming the audience up after the initial performance. This is in order to establish that this is to be a very different type of performance and that the audience will be required to do some work. It also ensures that they are less rooted to their chairs.

Then they explain the 'rules of the game'. The audience are told that they can stop the action whenever they feel that a character has said or done anything that is not helpful. This is done simply by raising an arm in the air and shouting, 'Stop!'

Finally, the facilitator handles these 'stops' using the *recognise, challenge and change model*. First the audience should be able to recognise mistakes that are being made or what motivates a character. Then they are encouraged to challenge the characters 'in role' about their behaviour (at times, the characters challenge them back by saying things like 'that's easy for you to say'). Finally, they coax the audience up on stage to try their solutions in place of the actors.

It takes a lot of confidence to be able to step up on stage in front of a large audience and many of our audiences are made up of people with low confidence. On one occasion an audience member came up on stage early in the first scene to propose a good alternative way of behaving. Thereafter no one put their hand up, knowing they'd be invited up on stage too. On other occasions only a small number of confident people regularly get on stage and the vast majority remain quiet.

Our initial aim to 'recognise' what is going on has the other benefit of getting lots of people talking very quickly. We also make a point of valuing everything that people say, so that no one feels that their views are less important than anyone else's.

The play in practice

Recognise

Scene 2

Maureen has just been examined and is buttoning her blouse.

MAUREEN: How serious is it?

GP: Well, there's a definite lump there, isn't there? I think it's impor-
               tant that you're seen quickly by the hospital, so I'm going to refer
               you straight away and ensure that you're seen in two weeks.

MAUREEN: Could it be... [*pause*] you know?

GP: It is possible.

An audience member shouted 'stop!'

Immediately this created a lot of debate. Maureen is scared and unable to say the word 'cancer'. The GP is being sensitive, allowing her to use her own language. However, the GP doesn't get her to actually say the word and so it is not absolutely clear what it is she is scared of. The audience thought that there is a benefit of talking about cancer openly and not avoiding saying words that for some people carry very negative connotations, but are not necessarily as serious as the patient may think.

A subtle subtext here is that the GP, by not being open, inadvertently hints by their behaviour at the seriousness of the matter, rather than dealing with it openly.

The scene finishes with the GP asking Maureen to make another appointment, because there are other patients waiting.

GP: What I'd like is for you to make another appointment to come
               back and see me in two days, so that we can talk it through. If you
               can manage it, you might want to bring your husband too.

The focus moved to the receptionist in Scene 3.

RECEPTIONIST: [*She has answered the phone and is making an appointment for someone. At
               the end of the conversation she puts the phone down and sees Maureen*] Mrs
               Beck, isn't it?

MAUREEN: What?... Yes.

RECEPTIONIST: I'm Mrs Jones, Paul's mum.

MAUREEN: Oh, right.

RECEPTIONIST: Paul said that Toby wasn't at football last night.

MAUREEN: No.

RECEPTIONIST: Is he all right?

MAUREEN: Yes, he's fine.

RECEPTIONIST: Good, cos I know that him and Paul get on really well…

MAUREEN: Look, I'm sorry, I need to make another appointment.

An audience member shouted 'stop!'

The discussion here was about the balance between maintaining a welcoming and friendly atmosphere in the reception area, whilst also appreciating that some things are inappropriate to say. The receptionist has probably been looking for an opportunity to say hello to the mother of her son's new friend. However, this recognition at a point of anguish for Maureen is not only confusing but also embarrassing. Maureen is probably feeling a mixture of emotions, one of which is to do with feeling very self-conscious and now everyone in the reception area knows her name. As the scene develops the receptionist is unable to make her an appointment on the day she wants and Maureen explodes at her.

MAUREEN: I don't believe this… I don't bloody believe it! [*She bursts into floods of tears*] It's not as if I want to… [*Sob, sob, sob*] There's other things… [*Sobs*]

Maureen has started to feel that things are out of her control. She is worried about bringing her husband to an appointment with her, she feels that everyone knows who she is and she feels like they are not listening to her: all of which could have been avoided.

There is also a difficult situation of the receptionist not feeling able to release other appointment times without the say of the practice manager.

RECEPTIONIST: When do you want your appointment for?

MAUREEN: Dr Hall said for two days time. Early in the morning if you can.

RECEPTIONIST: We're full that day, I'm afraid. I can do you one next week?

MAUREEN: No, that's no good. Dr Hall said in two days.

RECEPTIONIST: I see, well, unfortunately…

Unfortunately, as the practice manager has popped out, the receptionist is left in a very awkward situation. She also thinks that Maureen has been slightly rude to her in ignoring her chat about their children and now feels uncomfortable. As a defence mechanism she adopts a slightly officious 'jobs worth' manner, thus missing a simple solution such as 'let me do what I can and give you a ring' or, even better, taking it upon herself to release an emergency appointment time. If anything, the learning outcome here was to listen…and listen…and listen and let the patient set the tone of the conversation.

Challenge

Scene 5 involved a home visit by a DN. Things start quite well.

DN:	How are you feeling, then?
MAUREEN:	It's not as sore as it was.
DN:	[*She gently probes in order to get Maureen to speak*] Right? [*Pause*] Any other feelings? [*But as there is no response*] Have you looked at yourself?
MAUREEN:	[*Hurt*] Of course I have.
DN:	Properly?
MAUREEN:	[*Hurt again*] I do bath, you know.
DN:	And when you look in the mirror…?
MAUREEN:	[*Changes the subject*] It's funny, isn't it? Because with a jumper on you'd never be able to tell. And Graham's been superb. I suppose it's just me… [*longer pause*] Well not me.

The DN is trying to get Maureen to talk about her feelings, but somewhat mechanically. The audience were asked to challenge the DN about her approach. In character the actress replied, 'I know it's important to get them talking about their feelings'.

Although the other DNs agreed with this there were differing opinions about whether it was Maureen's right to talk when she was ready or if it was the DN's role to prompt her. The DN in this piece is experienced, but gives the impression that she has seen it all before and is doing her job by numbers. 'On this visit I will get her to talk about looking at herself in the mirror.' She attempts this in a sensitive way, but there is a hint of the school teacher when she says in the script 'properly'. It is as if she doesn't trust Maureen's answer.

The scene continues:

DN:	It must ease things when you can rely on your husband.
MAUREEN:	Yes well he's been great…and great with Toby, but…?
DN:	What?
MAUREEN:	Nothing. [*Pause*] He broke a glass washing up last night and…
DN:	Yes?
MAUREEN:	He started to cry. I mean we've got plenty of other glasses, but they're crystal…we were bought them for our wedding… [*Pause. She looks upset*]
DN:	We were bought crystal for our wedding too. I don't think we've got any left. We end up drinking wine out of tumblers.

An audience member shouted 'stop!'

This moment caused outrage by most of the audience and they demanded to know from the DN the reasons for her relating the situation to her own life. The actress in role responded: 'I wanted to tell her that I sympathised and to let her know that everyone breaks their crystal glasses.'

Of course, the point here is that the DN had picked up on the wrong prompt. The breaking of the glass is not the most important issue here, but rather that Maureen's husband was letting his feelings out. This was such an opportunity to discover more about Maureen's relationship and how she and her husband were coping. When challenged about this the actress responded: 'I know it's important to listen, but I'm not a psychologist. And so, I have to be careful not to expose myself to situations I can't control.'

Change

Finally a DN from the audience offered to become a spect-actor and replace the actor on stage. The scene was replayed like this:

MAUREEN: Nothing. [*Pause*] He broke a glass washing up last night and...

DN: Yes?

MAUREEN: He started to cry. I mean we've got plenty of other glasses, but they're crystal...we were bought them for our wedding... [*Pause. She looks upset. Long pause*]

DN: Go on.

MAUREEN: [*She starts to cry. Through her tears she speaks*] He's scared. I can see, he's scared. I've never seen him like that before. He's always been my rock. I'm the one who cries not him... I wanted to tell him not to worry...that everything would be all right...but how could I?

Suddenly Maureen was able to tell the DN all about her relationship with her husband. It became clear they loved each other but didn't talk and that Graham needed some support too. It also became clear that Maureen, through her relationship with Graham, found it hard to say how she was feeling or to see him expressing his emotions.

In Scene 7 Graham visits the GP. We join the consultation near the end.

GP: Okay, I'll write you out a prescription for some steroids for your eczema. You need to rub them on the affected area twice a day. Try and make sure you wash your hands so that you don't infect the skin. There's one cream for your body and the other for your face. All right? [*Pause, he looks at Graham knowing that there is something else*] Is there anything else you wanted to talk about?

GRAHAM: [*Pause*] You saw Maureen yesterday?

GP: Yes I did.
             [*He knows Graham wants to talk about it*] How is she today?

GRAHAM: Not much different.

The discussion started around the intentions of the two characters and both were questioned in character. The GP knows that Graham wants to talk about Maureen and probably came in to do so. The eczema in a way was a piece of shadow puppetry before the main subject was raised. However, they have now used most of the consultation time. The GP has adopted a perspective of dealing with each patient separately and allowing them to direct the consultation. So Graham has come in about his eczema, which has flared up, and the GP thinks they must deal with that, even though the cause of the flare up might well be stress. There is once again the fear of opening Pandora's box.

The consultation continued:

GP: [*More sensitive territory*] Have you talked to each other?

GRAHAM: About what?

GP: How are you both coping?

GRAHAM: I think she's coping better than me, to be honest.

GP: So you have talked about it then?

GRAHAM: [*Pause*] It's difficult.

GP: I know it is, but don't you think it's important?

GRAHAM: Why?

GP: [*Pause*] You might surprise each other.

GRAHAM: What am I meant to say? Goodbye?

GP: It depends on what you want to say.

GRAHAM: And what should I say to our son, eh? What should I tell him?

GP: Maybe that's what you should discuss with your wife.

There were a number of interventions in this scene. It is a difficult scene for a GP to manage and there is no definitive right or wrong approach. Clearly the GP needs to be sensitive to the confidentiality of his other patient, Maureen. The GP can't make a judgement about whether Maureen wants her husband to know or not and in any case it is not appropriate. However, by not answering any of Graham's questions the GP is making Graham feel unimportant and frustrated. One approach was to give credence to Graham's feelings

GP: [*More sensitive territory*] Have you talked to each other?

GRAHAM: About what?

GP: How are you both coping?

GRAHAM: I think she's coping better than me, to be honest.

GP: It must be hard for you.

GRAHAM: Yes it is… [*Pause, which the GP doesn't fill*] I don't know what to say to her. What should I say to her?

GP: What do you want to say?

GRAHAM: I don't know.

GP: It's not easy, I know.

GRAHAM:	Do you?
GP:	It's important, though...to try. [*Graham is silent, the GP fills the gap*] I'm sure there's a lot she wants to say too.
GRAHAM:	Like what?

The GP who replaced the actor quickly saw that by saying the last line they had cornered themselves and the consultation stopped. In discussion, it was thought that progress had initially been made, but with Graham desperate for any news about Maureen it was best to keep the focus on his feelings and not hers.

In the next attempt the starting line was amended from 'How are you *both* coping?'

GP:	How are *you* coping?
GRAHAM:	Not good. I think she's coping better than me, to be honest [*Pause not filled by GP*] But then she's a fighter. [*Pause not filled by GP*] She gets on with it.
GP:	And how about you?
GRAHAM:	What?
GP:	How do *you* cope?
GRAHAM:	I get through one day at a time. If you can call that coping. But then it's easier for me, I'm not dying.
GP:	You still need to look after yourself, as well. [*Graham scoffs quietly under his breath*] *You* need to stay well.
GRAHAM:	Just like that.

Graham is feeling hurt and is looking for opportunities to be antagonistic. In this one the GP is more insistent on keeping the focus on him and away from Maureen. However, Graham should still be able to ask the difficult questions rather then being steered away from them.

The scene ends with Graham demanding to know how long Maureen has to live.

GRAHAM:	And what should I say to our son, eh? What should I tell him?
GP:	Maybe that's what you should discuss with your wife.
GRAHAM:	Why don't you come down off that fence? What can I say?
GP:	It's hard to know what's right… But children usually pick up a lot more than we give them credit for…
GRAHAM:	He's only eight. What can I say to make him understand?
GP:	The truth, perhaps.
GRAHAM:	Well, in that case, what is the truth? Maybe you can tell me that. I mean how long has she got?
GP:	That's really hard for me to say.
GRAHAM:	Why, don't you think I have a right to know?
GP:	It's not that, it's…

GRAHAM:	Don't you think it would be easier for us all…
GP:	It's not that easy…
GRAHAM:	What, a week? A month? A year?
GP:	I wish I could say…
GRAHAM:	Or do you just not want to?

The GP clearly can't say. They genuinely do not know. It's difficult to convince Graham of this point, however. He is desperate for someone to help him. This was another attempt:

GRAHAM:	How long has she got?
GP:	I really don't know.
GRAHAM:	Or don't you want to tell me?
GP:	No. I really don't know. It's impossible to say.
GRAHAM:	What, a week? A month? A year?
GP:	I know that it would be easier for you to know. But each person is different. It could be any one of those options.
GRAHAM:	I see.

But the real point here is that Graham and Maureen have to be able to talk the issues through together. Who else can make decisions for them? A counselling service or a local hospice might be able to help them communicate with each other.

The final scene (8) finishes like this:

The receptionist has been chatting with an elderly gentleman on the phone.

RECEPTIONIST:	All right, love… Thanks a lot… Bye! [*She talks to Graham without looking up*] Hello, can I help you? [*Looks at bag*] Few provisions?
GRAHAM:	No. I'm bringing these back.
RECEPTIONIST:	Oh yes, what are they? [*She looks up*]
GRAHAM:	I'm Mr Beck. They're my wife's medication. Dr Hall asked me to bring them in.
RECEPTIONIST:	[*Now she's embarrassed*] Oh yes, I see…well, thank you… I'll let him know… That's very good of you.

By this time we had already seen the GPs and DNs step up and replay their scenes; now it was the turn of the receptionists. The first intervention was straight to the point. The audience member/spect-actor toned down the joviality of their phone conversation and then waited to look at Graham before speaking. When they spoke, they spoke to him politely and without embarrassment. The final question was put to the audience by the joker.

JOKER:	'Was that progress?'

And the answer came back a resounding 'yes'.

Conclusion

I commented earlier how the theatre offers immediate feedback. This piece has now been performed on three occasions and audience reaction has always been positive and warm. Although few people now think of going to their local theatre to see a play, when a piece is presented to them with direct relevance to their everyday lives the real power of the medium (to offer stimulation to the eyes, ears, head and heart) can still be harnessed.

To gain clearer understanding of the performance's usefulness, we used audience feedback forms. Ninety-seven per cent responded that the piece was relevant. Some added further comments:

- 'A good way to look at patient reactions and how medical staff can interact better with them.'

- 'V. good exploration of sensitivity, confidentiality, responding to verbal and non-verbal clues.'

- 'Helped me reflect on how I handle certain situations. I don't have a formulaic response, but feel one's way through consultation.'

They were also asked to comment on the effectiveness of this approach as a learning tool. Once again the response was extremely positive with comments such as:

- 'Excellent. Really draws out the issues and the differences in approach.'

- 'It's evocative, thought provoking and an excellent learning tool.'

- 'It was very true to life and showed different ways of dealing with a situation.'

- 'It made all the professional groups think about how they approach patients.'

- 'It's a very powerful medium.'

- 'Can be threatening and uncomfortable. Can open cans of worms.'

- 'It was a very different and more realistic way of looking at the issue.'

It is often difficult for the arts to provide real evidence of benefit; longitudinal feedback was not possible, say, six months later. Nor would it be relevant. This type of 'training' is not prescriptive, saying that the correct way of doing something is A then B then C. Instead it allows for the audience to take away personal learning points corresponding with their own set of beliefs and behaviours. To truly change someone's behaviour would take considerably longer than one hour, but we have to start somewhere. Surely this work says to the audience: 'it is possible to change', 'there are other ways of carrying out your job' and 'you can improve the experience of patients by trying to understand the situation from their perspective'. And that, for me, is real progress.

5. Visual Art for Professional Development

Sandra Bertman

The arts – literature, art, photography, pop-culture (cartoons, greeting cards, folklore) – invite us into the world of human suffering and bereavement in a manner different from but no less penetrating than clinical analysis (Bertman 1991, 1999). Paradoxically they both reduce and at the same time heighten reality by giving it another dimension. For reality is not rational, explainable, knowable. Intuition, awe, wonder, love and human connection retain auras of mystery, incomprehensible to full understanding.

Can you look at a picture (painting or photograph) without imagining a story? A visual study, mindful staring, is an immediate invitation to dialogue with oneself and by extension with the picture. It is an invaluable prompt for contemplation, insightful conversation and action. For even the most linear thinker an image evokes curiosity: shifting the wheels of problem solving into high gear. One does not have to have taken an art course. What matters is one's own perceptions, queries and responses to the picture. The opinions and observations of professors, scholars or attending physicians are no more valid or correct than those of a patient or client.

Such an exercise can be used almost anywhere in public and professional forums. Perfect as a trigger for discussion, I have used it for workshops and lectures on psycho-social and spiritual concerns, communication skills, and grief and bereavement in many courses and training on end-of-life care for physicians, nurses, social workers, clergy and volunteers. Often I have distributed and at the same time projected several artistic images on a screen allowing participants to choose one that spoke to or disturbed them. More often than not, I have supplied 'probe' questions: 'If the image could speak, what do you think it would say?' or 'How does the image relate to your experience?' Five to ten minutes is ample time for participants to immerse themselves and jot down spontaneous reactions.

Invariably, group members are drawn to different images. And the reasons for their choices are individual and varied, more often than not related directly to prior personal experiences in their own lives or memories.

Participants in public or professional audiences are invited to share their responses in dyads, small groups or even auditorium settings. Quite often, totally opposing interpretations and associations are voiced. With each recitation, we shift our blinkers, and respectfully acknowledge coping strategies and where another is coming from, without judgement though often with awe. The caveat of not projecting our own assumptions or readings, and of carefully listening to another's, is forcefully brought home in such an exercise.

For our purposes here, however, let's just consider one picture. Reflect on the image below. Let yourself be drawn into the visual: what are you thinking? Feeling? Sensing? Seeing?

Figure 5.1: Kathe Kollwitz, 'Kindersterben'. Copyright © 2006 Artists Rights Society (ARS), New York / VG Bild-Kunst, Bonn

A random compilation of healthcare practitioners' responses from a variety of disciplines to this single image is proof enough of the power of art to communicate, to enable people to connect with their feelings, experiences and thoughts, and to refuel compassion. For some, the image evoked personal specific memories.

> How many times have I 'carried' infant coffins down aisles and up aisles and off the hearse to the grave...myself or with mothers and fathers, including my own brother.
>
> (Priest, 61, M)

> My mother died two months after my brother. My brother Tom had been cremated but not buried because the ground was frozen. I asked the funeral guy if my brother could be tucked into the coffin with my mother. Then she could take him back to the earth with her. (Anonymous)

> I waited so long for you to come to me. You arrived, but it was too quick, without warning, my heart is heavy and everything is so black. I want to caress and hold you, I hope that you'll come back. Still, I can't see you. Who are you? How can I fix this? (My wife and I had a miscarriage 14 years ago.) (Social worker (SW), M)

> Nobody ever told me this is what a father would be all about. The wood I hold has made me wonder. The child I hold has made me whole. I bury my wholeness with my child, never again to be a father. (Clergy, 52, M)

Other responses were more general, often in the third person.

> Face – ageless and genderless. The loss – unspeakable. Eyes emptied by grief. The hands hold everything but also seem empty, powerless…to change the fact of death.
> The artist's simple black and white pares the message down to its essence…no distractions by flourishes. In the blackness I see the aloneness. And the blackness speaks to me of the totality of the impact of the death of a loved one. (SW, 59, F)

Still others saw the image as the personification of Death itself, neutral, emotionless, all pervasive. Some invite us to reverse roles with death…

> A mother carrying her most prized possession – her child. In death, the mother wants to hold her child's body close but yet knows she must present it to a being greater than herself. Reluctantly, she let's go and hands over her child. (SW, 59, F)

> Death encompasses our life. It is a reality that knows no particular age or social group, and wraps its arms around our collective accomplishments, failures, and all that comprises our 'lives' when the appropriate time arrives. Death is bigger than us (the large figure versus the small casket). It shows no joy in thinking (facial expression) but simply carries on the task it was dubbed to do. We need to embrace death as this face has accepted its duty. (Anonymous, F)

> Precious
> Being Still
> Sacred
> Not wanting to let go yet
> Deep anguish
> Treasuring
> Remembering
> Physical offering
> Keeping
> Giving back
> Holding, Open, Precious, Experience. (Nurse, F)

Empathy helps us to know who we are and what we feel. Strains of empathy are apparent in just about all the above responses. Physician and literary scholar Rita Charon postulates that the effective practice of medicine requires the ability to absorb, interpret and respond to the meaning of stories and, for our purposes, images (2001). What better (vicarious) way to practice than by close reading of a picture or story or text?

One counsellor saw herself as the figure in Kollwitz's picture, hopefully holding 'hope' along with counselling techniques in a kind of Pandora's box. Another psychologist, Dr Judith Stillion (2006, personal communication) composed an acrostic as part of her commentary:

Harried by death she stands
Opening heart and soul to the eternal through the closed casket
Perpetual caregiver, lover of life lost
Entirely enveloped in sorrow

Touch her physically, psychologically, spiritually. Work with her on HOPE to survive the death – listen, listen, listen with Love.

Discussion and role-play

In discussion, we flesh out what this therapist might be thinking. We set this image up as a role-play, knowing the banality of glib consolations intended to be comforting ('He is in bliss with God', 'You're young, you'll have another child', 'At least he was so young', 'At least you'll be spared the grief of his dying in adolescence!'). What would a counsellor say? Specifically, what words would she use at this very moment? How would a practitioner work with a suffering soul towards hope to survive the death?

Medical and healthcare professionals are trained to solve problems: to assess, diagnose and treat. For them, a journalistic approach of a mantra of five questions (What? Why? When? How? Where?) can be an unintimidating way to initiate involvement with a visual image.

In one group a participant took the role as the grieving mother standing or sitting in silence, eyes fixed on the box, or on a photograph of a mother and child, or on a printout of this Kollwitz image. One novice therapist introduced herself, and asked gently, 'What are you holding?' There was no response from the professional role-playing the mother. Self-conscious and having no idea how to respond, the flustered volunteer stepped out of role and asked if someone would please 'double' for her. Another group member took her place, introduced herself and then sat down close to the 'bereaved mother' – in silence. For what seemed like an eternity, not a single word was spoken by either party. Eventually the 'bereaved woman' still staring at what she was holding, spoke softly, 'My boy would have been one year old today. Obviously he's not here now. But I still don't want to say goodbye. I won't say goodbye.' For the first time making eye contact with the therapist she raises her voice and adds angrily, 'Why should I?'

The group responded, continuing to role-play. One therapist gently queried, 'Why do you think you should?' Another continued with 'Tell your son that.' Suggesting she keep her eyes focused on the box, or photograph, a third volunteer took the conversation on a different tack: 'If your baby could speak to you now – from within his casket...or from heaven...or wherever...what would he say to you?'

I'm reminded of experienced colleague Carol Wogrin's talk of our responsibility to hold the hope for clients when they are unable to believe there is any. For her this means holding in her consciousness and awareness that clients do manage to find a way to hold the loss *and* to build a life again that can also embrace joy. The hope is that eventually the grieving person would come to accept that yes, it will never be 'OK', and that there might always be eruptions of pain; but a future time can be imagined when both seemingly opposing realities can exist in the same space. The therapist can't tell how, or in what form, this 'healing' can happen, for clients will come up with their own meanings and rituals. But she can acknowlege, as Dr Wogrin does, that she has witnessed this phenomenon time and time again.

Discussion

This exercise demonstrates how the arts can challenge, instruct and literally buttress us in our endeavour to stay present with another's suffering and to better understand our own. The beauty of requesting responses to a picture is its openness to interpretations. Any of us personally and professionally as therapist, educator, client or caring human being can take it in and use it for ourselves or with those entrusted to our care.

I would go so far as to suggest that there is an unmistakable synergy between therapeutic and aesthetic competence. Both involve grappling with understandings of ambiguity, nuance, metaphor and comfort with the inexpressible.

The arts understand that we need to speak our afflictions. Physical constraints of life may be shaped by illness or loss but in re-telling the experience artists and writers shape meaning. The creator of the image is a vital being amongst us. Probably we are curious as to why the artist painted this particular image. Is there a message or some event in their personal life that is being grappled with, acknowledged or commemorated?

Art releases unconscious tensions and purges the soul, said Aristotle around 330 B.C.E. (1996; Schaper 1968). The catharsis function is based on the premise that the expression of a concern itself provides relief. The artistic process itself is often sufficient for the working through and release of tension; the function is not dependent on verbalisation. Artists perhaps are able to be liberated by their creativity – or at least distracted – in the very act of painting. They can transfer hopelessness and grief at least for a period of time to the canvas or page.

What makes something art is whether it has a life of its own or not; whether it speaks effectively to someone who doesn't know the artist. You or I or anyone viewing such a work can take it and use it for ourselves. As we see from the brief sampling of responses, discussions and role-plays, there are many interpretations. It isn't a question of which is right or wrong but of what we do with what we've seen, read, heard or thought about.

Kollwitz's 'Kindersterben' captures the more amorphous expressions of grief: the intensity, the emptiness. Juxtapose the American W. S. Merwin's tiny poem, *Separation* with this monochromatic woodcut: 'Your absence has gone through me like / Thread through a needle. / Everything I do is stitched with its color' (1995, p.15). Or, in this case, its lack of colour.

In the role-plays we got away from abstract and academic speculations and asked what would you say to Kollwitz's figure? How might you use this image practically and therapeutically in clinical or educational contexts to discuss theories of grief and bereavement? Sigmund Freud (1913) stated that the task of mourning is psychical and goal oriented: specifically, to detach the survivor's memories and hopes from the dead. Traditional medical models stressed the idea of healthy or normal grieving as a trajectory progressing to a resolution. But *resolution* implies an endpoint. Contemporary models validate oscillation, the idea of continuing bonds, and the healing power of memory. If anything, for artist and viewer this picture is documentation that to celebrate is not necessarily to rejoice over an event but to mark its significance.

I rest my case with another juxtaposition, my adaptation of a two-stanza poem by the Victorian poet Alice Meynell (1847–1922):

Maternity
One wept whose only child was dead
New-born, nine days ago.
'Weep not; he is in bliss,' they said.
She answered, 'Even so.'

'Nine days ago was born in pain
A child, not now forlorn.
But oh, nine months ago, in vain
A mother, a mother was born.'

(Meynell 2007)

'But oh, nine years, …nine days, nine months, ninety-three years ago, in vain, / A mother, a mother was born.'

Nine months instead of the original poem's 'nine days' (my adaptation) captures the poignancies of a pregnancy loss, a neonatal death, the loss of a stillborn, the loss of a child at any age. Thankfully, abortion, still-birth, neonatal deaths and pregnancy losses are no longer disenfranchised griefs. This brief selection of responses cited above encourages sensitivity to griefs still too often unacknowledged. A mother, a father, a sibling, a grandparent was born.

The arts provide invaluable entry points into the diversity, particularity and commonality of grief, dying, death and loss. The arts invite us to uncover, express, revisit and appreciate not only others' stories, but our own as well. In every one of the arts grief is not pathologic, but part of the natural life cycle. The simple technique of visual study has the power to heal: to document and affirm where one is in the healing process. To let it be. Revisiting the same image at another time will be just as informative and revealing. The great power of the arts is to activate, renovate, transform. Indeed the arts – as the process of grief – can thaw what trauma and suffering freezes, or at least can help us better appreciate and endure the sorrows as well as the joys of life.

6. Healing Arts in Palliative Care

Christina Mason with the assistance of Chris Davis, Gina Langley, Bridget Lee and Cinzia Verduci

It was called 'soul pain' by Michael Kearney (1996, p.13) and 'total pain' by Dame Cicely Saunders (1964, pp.vii–x). Both make reference to something profound, all encompassing and often inexpressible through ordinary everyday language. It is these concepts that I am going to examine through some of the arts work done at an East London Hospice for the past eight years.

The chapter is in two sections: the factual and the more theoretical. The factual is partly based on conversations with paid staff at the hospice. All of them have an important part in therapeutic arts work. I then explore some of the theory underlying the arts in palliative care. But before anything else I need to give some personal history and talk a little bit about the social context of the hospice.

Some history

My route into caring for people at the end of life and in grief is complex, perhaps even tortuous, with twists and turns, choices and decisions that some described, at the time of their making, as very odd. And it is actually only as I am writing this that I realise that the journey begins very early on: with the arts, in my case music. For as long as I remember, it was listening to, and later playing, music that gave me the greatest joy and solace: a way of expressing private things that were troubling to a young child and adolescent.

Coupled with this passion for music were the formative experiences (and since there were a lot of relatives there were a lot of experiences) of bearing witness to the process of dying and grieving. These were the days before palliative care and hospices and I watched people, both patients and their family carers, in a great deal of distress.

Rolling forward a lot of years, in 1995 I applied for and was successful in being appointed to the post of social work manager at a hospice in the East End of London. I was enormously happy to accept the post. It felt in many ways as if I had 'come home' and during the next five years I worked towards building up a staff group that I hoped would be fully sensitive to and who would respond therapeutically to the 'soul pain' experienced by some of the patients under our care. During the last three years I have had a different role at the hospice but feel that I have left behind a team in which there are several members who are fully qualified to work with patients and their families and friends using different arts therapies.

This hospice, begun as long ago as 1905 and unlike many hospices built later, fronts onto a main street. Six different buses stop by the gate and there are always many people walking, running, cycling and driving immediately outside the front windows of the hospice wards. This location is an important symbol of the area served by the hospice. Hackney and City, Tower Hamlets, Newham; these are some of the most poverty-stricken areas in Britain. They are also boroughs rich in history and with a great deal of immigration in earlier years. At the last count, there were 76 distinct languages spoken in the area; some first-generation incomers speak only in their mother tongue although subsequent generations have fluent English.

The practice of the arts therapies

Clients are generally referred to the therapists by other staff members. Some are ill and are coming to the ends of their lives; others are trying to cope with loss both before and after the death of relatives or friends.

Creative writing

Bridget, one of our social workers, is employed as a counsellor, having completed a number of therapeutic courses, including creative writing. Bridget works with both individuals and groups, and the context can be by the bedside, in the counselling room, in the day hospice, in fact anywhere with a quiet space. One of the hallmarks of arts therapies in palliative care is the requirement for maximum adaptability.

A creative writing open group meeting lasting 1.5 hours has taken place in the day hospice most weeks since June 2001. Ranging from 3 to 12 members, with an average of six, a core group attend regularly, with others coming when well enough and free of competing hospital appointments.

The group aims, which are openly shared, include helping its members develop a greater sense of connection with one another, thus reducing the sense of social isolation which often accompanies serious illness; providing a means whereby, through the exploration of particular topics, individual members can 're-member' aspects of themselves lost in the process of becoming a 'cancer patient', particularly their sense of personal agency and productivity; creating a contained physical and emotional space in which fears and anxieties can be discussed.

These aims are achieved through the selection of topics which stimulate personal memories, thoughts or feelings, written about and shared within a relaxed, playful and supportive environment.

There are only a few attendance criteria, including willingness and ability to participate. The level of participation can vary according to individual situations, with volunteers helping those unable to write or speak for themselves. One long-standing member with motor neurone disease, who had always enjoyed writing poetry, came regularly with his electronic light writer and a nurse or volunteer was his mouthpiece. The only people who cannot be catered for within this group have been those with serious dementia who cannot follow its task or process.

The following example was written by a former screenplay writer in response to a question about smells from childhood. He rediscovered his motivation for writing and became an influential founder member. It has been reproduced and used in subsequent groups with his written permission.

> Different days meant different smells in our house. Monday and Tuesday were Sunlight Soap, Wednesday and Thursday blacking and Brasso. On Friday it was fish and on Saturday, Mansion House polish and disinfectant. For the rest of the time it was an amalgam of those smells and food.
>
> Saturday evening always started the same way. First the semi-bribery, then the praising, then the promise that would never be held to. You do it just this time. I'm sure if my father had been at home the treats would have been part of the liturgy.
>
> I knew that if my mother's knees weren't what they were, she'd never ask a man like myself to polish the hall lino. But I always ended up arguing and doing and being quite proud of the shine I could waken from the fibre. And sometimes during the week there was the benefit of someone slipping or sliding on the floor. However, above all this there was the smell that came from the small flat tin, a sort of welcome, comfort and continuity that is rarely evoked today. (John Davis)

When he first read this out he was pleased to have sparked a lively discussion about the importance of the distinction of different days of the week, a distinction that group members felt had been gradually eroded. In a later group, sometime after John's death, it became a springboard for discussion about memories of Mansion House polish as a symbol of a bygone era where domestic work was hard but satisfying.

In a similar vein, an extract from a book about a 1920s childhood which mentioned Sunlight Soap led to a lively sharing of childhood memories of washing and bathing, with members from as far apart as Poland, Ireland, South and West Africa attesting to the ubiquity of the brand and their preference for it over carbolic soap.

Sometimes the group will work together on a piece of writing, a task that always brings much joy and satisfaction. Three members wrote a lively poem during the opening week of the 2006 World Cup. A much larger group, including men and women aged 37–84 from Belgium, England, Ireland, Nigeria, Sweden and Zimbabwe, wrote this poem. It started with a series of statements elicited from members about the things they felt were important in life. These were then threaded together around the repeating phrase 'it's a wonderful feeling'.

It's a wonderful feeling
to hear the birds sing
and children's bright chatter
before the bell rings

It's a wonderful feeling
to nuzzle a tum-tum.
Turn baby over
and nibble its bum bum

It's a wonderful feeling
when cool ocean waves
come tumbling against you
washing problems away

It's a wonderful feeling
when people are kind
It helps you to leave
all your troubles behind

It's a wonderful feeling
when tolerance works
against all the odds
and the efforts of jerks

It's a wonderful feeling
when people give care
to loved ones or strangers
to care is to share

It's a wonderful feeling
to hear those you love
are healthy and safe
and, though distant, still close

It's a wonderful feeling
when friendship survives
the years spent apart
living separate lives

It's a wonderful feeling
to write of the past
and the friends we forget
Life is going so fast

It's a wonderful feeling
that home is the place
where you start and look back
upon life's busy race

Creative writing with individuals generally takes place within an ongoing counselling relationship with people using writing as a means of uncovering and expressing buried thoughts and feelings. The following was written by a 50-year-old terminally ill German woman who wanted to express her thoughts in a way which could be widely shared. It was particularly important for her to do this as she feared that her cancer would move into her brain and affect her ability to communicate.

A Way With Words

A way with words (they say I have)
AWAY WITH WORDS!
I say now
Language for death does not exist,
I only ever seem to have listened to (and uttered) platitudes.
Language I have used to cover up feelings –
PAIN AND FEAR

Patients have been supported to write letters for family members, particularly children: a task which can feel almost impossible without advice and support. These letters, or other pieces of writing such as memories of specific events, have been treasured by the family members to whom they are given following a person's death.

Finally, there is the more general use of narrative techniques within counselling: for example, asking clients to describe the way their lives fall into chapters as in a book and to allocate titles to the separate episodes as well as the whole. This is a narrative approach to therapeutic work, helping men and woman to talk about and make sense of their lives and changed circumstances. The narrator can begin to explore some of the choices they want to make about its ending.

Arts psychotherapy and counselling

The work of two fully qualified arts therapists is supported by several volunteers, most of whom are developing their work as part of a training placement. Media used include all the painting and drawing tools, modelling clay, sand trays, stones and shells, small figures and play equipment.

Adult clients generally lack confidence in these activities; sometimes they take time to understand that a good finished product is not the goal. Children are much less inhibited and readily express thoughts and feelings through painting and drawing.

Chris Davis, a social worker with further therapeutic qualifications whose journey into psychotherapeutic arts is grounded in her own experience of working in groups, finds arts to be immensely helpful in expressing thoughts and feelings. In addition to individual and group work with patients and relatives, she has a passionate concern with the well-being of staff, and the sometimes very difficult work in which they are involved. In March 2006 she ran two workshops with Michele Angelo Petrone (see List of Contributors) for staff and she wrote this afterwards.

There are so many complex and painful issues relating to serious illness and the workshops provided palliative care staff with an opportunity to express a broad range of feelings through their own images. It wasn't necessary to have any artistic skills to take part and yet staff produced the most moving images that powerfully illustrated the therapeutic value of this form of expression and the emotional impact of working in a hospice setting. A nursing assistant who took part in the workshops spoke about her experience:

> The workshop gave me the opportunity and space to express my feelings, feelings that do not dissolve like sugar cubes; a residue of emotions sometimes remains with me when a patient dies. I was so pleased to have the chance to express myself by putting my emotional self on paper with paint; it was most therapeutic and satisfying. (Davis 2006)

Therapeutic artwork is also used for introducing palliative care to new members of staff who have plenty of experience, but in other specialties. For example, each year new doctors arrive to work in the hospice as part of their training to become consultants or general practitioners. During their induction programme, they take part in a two-hour workshop on using art therapeutically. Chris begins with a relaxation exercise which enables participants to feel free enough to try creating an image. The feedback from the young doctors is that they find this to be extremely beneficial and are able to identify experiences and feelings that might otherwise be standing in the way of their work with patients who are very ill. This is just one example, and workshops such as this are part of the regular programme of multi-professional educational activity.

Therapeutic arts in the Children and Young People's Service

The Children and Young Persons Bereavement Service, active for around five years, is not restricted to families where a member has died at the hospice. Some children and young people have experienced trauma: the sudden death of a close person from causes such as road traffic accidents and suicide. The service also offers to help relatives caring for children who are unsure of how to react or manage their grief. Information, advice and workshops are also available to health professionals; teachers; anyone working with children in the difficult circumstances of death and trauma.

The service is available for children from the age of three into the late teens. The borderline when art play becomes art therapy is around ten. Children and young people are referred by any agency in contact with children. Although children can come at times of crisis, they are usually seen around six to eight weeks into their bereavement: to give the child time to settle into new arrangements following the funeral. The service, unlike many for children, is not time-limited although there will be regular reviews of progress.

Gina and Cinzia, salaried therapists responsible for the children's service, work with several volunteer therapists on student placement. All use art at some time, and, quite apart from the therapeutic effect of this, it gives the children something that they have created to take away. On entering the therapy rooms after a child, it is the 'mess' that frequently meets the eye. The mess might be seen as a metaphor for the internal world of the children; it is part of the therapist's task to initially contain and later help children themselves to contain the confusion and pain of difficult feelings.

A striking event in the history of the service was the formation of a therapeutic group in a school at their request, following recognition of the number of bereaved children which teachers encountered. Later a similar group met for ten weeks in the hospice. Particularly noticeable in the latter was the seriousness with which the children saw this work. They realised what they needed and with scarcely a word amongst them while they created their images, they got down to the task the moment the sessions started. There was tacit agreement amongst them that this was what the group was about.

Reflections on the therapeutic use of arts

The theoretical basis underlying the use of the arts in therapeutic endeavour is rich and complex. Here I restrict myself to citing a few examples of the way in which this form of therapy can help individual members and whole families approach the end of life. I look at the question, how does it work?

Many coming for therapy are troubled, and not a little frightened, even though they may not express it as fear. The early pioneer Elisabeth Kübler-Ross (1970) identified five stages in coming to terms with one's own mortality: denial, anger, bargaining, depression and acceptance. Our experience at the hospice is that every person's approach to their death is unique, although there may be recurring patterns, such as observed by Kübler-Ross.

When people think of cancer they often think of unrelieved pain and distress for both patient and relatives. However, as a result of their work, initially that of Dame Cicely Saunders, palliative care practitioners have made enormous strides in the relief of pain and other distressing symptoms. But occasionally there is pain that does not respond to the normally effective drugs used, and when this happens there is a suspicion that the pain may be exacerbated, or even caused, by a deep and frequently unconscious issue: an inexpressible fear or dread, or guilt over some past event. These are examples of the 'soul pain' and 'total pain' referred to above.

> Soul pain in another can be recognised in a number of ways… We may find ourselves using words like suffering, anguished, or tortured… Because soul pain results from an alienation from the deepest part of ourselves, there may be an all pervading sense of emptiness, hopelessness and meaninglessness. (Kearney 1996, p.64)

The creation of an image can move the sufferer to a different level of awareness. The therapist does not interpret the image, but rather helps clients to discover in their own time what is being communicated. 'Once it is out there, I can get to know it', is a core idea of the arts psychotherapies, and from such depths come ways to communicate the hitherto inexpressible.

And of course there are the people who are left behind. Although not an illness, the grieving process can often feel like one. Common physical sensations are headache, loss of sleep, experiencing the same symptoms as the one who has died, loss of appetite and energy, and these are without considering all the emotional pain of yearning and searching and at last recognising that a person will not be returning. The therapeutic arts, together with counselling support, are used to help people in their pain: putting into words all that they have lost, helping to define who they now are as a person without the one who has died. Painting the anger, the rage, the sadness and the emptiness of their grief can feel like lifting a huge burden from their shoulders.

Any serious illness creating change in physical functioning or sensations within the body can affect self-image. Cancer, particularly when treatment has been disfiguring, can be extremely difficult for people to bear. They need to confront a new appearance as well as different capacities. 'Who am I' is a frequently asked question as people struggle to find their identity in the changed circumstances of their lives. The therapeutic arts can help people not only to express their fear, anger, sadness, and bewilderment, but to find themselves: the person that they were and the person that they are in the process of becoming.

Sontag (1978, pp. 54–61), amongst others, has drawn attention to a commonly held belief that in cancer it is vitally important to keep alive a positive attitude and, in that frequently expressed phrase, 'to fight' the disease. Obituaries reiterate the battle metaphor: 'he fought bravely', 'he lost the fight'. Many patients that I have had contact with express how important it is for their families to keep up a positive attitude and I have sometimes heard relatives saying, rather crossly, 'she's given up'. The space created by arts therapists may be the only safe place where patients can chose to express their negative thoughts and feelings freely. The meaning of their images, both poetic and visual, does not have to be declared to anyone, but with their expression frequently comes relief.

Loss, not only of physical function and independence but also of people, is painful to face. People have to find a way of coming to terms with the prospect of not seeing children into adulthood, or grandchildren achieving their chosen career, of ever again being with a much loved partner. It helps to externalise the pain of these feelings. The words, frequently unspoken in life, can be written in the form of poetry, letters, autobiography, reminiscence, to a partner, a child, a friend.

How does the therapy work?

There are many different schools of psychological therapies, and much research has been carried out on the effectiveness of different approaches. Over and again results have pointed to the relationship between client and therapist as being crucial for success: much more important than the mode of therapy. Perhaps we should not be surprised. The concept of the healer has a long history in fact and in myth. For example, we read in the New Testament that people flocked to Jesus and were healed by touching his cloak.

> And wherever he went, into villages or cities and farms, they laid the sick in the market-places, and begged him that they may touch even the fringe of his cloak; and all who touched it were healed. (Mark 6: 30–4, 53–6)

I believe that arts therapies, like counselling and psychotherapy from which they derive, are, at their heart, relationship therapies. What heals is a relationship in which the person is fully valued and accepted. So many clients say that they have been attended to for the very first time in their lives and that they leave a session feeling much better in themselves as a result. Part of this healing process involves an empathic understanding of what they are attempting to communicate. Empathy is one of the Core Conditions identified by Carl Rogers (1961) as necessary for effective therapeutic work and there is a connection between Rogers' understanding and that of Martin Buber who, reflecting some of our understanding of psychological development, wrote:

> When a human being turns to another as another, as a particular and specific person to be addressed, and tries to communicate with him through language or silence, something takes place between them which is not found elsewhere in nature. (1973 (1947), p.72)

Buber called this meeting between humans the sphere of the between. This relationship takes place when each person has in mind the other in their present and particular being and turns to him or her with the intention of establishing a living mutual relation between them.

It is important that the visual image of a person is not interpreted by the therapist. The therapist is there to enable what the client has created to be understood in his or her own terms. We need to avoid fitting what is being created into a category of the known, and to allow the strangeness and newness of a person's unique experience to occupy our attention. We can than perhaps deal more ably with the immediacy and reality of their unhappiness, perplexity or fear.

Work with staff

Arts in palliative care can help staff deal with difficult care situations. Professionals dedicated to care can better empathise with clients' situations if they have examined, come to terms with, and attained a degree of understanding of their own values, feelings and previous relevant experience.

This development of awareness is a key element in the process of reflective practice where practitioners can consider both the 'wounds' they bring with them from their own past experiences, which inevitably impact on their work, and also those arising from their often stressful work. Every day those in the caring professions will encounter situations of disease, distress, disablement: people who are broken hearted, anxious, depressed. How are they to respond?

> For that element of tragedy which lies in the very fact of frequency has not yet wrought itself into the coarse emotion of mankind; and perhaps our frames could hardly bear much of it. If we had a keen vision and feeling of ordinary life, it would be like hearing the grass grow and the squirrel's heart beat and we should die of the roar that lies on the other side of silence. (Eliot 2003)

Practitioners rarely fully grieve the losses experienced in their work. Remen tells of caring for children, many of whom died. Years later she experienced disturbing dreams. With help she began to realise that the care and concern she had felt for these children, and her sadness when they died, had never been acknowledged.

> The expectation that we can be immersed in suffering and loss daily and not be touched by it is as unrealistic as expecting to be able to walk through water without getting wet. (Remen 1996, p.52)

The way we deal with loss can shape our capacity to be present in life and be present to clients in their pain, for sometimes clients will impact on us at a very deep level. On occasions such as these, therapeutic arts can be extraordinarily helpful.

I began this chapter with Cicely Saunders's important concept of 'total pain' that took shape when she was working with hospice patients in 1964. This has been a central tenet of end-of-life care for both patients and their carers. We discover the many facets of this pain by being in relationship with people and using every one of our senses as well as our therapeutic tools, including the therapeutic arts, to understand and bring healing to their experience of suffering.

7. Imagination and Health in Cancer Care and Palliative Care

John Graham-Pole

Thursday morning rounds at Alachua General Hospital. But not like any hospital rounds I am used to, where doctors and nurses pore over charts of patients referred to by last names, even the infants, amid a melee of *H and Ps* (histories and physicals), arcane laboratory data, and several voices raised at once as though we were all out in the ward corridor at a dead run. This is a gathering of ten artists-in-residence from our university hospital's Arts in Medicine program (www.shands.org/AIM). We set aside the first 30 minutes of rounds for each to "check in," while the rest listen without interruption to vignettes from personal lives, wrapping an intimate space about us. This is the space, I think, where human imagination locks into something beyond physical reach. The subtitle of theologian Matthew Fox's book *Creativity is Where the Divine and the Human Meet* (2002). His thesis is that the highest communion with the original source of our being is reached by simple expressions of creativity, and that this is key to our holistic health. Philosophers, psychologists and poets also see this urge to create as the very core of being human: in the act of creating we give birth to ourselves.

It is this understanding that these artists-in-residence bring to their chosen work of adding art to the sum of human health, individual and collective. These Thursday morning rounds are also a time for "patient sharing," another concept alien to medical rounds. The stories are poignant. Janet tells of Mrs P, resident on ward 7B and dying of leukemia. Janet first met her when she was delivering a bunch of sweet peas from her daughter who lives in another city. Mrs P is 92; she wears a pink chiffon nightgown and a matching hair ribbon. In the 1930s she was a model in New York and saw Isadora Duncan dance. Yesterday Janet and Claire danced Duncan dances for her: "Cherubim," "Narcissus" and "Blessed Spirits," and in time Mrs P got up and joined them. Mary tells the story of H, a 22-year-old woman who has had a bone marrow transplant, recounting tearfully that the doctors have told this woman's husband the outlook is grim. H loves the beach, so

Mary and her students have decorated a long silk scarf with seagulls and shells of all shapes and sizes, and draped it over the top of her bed. Gabrielle speaks of the poem she has created with L, a 14-year-old boy with sickle cell disease admitted to the adolescent ward in a severe pain crisis. Their subject was friendship; they composed alternate lines, and afterwards L helped Gabrielle set it to music. She thinks he is going home tomorrow, so has printed a copy for him, complete with musical score, to recite to his classmates.

Reading and writing poetry together bridges the gap between healer and heal-ee, in a way the traditional American resident doctor's "SOAP note" (*Subjective, Objective, Assessment, Plan*) cannot do (Graham-Pole 2005). We doctors pay lip service to this "S"; but it is only the patient's subjective experience of their illness and its treatment that deepens communication, helps us remove our masks. Cecil Helman, general medical practitioner for 27 years, speaks of the "mingling of narratives among doctors, and between them and their patients" as the only way "to understand the storyteller, as well as the story" (2006, p.12). *Communication* shares a root with *community* and *communion*, so it has spiritual as well as emotional overtones. Stanley Kunitz calls poetry our mythology, "the telling of the soul's passage through the valley of life," with the poet the "bearer of news from the gene pool"(personal communication).

Poetry has turned out to be a way for me to humanize my encounters with those I serve. As a children's hospice director, I have found it can help to write a poem about a patient who has died, for my own mental health and to bear witness to a short life well lived. Sometimes I share these poems with families or colleagues, but mostly they are my own requiems: a way to deal with my feelings of grief or failure. At times, though, they feel almost like celebrations. I remember "Laura," a 16-year-old girl who died on a respirator. I spent the last 36 hours of her life at her bedside, and it felt almost as though we exchanged something of our core cellular structure (Graham-Pole 2002, p.41):

Cell shed
I lean in among
the plastic tubes besetting you,
my breath voluntary,
yours urged.
Our cells mingle each with
each other's, spilling in spindrift
of air-ice-water
between mouths.
You, going, dying,
take my life to rest.
I, living, left, draw in,
exhale your seed.

Close to the last gasp of this young woman's life, I sensed something passing between us. Leaning in through an armamentarium of modern medicine, I got a sense of her cells being shed into my breath. At the same time I was breathing my own cells into her. It was as if I was salvaging something of her immortality for our earthly world as she carried a few of my mortal particles to heaven.

I wrote a requiem for "Janet" too, a 21-year-old patient I had felt strong love for. She had won a graduate scholarship to the University of Chicago's MFA program, so once she knew the score she made a deathbed gift of her savings to her needy parents to pay for the funeral. Shortly before she died she told me with typical bravado that she wanted to go out in style. In this poem, written five years after her death, I was still trying to voice my feelings toward a patient I had come to know as a dauntless and witty young woman trying to face down the savagery of her cancer. Across the generations a close friendship had sprung up between us, even though we both knew it would be brief by the world's measure (Graham-Pole 2001, p.19):

> *Cartoons*
> Janet said: "Dying I don't mind
> but not please in diapers, doctor!"
> (She thought, did she, I'd some
> Hippocratic power to veto that?)
> For diapered in due time she died,
> Greg changing her like his own baby
> in the Disney parking lot through her
> last weekend between carousel rides
> until sunset, two 21-year-old lovers in
> the best of humors, and still my friends,
> who wouldn't let me back off and do
> my doctor stuff.

Our AIM artists are at pains to claim no credentials as "therapists," yet their work is inherently therapeutic: we all want to tell our stories, to be listened to more, and especially in the extreme of illness. Art is always narrative, whether music, mask-making, poetry or pottery. It has a problem-solving aspect, too: from the interaction emerge themes and directions for how to move forward. Meanwhile the doctor's H and P focuses almost entirely on pathology, what's *wrong*, not what's *right*. The same was true among psychologists, at least in America, until the Positive Psychology movement emerged (Seligman 2002). In medicine, the strengths that emerge from within a patient out of an illness experience, and how carers can build on these, are still little stressed.

My interest in arts medicine goes back at least to 1990. Until then I had been publishing the kind of academic research that doctors favor: for example, strictly quantifiable randomized clinical trials (RCTs). I was deep into the third or fourth revision of a paper that was finally accepted by *Blood*, a hard journal to get into. Somewhere in that year-long process, I had a simple insight: the scientific data bored me! I realized how much more interested I was in the way things were said. From that point it was a short jump to acknowledge to myself I was no longer "turned on" by the diseases the patients were suffering from; my curiosity and concern were entirely with the patients themselves who were doing the suffering.

That led me to start describing my work in more storied form, including poetry. I thought of pediatrician-poet William Carlos Williams writing poems on his patients' charts during home visits, and that gave me heart. I would scribble fragments of poetry when I was at Institutional Review Board meetings where I was supposed to be listening to the ethical pros and cons of the month's host of research submissions. I felt I was passing through a gateway into a garden full of flowers; words became a new way to tell what I was seeing; they gave me new colors.

About that time nurse-painter Mary Rockwood Lane and I started AIM together in 1991. At first, we simply invited the artists we knew to volunteer at bedsides and clinics. No one in those days knew quite what to do with them; our first artist-in-residence, Leanne Stackpoole, set up her easel in patients' rooms and made portraits. Every so often someone would want to take a turn; that was all it took to embolden her to put a brush and palette on a bed table and urge: "Come on, you're an artist too!" It took a year of collecting testimonials from patients and family members about the program's helpfulness to get pay for artists' stipends. It speaks to the worth the hospital has since put on AIM that, despite deep cutbacks elsewhere, the budget for this "line item" has gone up every year.

Writing "creatively" most days led me to remember stories of dying patients I had known when I was a house officer in 1967 at St Bartholomew's Hospital, London (Barts) with Gordon Hamilton Fairley, Britain's first Professor of Medical Oncology; I found myself caring at any time for several dozen cancer patients. Those were days of highly experimental chemotherapy protocols, and it was rare for anyone to survive more than a few months. After failing to start yet another intravenous drip in what seemed a futile attempt to keep a doomed heart ticking a few days more, I would be barely functioning, and would retreat to the sluice for a good cry. Twenty-five years after the events it describes, I wrote *Venipuncture*: a memory swimming up unbidden from some dark well (Graham-Pole 1994, p.691):

Venipuncture
In the callows of my intern year of
sixty-seven, I kept the company of
big leukemia men, often so unstickable
I shrunk from them; stuck so often
without issue but blasphemy of
tears leaking from the both of us.

I pinioned once a nameless tributary vein,
harnessed thick of shoulder, elbow,
forcing a twist to the neck cords as
blue line on ulnar pulp bulged,
skittered squeamish, coy around my darts

until the time the hematoma sprang,
screaming its livid tracer on the passes
of ineptitude, pricked me to sacrilege:
he'll die anyway (they all did then,
the blasphemy of blame: God, why this
tiny vessel in this gargantuan frame?

The poem brought some long overdue peace to events thought gone and forgotten, so I could make sense of seemingly senseless things. It makes me wonder what else is skulking around down there! That particular problem got solved by the senior house officer on call that night with me swinging by and sticking a needle into the back of my patient's foot. "No football for you this week, sorry to say, mate," were his parting words, which taught me you can say – and write – funny things too to capture sad moments.

I came to art after years as a medical researcher, tempered by doctors' very quantitative approach to research. I never thought of myself, or any of the artists who worked with me, as doing anything that could be called research with art. I was just telling stories in prose and poetry of my work with mostly very ill children and their families. Then I heard of the work of Dorothy Lander and others, who were using the qualitative arts-based research methodology called Appreciative Inquiry to look at the subjective side of illness (Lander 2006). I finally got it: my stories of illness were research data in their own right. Qualitative research is better than quantitative at understanding people's social and cultural contexts, the "texts" of their lives – stuff you don't get from RCTs. A good way forward will be to weave quantitative and qualitative research together (Kaplan and Duchon 1988). This way we can uncover the nuanced or hidden health benefits that come from viewing a Van Gogh or listening to Bach or watching Shakespeare performed – or just doing your own thing, be it singing or dancing or journal writing or rolling down the hill in the park.

People ask me how I can care for very sick children, many of whom die. I say it is tragic that terrible things happen to good people, especially young ones. Given that they do there is no better work than to try to be of service. I don't believe in altruism; I do my work – a bedside vigil or the draft of a poem – for my own benefit. When I'm having a tough day, giving someone else a hand, casually on a railway platform or mindfully at a deathbed, always lifts me up.

8. Visual Art in Cancer Care and Palliative Care

Anna Lidzey, Michele Angelo Petrone,
Julie Sanders and Gillie Bolton

Visual art is a way of expressing and relating to images with or without words. Memories and experiences are often retained in the mind as image, rather than verbally. Exploring and expressing them non-verbally can therefore be very powerful. Anna describes how she encourages palliative patients to visualise their own personally vital images, and then to express them. Michele vividly shows how his own experience of cancer, which he painted his way through, was turned into an organisation to help other cancer sufferers through art. Julie Sanders tells how the arts helped her through her own breast cancer.

The power of personal imagery and visualisation within art therapy   *Anna Lidzey*

Art therapy is a powerful medium that can help hospice clients from the moment of diagnosis through to their last days. My clients with less advanced symptoms benefited enormously from the hours spent drawing and sculpting in the art therapy room. However, those in later stages of illness would often struggle to summon the physical energy to sit at a table – let alone pick up a paintbrush. The illness was playing havoc with their bodies, battering their self-esteem and robbing them of any creative resource. It often felt impossible to facilitate an exploration of the psyche in those who wished simply to bury their head and wait for the pain to pass.

In palliative care, as the body and conscious mind become weakened, the unconscious is the main resource to nourish and assist the soul in its vital role supporting a client to their death. Art therapy utilises image-making, symbols and metaphors to help the unconscious become conscious. To discover and harness unconscious knowledge and strength brings us to a greater awareness of who we are and what we might need on our journey through life.

On a one-to-one basis and in groups, I began to use visualisation as a means to connect with the exhausted clients who were nearing the end of their life. Visualisation gave those retreating from this world an opportunity to close their eyes and gently and quietly imagine a beautiful world opening up to them supporting them through their turmoil, exhaustion and beyond.

My aim was to offer each client a unique visualisation tailored to their particular needs. This differed from other approaches to visualisation, where clients would be led from a prescribed text. Initially I spent time establishing what specific need to address, be it a physical pain or troubled feelings. Next the client would be encouraged to imagine an image to describe this pain or feeling, and then to find an image to act as an antidote to this pain or feeling. This antidote would become the core of their visualisation.

In the quiet comfort of the art therapy room sat Sally, having arrived with the beginnings of a migraine attack she described as a bright, piercing light, twisting and turning her inwards. Her imaginative remedy was to visualise herself in a woodland, beside a trickling stream. Using the five senses and the various natural elements, I'd ask clients to explore the qualities of their image. So Sally went on to describe the woodland's healing qualities: in a cool glade there was a small, mossy bridge where she could sit and dangle her feet in the fresh water. In particular she liked the idea of the cool air soothing her and the water washing away her tension. She mentioned that she found the dragonflies uplifting. With the healing qualities of air, water and dragonflies, there was plenty of material here to help ease Sally's pain.

Clients would at first be asked to simply imagine themselves in their landscape, to walk around and explore its various sights, sounds, smells, textures and tastes. As they relaxed into their landscape and the visualisation, they would be encouraged to slowly become their landscape. In the case of Sally, the coolness of the woodland shade infused her skin until it touched her very core. The water of the stream washed away the penetrating pain of the migraine. Then as Sally began to deeply relax and connect with her calm, centred self, the dragonfly was introduced into her visualisation to bring renewed energy. Hours later Sally's migraine faded and was replaced with a sense of tranquillity.

After a visualisation I would encourage clients to find or make an image that reminded them of what they had experienced. It was often as simple as choosing a polished gem stone or picking a feather. Encapsulating the visualisation in a tangible form allowed for artwork to act as a talisman.

Many of the clients who used visualisation chose landscapes or seascapes to help instil a state of harmony. The seascape in Figure 8.1 below was made by a client who regularly attended 'The Art of Relaxation' visualisation group run for all hospice patients and relatives. The inspiration of a seascape soothed troubled emotions; and the warmth of the sun in particular was used to melt the client's tension. Like most of the suns made by hospice clients, this one is a setting sun. There are many images which could be chosen to paint the ending of life. A sunset portrays tremendous harmony and openness as well as closure. When the mind and body struggle to function, it is important for a person's soul to connect with harmony. The soul yearns for this type of nourishment. As Thanatos – the Greek god personifying pain, grief and death – begins to take hold of our being, we yearn for the strength of Apollo. Apollo – the god of harmony, creativity and order – is called upon in these times to inspire and stabilise our being. We cannot simply assume that flowers at a bedside table will suffice in inspiring our soul in this way. The psyche and soul are totally idiosyncratic in their appreciation of what is beautiful and harmonious. Art therapy is able to help us access and understand our expression of Apollo's qualities.

Figure 8.1

Those with a strong faith often chose iconographic images of saints or angels to feature in their visualisations. However, Figure 8.2 was made by a client who claimed no previous faith or belief. This image of an angel radiant in light therefore represents a very personal figure. In future sessions we were able to refer to the image as a source of guidance and inspiration.

It was important for clients to consider how the visualisation could inform or change their life. Time was set aside for a sharing of images and experiences: one lady who had chosen a white feather spoke about needing more softness in her life. She was a retired school teacher who always appeared to be very strict with herself. Through the visualisation, she had found the need to be a little more gentle.

Figure 8.2

Not everyone is able to benefit from visualisation. Some people simply feel too vulnerable or silly to sit with their eyes closed. For other hospice clients the idea of relaxing can be unnerving and even hazardous. In visualisation when the ego is relaxed its defences dissolve and a door into new possibilities is opened. It is possible that material arising from the unconscious may be released at a time when the client is unable to cope with integrating this new information. What could result in this case is a deep state of inner turmoil and confusion. Working with unconscious imagery and visualisation requires skill and sensitivity. Visualisation with hospice clients should be used by those experienced or qualified in working with the unconscious (Help the Hospices 2005).

Art therapy is a versatile discipline equally at home with images of chaos and destruction and harmony and relaxation. Many hospice clients in the latter stages of their journey need a gentle supportive approach that honours their struggle, yet guides them through its rocky terrain. The visualisation offered has found a way to work with the client's suffering, instead of attempting temporally to distract them from its presence. Furthermore, art therapy clients have been empowered to discover a medicine unique to their body and soul's needs.

The act of discovering our own antidotes to physical, emotional and spiritual sufferings offers a new approach for many hospice clients. A shift is made from medicine being administered by the expert, to the client becoming the facilitator of their own healing. It is they, in this case, who are experts in knowing what images inspire in them a sense of relaxation and harmony. This is an ancient form of medicine and wisdom used by our ancestors (Kearney 2000) and overshadowed by modern medicine. This timeless wisdom is as effective today as it was thousands of years ago.

MAP Foundation: creating a language for living
Michele Angelo Petrone

The MAP Foundation uses the creative arts to promote expression, communication and understanding for people affected by serious illness and dying.

Figure 8.3: 'The Healing Touch' from The Emotional Cancer Journey *by Michele Angelo Petrone*

> I need to know that this body is my body. And I need to know everything that is happening to my body. But most of all I need to know that you know that within my body there is me.

Healing is brought about not just by medicine. It's not just treatment which cures you, but all that encompasses the human touch.

The MAP Foundation builds on my artistic work following the diagnosis of Hodgkin's Disease in 1994 and subsequent treatment. I painted *The Emotional Cancer Journey*: 21 pictures and prose, it expresses my feelings of isolation, pain and loss, as well as love and hope. This exhibition spawned a massive reaction from the medical and psycho-social community, and today it still tours hospitals, hospices and other public venues.

Figure 8.4: 'Touching the Rainbow' by Michele Angelo Petrone

> Michele demonstrates the power of arts as a channel for communication. It would be difficult for anyone who sees his work not to be touched by it. I believe that his paintings have a valuable role in educating health professionals and society more widely about the emotional aspects of cancer. (Professor Mike Richards, National Cancer Director, personal communication)

Since 1998 I have facilitated art workshops, initially for patients and carers, but more recently for health professionals also, to help express and explore their feelings and issues. The first project, a two-month hospice residency working with cancer patients, relatives, friends, health professionals and volunteers, has been exhibited and published as *Touching the Rainbow* (Petrone 1999).

> Beams of rainbow colour radiate from a circle of solid black over a green landscape. This was one of the ways Wally Backshall coloured his feelings about his illness – cancer, 'A black hole and then coming through to light, a coming to terms with the illness', is how he explained his painting. 'It's surprising how talking about the illness and then putting thoughts into colour worked', added Wally.

Colour Our Feelings, two months of free hospice art workshops, resulted in a two-week public exhibition including over 200 paintings, prose, decorated stones that will be a permanent feature of a new hospice garden, masks and a Tree of Life. It was a unique collaboration between myself, the local health promotion department, health authority, the hospice and the district council. Being 'artist-in-residence' at the hospice and working with people of all ages, backgrounds and a range of experiences of the illness was very rewarding. People used the workshops for different things. For some they were a form of escape and recreation while others wanted to think and talk about different aspects of their illness and to explore ways of expressing their feelings about what is a life-threatening illness. My aim was to help people feel at ease and to guide them so they felt free to express whatever they wanted.

Sister Margaret Scully said the workshops and exhibition were very positive experiences for the hospice patients, staff and visitors. 'People were so open with Michele, perhaps because he has cancer himself. There was an immediate rapport between him and those taking part in the workshops. One man said the experience had done more for him than anything else and many people were given a real lift.' Health Promotion Adviser Margaret Felton said the workshops were a way of raising awareness about cancer and giving people the chance to think about the illness in a creative way. 'Cancer can be a difficult and painful illness. There can be a lot of fear and isolation. The workshops were an opportunity for people to explore and express their feelings in a safe and supportive environment', added Margaret. Eighteen participants talked about their paintings in a series of recorded interviews. The result is this unique combination of pictures and words *Touching the Rainbow.*

Figure 8.5: Tracy

Tracy: This painting is a description of how they saw me, the me in the hospital bed. I was considered to be a patient and I was treated like a patient and this rather negated the rest of my life – the life that had been going on outside up until the moment I was admitted. As soon as you're diagnosed the medical profession sees you as being the illness with a person attached. Actually you are an ordinary person, with something dreadful that has happened to you, absolutely dreadful. That doesn't mean that all the rest of your life isn't carrying on.

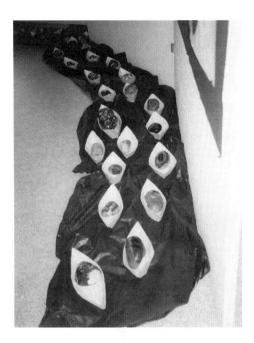

Figure 8.6: Painted pebbles created by the participants

Margaret Felton, Senior Health Promotion Officer, said:

Despite the fact that one third of the population will experience cancer in their lifetime there is still a reluctance to discuss the subject. Having cancer can be a difficult and frightening experience. People are often trapped by their fears, their isolation and their secrets. Overcoming communication gaps is an important aspect of health education and health promotion. All too often cancer is perceived to be fatal, a punishment, infectious, a no hope situation. This is in part due to people affected by cancer not having their voices heard, not being given the opportunity to express the emotional impact of their experience. Too often we hear about losing the battle, as if dying was a personal and ultimate failure of individual people to defeat cancer. Less frequently do we hear about people living long and fruitful lives having had cancer, with cancer or with episodes of cancer. The exhibition of *The Emotional Cancer Journey* raised many important issues. Patients and people affected by cancer filled in evaluation forms and wrote to us with their own experiences.

On analysis it was very clear that people were saying that they do not want to be isolated and marginalised with their fear and loss. They want to share and learn from the experience of others and they want to be exposed and have access to images and writings, which relate and reflect their own experiences. Health professionals expressed two basic issues, some were relieved to be able to learn and understand better the emotional impact of cancer, and some felt it was their responsibility to protect people from these powerful emotions. It was also clear that health professionals needed to be better supported if they are to allow people to express their emotional needs. Michele took up a residency at the hospice, putting to the test people's desire to make visible their emotional response to cancer. Enormous barriers were broken down; people were able to communicate with and without words and expression was given to these feelings.

The publication *Touching the Rainbow* will help bridge the gap in communication between the carer and the cared for; demystify the cancer experience; help us to cope with living life to the full when everyday is a bonus and dying a real possibility; help us believe in recovery and life after cancer; remind us to take nothing for granted; it will help us develop a language and a dialogue around cancer without which we cannot begin to share responsibility with health professionals for our treatment and care. These pictures and words are invaluable to our understanding of the totality of the cancer experience. The people represented in this book wish to share their emotional cancer experiences in order to help others. The openness, honesty, beauty and hope expressed in this book took great courage.

Figure 8.7: 'Tree of life' produced by the workshop participants, their friends and families

Celia, a patient, appreciated the experience of coming together with people of different ages who had different types of cancer, and enjoyed that they could share an activity together. She described herself as 'useless at art' and yet felt safe in the workshop to explore, and found it a real pleasure. It gave her the courage to try to do something different. She said it was a starting place to find her own voice and that it was exciting to have her experience published, she felt it was very empowering, and has led her to new arenas. 'I have taken on new challenges, speaking publicly to health professionals to communicate the patient experience. The workshop was an empowering step in my cancer journey.'

Pieta, a carer of a husband with cancer, came to the series of hospice art workshops, four years after her husband, Iain, had died from cancer. The workshops provided her with the opportunity to be creative in a space where she felt safe enough to express her feelings. An emotional woman, Pieta had learnt as a child that her tears caused discomfort and embarrassment to others and so, feeling ashamed of showing emotion, she tried to control her tears. In the workshop space, however, warmth and openness provided the sense of safety and support which enabled her to look at some of the painful issues around coping with her husband's illness and death that she had held deep within. 'I learnt self-acceptance from Michele: that it's OK to express my emotions. I recognised that each person's response is unique and valuable.'

Like many others, Pieta felt privileged to be part of the group and that the opportunity to share personal stories and experiences was supportive, rewarding and enriching. It powerfully reduced the isolation of her husband's illness, which had continued after his death. 'I see Michele's workshop as a very important step in my journey towards self-acceptance and an important step in walking forward into my life.'

Sue, a breast cancer patient, is completely convinced people need to talk about what is going on for them with their illness. People need to address issues of their own mortality and to communicate. It does so much damage when people don't talk about what is going on. Cancer affects more than just the individual. It's essential that we educate people into a new way of thinking about how do they talk about what is going on.

A series of workshops, *Moving Pictures*, enabled hospice health professionals to express issues they faced in 2001. What does it feel like to break bad news? To be with someone when they die? To lose a patient? What happens when medicine no longer has the answers and when things go wrong? How do they manage to elicit empathy and understanding with ever increasing workloads? These paintings are being exhibited to increase the awareness of the issues and feelings of health professionals, and the lack of emotional support they face in this area.

Vision

The MAP Foundation works to address our own mortality and our feelings around life and death and illness. Our bodies do wear down, we get old, get ill and we all die eventually. Why do we have so much fear about addressing these issues in our society? Why can't we prepare ourselves? This work has spread to schools, to the future patients and carers. By providing creative space for people to contemplate their feelings of fear, pain, sadness, anger, hope and love, the MAP Foundation creates a visual and verbal dialogue around the issue of illness.

The nature of illness, loss and dying will always be difficult and painful. But perhaps we can reduce some of that pain, fear and isolation if we are able to communicate more. How many of us find it difficult to talk to someone we know is dying? Too often we hear stories of the neighbour who crosses the road, or the friend who stops calling. And this increases the isolation and hurt. Yet no one is to blame. And this seeming lack of compassion exists within healthcare for the same reasons; fear and lack of understanding and education.

A registered charity since 2002, the MAP Foundation is run by a board of trustees supported by a group of professionals who advise on strategic direction. It is dependent on grants, donations and sales of publications in order to extend its work to the wider community. Creative expression can help break down communication barriers and contribute towards a healthier society and workplace. Arts-based activities, promoting emotional and spiritual well-being, help reduce isolation and marginalisation and change public and professional attitudes to the emotional impact of life threatening illness.

The MAP Foundation develops arts-based workshops using trained facilitators for patients, carers and health professionals to explore and promote expression of the emotional and spiritual aspects of serious illness and dying. It fosters emotional literacy in healthcare professionals and other relevant groups, and communicates the learning and insights from arts-based activities through conferences, workshops, exhibitions, publications and the dissemination of educational material. Links are made with academic and other institutions involved in similar work both nationally and internationally to contribute to the growing body of research into the effect of art and communication in patient care. The MAP Foundation aims to bring light to this difficult area by 'creating a new language for living'.

Art for recovery   *Julie Sanders*

I had a breast cancer lumpectomy and later went into hospital to have some lymph nodes out to see if the cancer had spread. The registrar advised me to have a mastectomy; I was alone when he gave me this news, telling me he wanted to operate that afternoon, which he did because I was so scared by that time I would have agreed to anything a doctor suggested. That November my husband said he didn't love me anymore and he left; my children were five and three. Nine years later I underwent a harrowing surgical procedure which traumatised me, and then had surgery again that afternoon.

I was unable to return to my job as a teacher, became depressed and agoraphobic and applied for ill health retirement, which was eventually granted after a great deal of support from the hospital. I complained to the hospital about the way I'd been treated and they offered me counselling, art therapy and massage. It was in art therapy that I began to explore what I was feeling especially in connection to being a cancer patient. I wrote stories and poems, painted and created other artworks such as batik and sculpture from wire and cloth, danced and used sandtray and plasticine.

I discovered themes and meanings in the images that emerged in my writing and artwork. I felt that gateways to new levels of consciousness were opened. For the first time I was seeing myself – that is, showing myself to myself – and making sense of what I found. I wondered whether it would have been possible for me to experience changes in my personality without using my creative imagination to express, through symbols, some of the content of my unconscious. Expressing my creativity through writing and painting changed my life and I began to experience love and other positive qualities in myself which I had not known before.

I began to feel whole inside, personally empowered, fully alive, able to experience peace, joy and love for the first time. I began to live creatively, energy flowed through me and my outer life changed. I trained as a transpersonal psychotherapist and continued with writing and making art. I realised these creative activities were crucial in maintaining well-being. Creative energy transformed depression, alienation, suffering into the rapture of life which seemed miraculous. There has been research to show that vulnerable patients working with metaphor which was developed without interpretations strengthened their egos because they did not have to tolerate direct awareness of powerful feelings but worked with them in symbolic form (Katz 1983).

The energy needed for transformation comes through images from the unconscious. Making images involves opening up to this energy, taking risks, dismantling defences, communicating feelings and this process strengthens the ego, provides personal power, self-knowledge and guidance. 'We can only correct what is in our consciousness; what is unconsciousness remains unchanged. Consequently if we wish to produce a change we must first raise these unconscious contents to consciousness so as to submit them to correction' (Jung 1954, p.153).

Blackness was the beginning and symbolised my condition of depression where I had lost the meaning and purpose of my life. I felt an extremely deep loneliness because in childhood there had been nothing for me to attach to and be nurtured by: my father had been mentally ill and my mother indifferent. At this time my feelings were not felt consciously but held in my body, unconsciously. The unconsciousness was present in my poetry later, but at that time I did not know how to relate to it.

When I worked in therapy with the creative imagination I became liberated from the constraints of the poetic form; narrative expressed itself symbolically, thereby facilitating communication with newly discovered parts of my self. It was as though my imagination came alive, enabling me to understand and express my inner being in a new way. I discovered that there are some feelings which can only be known through non-verbal evidence.

Figure 8.8 is a vital image of my life inside the cold, dark shell, which I carried with me for 20 years.

I drew a body map without a heart (Figure 8.9).

This was my first realisation that feelings were missing from my life. When I became conscious of my missing heart I added a cracked, clay heart. I worked with the image of a heart, writing stories, poems and making pictures. I wrote about a surgeon finding a heart bud which eventually rooted and grew (Figure 8.10).

Figure 8.8: Batik of woman on a beach (1976)

Figure 8.9: Body map (1996)

Figure 8.10: My rich leafy heart (1997)

Photography   *Gillie Bolton*

Photography acts to hold the moment, to be witness to things as they have been; by creating a record, it accords value to the person, thing or event photographed. Often used as aide memoire, as souvenir photographs can help remember holidays, dead loved ones, what people were like when younger. Photographs can transport us to these past scenes and places – often a form of reminiscence therapy. They are put in Memory Boxes created by the living – particularly children – to help remember their deeply grieved dead. Counterbalancing this is research which proves that a recollected scene or face is remembered in better detail than if a photograph had been seen (Leibovitz 2006).

The act of photography itself can also be therapeutic: 'in capturing the moment, an unconscious wish to somehow arrest the passage of time is stimulated' (Martin 2006, p.54). Photo-therapist Rosy Martin photographed her father's dying. Of these photographs' impact on her mother, she said: 'Photographs cannot heal the pain of bereavement, but they do offer a trigger to memories. I have always been concerned in my practice with challenging taboos and representing the un-representable. These photographs offer a means of thinking through feelings, feelings through thoughts' (Martin 1995, p.74).

Martin also photographed her childhood home following her mother's death (a series she entitled *Too Close to Home*), in an 'archaeology of the self' (Martin 2006, p.53). She asks how can a piece of photographic paper haunt her? And answers herself that these photographs evoke powerful personal memory-stories

(Martin 2006). She kept trying to capture the essence: 'I photograph in order to hold onto the moment, the place, the trace which I cannot stop, cannot keep, cannot hold. I know this, and yet however partial, incomplete and vain the attempt, I return and photograph again' (Martin 1999, p.73).

Photography invites us into areas we don't normally go, as does other art. In my research for this section, I've found reference again and again to some of the most deeply troubling images from the Vietnam war: they taught us so much, not only about what was going on which had to be stopped, but also about the 'inhumanity of man to man'. When reflected upon, photographs can reveal secrets missed at the time (Martin 1999, p.76), can reveal what is otherwise in the 'optical unconscious' (Benjamin 1977, p.48). Barthes explains that a photograph supplies a moment, a detail by accident – which would otherwise be lost. Tangential images will always be captured alongside the ones the photographer intended, as memorably explored in the film *Blow Up* (1966, directed by Michelangelo Antonioni).

Although 'in photography I can never deny that the thing has been there' (Barthes 1981, quoted in Benjamin 1977), it 'cannot be simply a transparency of something that happened. It is always the image that someone chose; to photograph is to frame, and to frame is to exclude' (Sontag 2003, p.41). Henryk Ross photographed the Lotz ghetto (1940–45). The photographs he chose not to publish, discovered after his death in 1997, challenge the image he built up of ghetto history: among them are images of happiness, prosperity, open spaces and greenery (Bush, Sladen and Harrison 2006). Photographs are as much an interpretation of the world as paintings (Sontag 1979).

Blake Morrison speaks of 'the [photographer's] balancing act between subjectivity and objectivity – the conflicting demands of being a participant, personally affected by the people and events in front of your lens, while also acting as an observer, coldly absorbed in the process of making a record or creating art.' This can create historical observations which are 'not a date but an image; not a textbook debate but a human face; not even a document but an emotional and intellectual complex in an instant of time' (2006, pp.12–13). Such can be the power of art, to give us 'language but no words' (Transtromer 2002, p.445). It must be remembered, however, that photographs do not have static, or even single, meanings: their significance will be different whether they are used in a police file, in a newspaper, for pornography or for advertising.

Susan Sontag discussed photographic images of horror and death, particularly relating to war. Do we become inured to them? Are they in fact brutalising? 'Something becomes real by being photographed. But a catastrophe will often seem eerily like its representation. The attack on the world trade centre on September 11 2001, was described as…"like a movie" in many of the first hand accounts' (2003, p.19). Or do these photographs help us to understand, to perceive elements otherwise missed, or to experience events otherwise non-experienceable? 'Although the camera is an observation station, the act of photographing is more than passive observing… [It is] to be in complicity with whatever makes the subject interesting, worth photographing – including, when that is the interest, another person's pain or misfortune' (Sontag 1979, p.12). This interest can have political impact, as in the way US military personnel's private photographs have been used to expose brutality in military detention centres.

What is the impact on the private lives of those depicted? Media exposure of suffering people by themselves, such as John Diamond's (1998) diary of his death from cancer, is becoming common. Perhaps these people seek witnesses for their suffering; perhaps they gain strength from feeling they share it with others. And audiences (readers, TV watchers, etc.) want to read or watch them. We need to know what suffering feels like psychologically, physically and spiritually. We are more than supportive witnesses: we gain insight and understanding, and, we hope, compassion.

Yet photography terminology is aggressive: shoot, take, blow up. Some peoples refuse to be photographed because they fear it robs the soul. Photography can exploit: images of brutality or extreme suffering and poverty exploit the victims. Paparazzi shots are not the only predatory photographs. Regulations concerning publication of images of people are rightly getting stricter, especially in medicine.

A series of photographs of a dying man – Michael Willson – opened this book. Michael wrote: 'These pictures are not for the album and later reminiscence; they are for now.' He wished to relate to the changing images of his own dying. He also wanted them used after his death to help those of us left behind to understand dying better. The photographer, Paul, said: 'His attitude to dying provides an alternative to the traditional stereotypes. It is possible to die well. Photography helped Michael define his identity and to deal with his terminal illness.'

9. Making Music in Children's Hospices

Lesley Schatzberger

No-one knows what music is... We know that it releases the human spirit into some solitude of meditation where the creative process can freely act; we know that it can soothe pain, relieve anxiety, comfort distress, exhilarate health, confirm courage...

Lucien Price (2004)

In the domed chapel of a convent we can hear wonderful songs from Ghana and Brazil, beautifully sung in harmony by about 30 people. Only a couple of days ago some of these singers were claiming not to have an ounce of music in them. We are coming to the end of the first weekend of one of Jessie's Fund's Music-Making in Children's Hospices training courses, in which we facilitate the use of music as a tool for communication and expression, and as a source of enjoyment for life-limited children. Very much a hands-on experience, participants (who need have no previous musical training) are amazed at music's effectiveness at breaking down barriers. Everyone, regardless of age or ability, can communicate through its common language.

By the mid 1990s there were eight or nine children's hospices in the UK, rising rapidly over the next decade to about 35. Those who have no reason to be acquainted with them may be vaguely aware that they exist, but will probably avoid the painful contemplation of the important part they have to play for a surprisingly large number of families. And so it was for us until our nine-year-old daughter was diagnosed with a brain stem tumour which was to rob her of her future within a few months: we spent the last week of Jessica's life at Martin House, the children's hospice in Yorkshire. As musicians, we quickly realised how important the creative use of music could be in enhancing the quality of children's lives in that setting. We discovered that at that time children's hospices had almost no experience of music as anything other than something to listen to passively, or as 'musack' – general background music which, at a conscious level, is barely listened to at all. Between 80 per cent and 90 per cent of children cared for by hospices are unable to communicate verbally, so it was clear to us that music had a much more vital contribution to make in providing them with an alternative means of expression and connection.

A new resource for children's hospices emerges

During Jessie's illness our colleagues in the musical world established a fund intended to pay for treatment in New York, but time turned out to be too short to use it for this purpose. Jessie's Fund became a charity in 1995, and after equipping the hospices with appropriate musical instruments our first thought was to identify a suitable training opportunity and then to fund care team members to take advantage of it. We soon discovered that this very specialised training wasn't available, so we decided to devise a course and engaged the help of the eminent music therapist Professor Leslie Bunt. A structure of two residential weekends separated by four or five months emerged. Between weekends participants incorporated their new skills into work with children, and identified where they'd need more guidance. This was shared at the second weekend.

> After our weekend in York I was cuddling a young girl who sometimes cried for hours. Remembering a discussion in York, I wondered if it was her only way of communicating. I maintained eye contact, trying with my voice to imitate her sounds. After a while she calmed, and I really felt as if there was a dialogue between us.

Each beginning of the course there have been choruses of 'I'm totally unmusical!', but as we say our farewells just two days later every single person is buzzing with the music he or she has produced, clamouring for more.

The first weekend starts with inevitable introductions, but introductions with a difference. We use an instrument to speak for us – handing one round in turn, or each playing one we have just chosen for ourselves – and we play it in any way we like. Already musical sound has eliminated any initial awkwardness. This tends to be a rather light-hearted session with room for plenty of laughter: we find out that one person may have chosen an instrument because it is shiny, another because it is tiny, and another because they've no idea how it sounds. The tone is set – this weekend we will spend most of the time playing music and we'll have lots of fun, though it will be intense and there will, of course, be much thoughtful and reflective work.

> I take up as many training opportunities as I can and, without a doubt, the Jessie's Fund course has been the most enjoyable, practical, thought-provoking and exhausting I have ever attended.

What happens in the course

There are four expert tutors, two of whom are music therapists and two of whom are 'animateurs' – musician/performers who specialise in education projects, often with a focus on children with special needs. The intensity and success of our course depends on the low student tutor ratio: about 7:1.

The first weekend takes place in York, where Jessie's Fund is based, and the second usually in either Kent or Somerset. This chapter covers the course, interspersed with a range of musical experiences inspired by participants' new skills.

Musical instruments

We dispel the myth that all musical instruments require years of lessons and dedicated practice before one can enjoy playing them. We look at the various ways in which different instruments can be played, their 'colour' (or timbre, quality of sound), tactile properties, visual appeal, range of sounds, range of dynamics, and their suitability for children with differing needs and abilities. All the simple but high quality instruments are very easy to play intuitively. We aim to give students the confidence to use them. Quality of sound is extremely important; cheap plastic toys should be avoided.

> Matthew has Down Syndrome and was dressed up in a soldier's uniform. He was marching around very seriously. I started to bang a drum to the rhythm of his marching; it really seemed to stimulate him and he took it very seriously, going faster and slower to see if I would follow his lead.

Simple keyboard techniques

We teach a few techniques which give a degree of facility even with no experience. Notation is not used, so there are no pleas of 'I can't even read music!' A piano, large as it is, can be an intimidating instrument, but by learning a few 'tricks' the students can get over their reticence to play it.

> We had a wonderful piano session. I utilised the black notes technique. Stan utilised a range of throwing, dropping, leaning and hitting keys randomly. Sitting side by side, we made music together.

Guitar playing

The guitar is a wonderful instrument, and we teach just three simple chords which can accompany all sorts of popular songs, or improvised songs. We also learn about 'open' tunings, so that the strings can be strummed harmoniously with the right hand without even having to finger the strings with the left hand. And we show how the guitar can be used in unconventional ways: the sides or front can be tapped, the wood can be stroked, the back can be held up to the face so that the vibrations can be easily felt, and it can even be drummed gently with a beater.

> Tim is usually restless and we find the guitar holds his attention. He has a degenerative disorder, so he can withdraw into a strange world of his own. It is lovely to see him enjoying the guitar, plucking at strings and using a drumstick. Others can see how he enjoys the experience of the guitar and they hear his vocalisations.

Improvisation

Almost all the music is improvised, as it will be when the participants take their skills back to work, so it can reflect 'the moment' and avoid the strictures of 'right' and 'wrong' which so often inhibit our musical impulses. The staff will be able to use this spontaneity to stimulate and respond to children's sounds.

> After November's Jessie's Fund course I got together with two teenage boys, both of whom had limited movement. I was on the black notes of the piano, Ned was on the drum, and Will was hovering around the chimes. As I played, Ned would answer with the drum, making Will jump and shake with laughter which caused him to catch the chimes. We got faster and faster until we couldn't play any more through laughing. It was so good to be able to share spontaneous laughter.

Structure

We can feel lost in music, as in life itself, if there is no structure. All composed music has structure, whether classical, jazz, rock or pop. Music needs shape: beginnings, development of ideas, repetitions, contrasts, surprises, climaxes, motifs and so on. Without a structure providing boundaries the range of possibilities can be intimidating to the point of suffocating any creative impulse. Even using a simple image or theme can provide a helpful focus.

> We had a 'sea' musical session. The chime bars on a stand were put within her reach. She was awake and smiled but made no attempt to reach for the bars. I played the softer sounding bars. She continued to smile. I played some 'sea' related songs on the piano and sang along. She was happy and calm for a long time.

Dialogue through music

A great deal of music uses 'question and answer' phrases: in effect, a musical discussion is taking place. The use of non-verbal sounds in one-to-one communication can be more powerful than words. We stress the important but too frequently overlooked qualities of listening, giving time and space, and allowing for silence within a musical dialogue. A child who cannot make himself understood verbally can fully engage in a conversation through music.

> I was with Joshua in the sensory room when I noticed he was concentrating extremely hard, drumming with his fingers on the surface of the bed. We began to have a conversation using our hands, drumming, tapping, slapping the surface, being loud and quiet intermittently. Both Joshua and I were enthralled. It was an interaction I had never had with him before. It was magical and so special. We had connected with each other just for a brief while. I don't think I would have recognised the importance of it if I hadn't been on the course.

Support

We can emotionally support children through and in musical activity. We give a safe framework in which to play and express themselves, allowing them to lead, responding with care and acknowledging their response. In this way a child may, for example, be able to express immense frustration or anger with no risk of offence. Indeed, she may be acknowledged and encouraged to do so in a way impossible in speech.

> One particular morning whilst on duty with an autistic child her behaviour became very unruly and she was throwing things around and being very abusive. I took her into the music room and for the first five minutes she went from instrument to instrument and I responded with angry gestures on the piano. She eventually laid on the floor and I sang calmly to her.

Negative feelings can change into positive energy when playing music. If we are sensitive in playing with and accompanying a child, his mood can be transformed in a short session.

> That morning Steve wasn't very happy. I tried to introduce different activities to him, but he wasn't interested in anything. Eventually I asked if he would like to play some music and he agreed. Steve was playing rhythmically on the drums. I played the tambourine, careful not to dominate his music. He was smiling throughout the session, doing something that was making him happy. He simply played music.

Use of technology

Various electronic equipment is now available, enabling everybody, regardless of physical disability, to participate in music. MIDIcreator and Soundbeam (www.midicreator.co.uk, www.soundbeam.co.uk), which can be programmed to produce a huge array of sounds, open the world of music to those with even the most limited movement. Imagine, for instance, the empowerment for a child with only a small range of very weak movement but now enabled to explore, compose and perhaps to create huge crashing cymbal sounds, and to use whatever movement is available when stimulated by such rewarding results.

> I set up MIDIcreator and put one of the sensors on the floor under his left hand, which was dangling down from the chair. Every time there was the slightest movement from this hand, musical sounds were made. He enjoyed the change of sounds and seemed quite relaxed. This session went on for at least 45 minutes. Later he was lying on the floor and very deliberately put his hand on a shaker and made it move and rattle. He also swept his hand along the row of chime bars, which he did repeatedly and with a lot of force.

Use of the voice

Singing and talking are only two examples of a larger range of vocal expression: excellent effect can be gained from more unconventional uses. Unpitched sounds like squeaks, grunts, whispers and rasps all have value in musical dialogue.

> John was playing with Duplo and became very excited, making lots of vocal sounds, pulling faces and waving his arms about. I copied the sounds, facial expressions and arm movements, and with great glee he repeated the process. The game continued for about ten minutes and then I changed the sound and he copied me. There was great enjoyment on both sides.

Acknowledging and responding to unconventional vocalisations gives the potential to develop and extend conversations.

Ian was particularly distressed today. Music played quietly and I hummed to accompany it. Ian lay down. I checked his pulse and tapped out his own rhythm on his back. He settled and visibly relaxed; this lasted for about 20 minutes. He sat up, all smiles and very vocal; he made sounds and I gave them back to him. He pulled faces, I pulled faces and he shrieked with laughter.

Group work

Much children's hospice music-making is one-to-one, but there is scope for the integration of several children of differing abilities into a musical activity. By careful allocation of roles and choice of instruments, a child with more limited ability, rarely (if ever) in a position of control, can be given a key part in the music.

> We had a very lively session. A 12-year-old lad with Duchennes Muscular Dystrophy played on the keyboard; a 10-year-old girl with Cornelia de Lange Syndrome played the metallophone, producing a good rhythm to accompany the keyboard; another 10-year-old boy with Hunter disease (profoundly deaf) banged merrily on the drums. Staff accompanied, using djembes and shakers to mirror the tempo and volume. I felt that the children connected through the session, and although they have very different levels of communication they were able to connect through the music.

For a child who normally has little opportunity to integrate with others in an activity, music can provide a unique chance to be part of a team.

> One child, whose condition causes her to flap her arms, enjoyed hitting the ocean drum in time to some other children playing on the karaoke machine. She was almost able to work out a rhythm and I found the workshops we participated in on our York weekend invaluable when thinking of new ways to involve the child in the music-making process. The look of wonder on the child's face when she discovered she could be part of the group was very encouraging. This occasion stands out because the child had not participated in this way before.

Role-play

By working in pairs, with one partner taking on the role of the child, we learn to be sensitive to the mood and pace of a child and to match it. We look at issues such as how best to aid a child in holding an instrument without removing control: finding a way of allowing her to beat for herself, or at least be in control of the impulse to beat. Students can be surprised at the frustration when they are 'being' the child and are physically compromised, leading to an even greater understanding of children's needs.

> I realise now how important it is to give a child time – I use this not just with music, but in the playroom. It was such a valuable lesson to have and something which I pass onto staff in the hospice.

Though we aim to unlock the musician within by means of our short courses, we don't try or pretend to turn our students into music therapists: in fact we are at pains to explain the discipline of music therapy precisely. Qualified state registered postgraduate training develops musical skills particularly in improvisation, and includes modules in psychology, psychotherapy, counselling skills and supportive clinical studies. One of the areas we look at is the difference between creative musical activity (which can be therapeutic) and music therapy. Many children in hospices are able to benefit from music therapy, and we guide carers to recognise those who are in particular need of the therapeutic relationship.

Jessie's Fund has actively encouraged and part-funded the appointment of music therapists in children's hospices because we firmly believe music therapy has a unique and positive impact on children's lives, especially in palliative care. In a children's hospice the therapist may see a child only once, several times in a short space of time, or once every few months. Sessions are often looked upon as self-contained units: the emphasis is on the present rather than on long-term thera-peutic goals more usual in other settings.

There are common benefits of therapy and the everyday musical activity which Jessie's Fund promotes and encourages. Perhaps the most powerful gain is the self-esteem in a child who may never have felt a sense of achievement. In a world where children, including siblings, are learning to swim, ride bicycles, taking part in drama productions, and generally enjoying the things kids do, the life-limited child tends to be totally dependent and rarely, if ever, has access to that glow of pride so important to a sense of self-worth.

> One experience I had was with a seven-year-old girl with a nerve disorder which affects her stability and ability to concentrate. She has no verbal communication. I gave the drum to this girl and she realised that it was loud and that the noise caught people's attention. She could bang it in any way and it always sounded good and loud. I started to copy her on my drum and then she replied. This went on until the whole group was listening to her and copying afterwards. She had the most amazing laugh and her eyes lit up with excitement. She was so pleased that she had achieved some-thing and now remembers her abilities in every drumming session.

Music is a great motivator. Children with extremely limited mobility are frequently stimulated to exceed all expectations: even a child deteriorating with a neuro-degenerative condition is sometimes seen to improve co-ordination skills. The immediate 'cause and effect' of striking or stroking an instrument and the sounds which result can induce effort far beyond that normally seen.

> It is so encouraging to see a child move arms or legs, which are usually stiff, to play an instrument. The concentration is immense and the look of success on their face when they manage to do it makes your day.

Children can be so engrossed and excited in new-found ability that they are greatly energised, despite their lack of strength.

> I was with a very weak 13-year-old with cerebral palsy. I helped him to bang a drum. This was repeated several times using an ascending verbal prompt. The child appeared to be enjoying the whole exercise, but after a 30-minute session seemed to be tiring, so I stopped. However at this point the child still had the drumstick in his hand and he repeated the action by himself (to our amazement). We resumed the exercise: the child was 'belly' laughing. *Wonderful!!!!!*

Many children cannot dress themselves, feed themselves, use the bathroom alone, or readily express their needs and desires. In music they can be given a chance to make choices and control the activity. Just by tuning in to the child's mood, a sensitive carer intuitively knows whether today is a day for energetic music or for gentle flow.

> Being inspired by our music course, I took a 12-year-old girl who suffers from worsening epileptic fits into the music room. I encouraged her to explore the instruments, but she showed little interest. I began to play the keyboard with a steady beat. She showed some interest but didn't approach. After a while she came over and started playing with me, choosing her notes carefully. As she became more involved she began leading the session and would move my hand to match her. We continued to play for some time in unison. For that time I felt very close to her and privileged to have been allowed into her world. I felt I had made a connection with her.

Whilst music can give a child an opportunity to control something of her environment, it can also provide an effective and non-drug-based means of pain relief and anxiety reduction. It can assist in slowing the rate of respiration and pulse, in reducing muscular spasms, and in inducing calm. For children who are already taking a carefully balanced concoction of drugs, any alternative interventions to alleviate distress are to be welcomed.

> We had a girl in who gets very upset and inconsolable. She was rocking furiously and crying out. I turned to her, took hold of her hands and started to rock with her and sing quietly – no words: just 'do do'. She slowed her rocking, stopped crying out and made eye contact. It seemed that she came to realise I was understanding her.

By fully engaging a child in an absorbing activity, music can distract from discomfort and pain, and care team members have found it helps through unpleasant medical procedures or physiotherapy.

> I use the musical instruments with children who are having physio. Using a beat is great and it takes their mind off the physio. It can also be very calming.

Amidst all this talk of the therapeutic benefits of making music, it is also so often a source of simple joy. Everyone enjoys the unique satisfaction of being creative, and this must be all the more intense when creative opportunities are so limited. Whilst music provides a superb outlet for communication and expression of emotions, it can also be pure fun!

> One young boy with cerebral palsy, but with quite good movement, was really enjoying playing loudly on one of our big drums. Every time I hit my drum he would roll on to his side and hit the drum with his arm, laughing in hysterics. He was definitely working hard at it and really trying. Great fun for both of us.

For most parents, looking after their life-limited child is a 24-hour-a-day strain: they have learned specialist skills, and cannot get a babysitter for an evening off. When the child goes to hospice for respite care, parents too are cared for and can relax. For a few days they don't have sole responsibility for dealing with the minutiae of everyday life. It is not unusual for them to become involved in musical activities.

> A child was visiting for a weekend, accompanied by Mum and Dad. I was playing my guitar to the child. Shortly after we had started his parents joined us. Mum took her

son and held him close, Dad sat opposite. I began to play songs that Dad knew on my guitar. For approximately 45 minutes, Dad sang to them and Mum didn't take her eyes off Dad for the whole time. She was really relaxed: this, in turn, transferred to the child, who fell asleep in her arms.

One of the joys of parenthood is pride in our children as we observe them reaching milestones and developing independent little personalities. We revel in their achievements, great and small. Our child may have been diagnosed with a life-limiting and debilitating illness, but the tendency is still to feel that sense of pride, perhaps even more so. Music gives unique scope for achievement, and parents can witness their children enabled rather than disabled.

> One of the greatest experiences I have had is being able to help an 18-year-old girl, Claire, who used to play the piano and sing in a choir before being struck down with Juvenile Battens disease, to rediscover music. What a joy to be able to 'accompany' her when I only have limited ability on the piano myself. To see the concentration and determination on Claire's face, but mostly the smiles as she has found an ability to play again – what a privilege to have been a part of that. To add to this was being able to 'perform' in front of her mum, sister and aunty, then to see the pride and joy on their faces, but also the tears of gratitude.

Healthy siblings, so often silent sufferers with a seriously ill child in the family, can also be given their own special space through music. Being able to show frustration or anger, without the risk of 'rudeness' which is implied in verbal language, can be a valuable release. Music may also provide a rare opportunity of shared activity with their brother or sister.

> I had a music session with Jay, a six-year-old who has cerebral palsy with complex needs and is also registered blind. It was a session with guitar, with plenty of time and no interruptions. I put the guitar across Jay's lap and strummed gently at first and then stronger and louder. Jay seemed uncomfortable with loud noise, so I continued strumming the guitar gently. His body relaxed and he appeared to be listening. Then his little sister appeared, and, although only four years old, picked up on the quietness and asked to play for her brother, which she did, strumming gently on the strings. She was very pleased that she was helping to provide sounds on the guitar which Jay seemed to enjoy. Their mum commented on this when she observed her two children sharing and enjoying an activity.

Families must inevitably face the loss of their child. When the time comes, the hospice offers support, and music can also come into play. Sometimes, just being there for families and allowing them space for expression is enough.

> I was sitting with a family of three generations. The just-bereaved Jamaican musician grandfather was strumming his guitar and singing, joined by the dead child's mother on a drum, and watched by his enraptured three-year-old younger brother. More members of the care team gradually joined us. This formed a beautiful, soulful but praising group who did not want to leave this special moment.

Young people, who may never have experienced a close bereavement, have huge difficulties in processing it. Children's hospices generally have mechanisms to support bereaved siblings, often during residential weekends some months later. Here children can be with peers who have had a similarly devastating experience.

Talking about their feelings does not come easily and is not forced, but they sense containment and safety in expressing themselves with musical instruments. They can even be encouraged to release some of their understandable anger in the days following the death.

> My most memorable music session was with two teenage siblings, aged 14 and 17, who had lost their younger sister a few days before. They had cried and looked pale and washed out. When music was suggested they came along with little enthusiasm and just tapped on a drum on their lap. I stood up and went to the drum kit and began a 'conversation' and looked at them and waited for a reply. Eventually they got up and I provoked an 'argument' on the drums with them. By the end of the session, we were all musically arguing frantically, a lot of anger had been released and the foot pedal on the big drum had snapped. We all looked at each other and smiled. I felt a real connection.

Life in the present

> Many people think that at a children's hospice our only focus is 'treating' a sick child's illness, but we do far more than that. We are concerned with improving the quality of life, however short that may be, and providing direct access to music helps raise self-esteem and dignity, provides a real sense of achievement, and it's fabulous fun!

When Jessie's Fund was established none of the children's hospices had experienced creative music's power: now, more than a decade later, many would say that children's hospices would be unimaginable without music. The value of music therapy is undisputed (Pavlicevic 2005). Enabling non-music specialists to engage through music has proved to be enormously enriching not only for the children, but for the whole community.

> For me this training has been life-changing, and if every student gets a fraction of the inspiration that I have what they take back to children will be invaluable.

10. Healing Writing in Palliative Care

Sheelagh Gallagher, Kate D'Lima, Kaichiro Tamba, Hilary Elfick, with David Head and Gillie Bolton

Writing is a powerful art, yet it needs only pen and paper, no extra space and can be done at home, in bed, in the dayroom, outside even. The first notes or draft of much writing, poetry in particular, is deeply personally expressive. Writers' success depends upon how well they can express experiences and observations from their exterior environment (such as nature), or their interior (memories, dreams, reflections). *The internal critic* often needs to be gently but effectively dispatched as it can be a powerful preventive.

The therapeutic writer is given permission to ignore all rules, or use or adapt as they wish, or as suggested to them. The different branches of literature have systems of rules and forms (sonnet, for example), as does everyday written language (grammar), to ensure effective communication. This writing is usually intended for a tiny audience, often only of one, the writer. Blog writing, which could reach audiences of millions (but is probably only read by a handful), is usually also written in a personal, non-rule-directed form: readers make what they can of it. Strict form such as the sonnet, used when needed, can however be extremely therapeutic (Hamberger in Bolton *et al.* 2006).

Literary published writers often use writing's initial stages to help with self-understanding, 'We write before knowing what to say and how to say it, and in order to find out, if possible' (Lyotard 1992, p.119). These exploratory writings are redrafted and edited. Therapeutic writers also sometimes undertake these later stages towards publication.

Writing to help prepare for death has good precedence: 'Montaigne wrote to heal himself, and those who attend to his Essays, of the pain and fear of dying' (Heitsch 2000, p.105). Sheelagh, Kate, Kaichiro, Hilary, David and I – from very different backgrounds – give very different perspectives.

Paying attention   *Sheelagh Gallagher*

The extraordinary thing about *Ways of Writing*, our creative writing group at the Hospice, is its very ordinariness. My aims and objectives were the same as for any other course, mostly to do with paying attention to language, discovering what we want to say and saying it in the clearest, most direct way.

The patients came the first morning because I was there. Some of them thought *Ways of Writing* would be calligraphy but stayed anyway. What has been different, or rather more intense, is the concentration with which we work, the combination of personal honesty and generosity towards other members of the group, particularly new members. As Barbara said very soon, 'We are sharing more than our stories.'

For the first weeks, maybe months, we used poems, stories, something in the air, to stimulate writing sometimes based on reminiscence but often on exploration of quite abstract ideas. We never ignored, we couldn't, the fact that some were very ill but we didn't confront that head on until we were preparing to write about choices one morning. The group was small and there was very definitely something in the air. Marion wrote about the choices she might have to make about treatment and how responsible she felt for the effect they would have on her family. After that there was a subtle change. We still focused our attention on writing, on the power of language, but there was much more discussion on the practicalities and implications of living with illness and the language used to make sense of that.

Poetry has been an extraordinarily powerful tool. When Liz asked me to read her poem out loud, I broke my own rule of always 'frisking' writing first to make sure I know what I'm dealing with. I felt a kind of panic as my eye ran ahead of my voice and saw 'We come here to die.' I'd forgotten for a moment what poetry can do. Two lines later I was confronted and calmed by the line: 'No, we come to learn not to panic.' 'Gotcha', she seemed to be saying, and something else too about how the experience of illness is as complex and full of paradox as any other.

Which brings me to something extraordinary. Of all the people in the room, I know the least about what is going on. In itself that's not so new for me. It's just that here it is clear to everyone. The staff know about treatment; the patients know about illness. And what do I know that's useful? I think I know about paying attention. If I'm offering anything it's something to do with waiting as the writers – and they really are writers, not students, or an audience – dig deeper, go further, come closer.

And there's more that's extraordinary. None of them ever said they wanted to write for other people. But they have, starting with stories and poems for their families. Marion's husband brought us a poem written in hospital just before she died, telling him without ever saying it directly, how much she loved him. Arthur wrote letters to his wife from various stages in their lives together, saying what he had never before put into words. And then something else happened. We read to each other: we read to visitors and then there we were reading to complete strangers in a library. Well, I wasn't. The members of our little group were now part of a larger, nationwide project, seeing their work published with great fanfare and celebrations to which I was invited, rather like a parent to an open evening, as I said at the time to hide the overwhelming emotion I felt.

So, was that it? Sweetness and light and a publishing deal for everyone. Better than that. At various times we have been asked, we have asked ourselves, what exactly we are up to and the answers have been as various and changeable as anywhere else. When Arthur said to his wife as they showed his folder to a visitor, 'You didn't know I was a writer, did you?', he was simply telling it how it was. Barbara characterised it as like the inhabitants of individual desert islands swimming out to visit other people's islands. Lol said it wasn't his cup of tea. He knew what I was getting at though; if we talked about gardens it was really like talking about life. Result! Mary has written witty, reflective, often hilarious, snippets about life as part of the Hospice Gang and always takes it upon herself to welcome visitors and new members, assuring them that we are noisy but harmless. Of her very first session she wrote that she felt 'as though I had achieved something most valuable to hold on to, in the couple of hours we had spent together' and, more recently, 'As my work says, giving up is not part of my life strategy.'

I think I'll leave the almost last word about the extraordinary ordinariness of what we do to Sue, who resisted joining us for so long. After all, she knew about writing. What she hadn't realised, but champions so eloquently now, was how we teach ourselves and each other, how we go on growing and developing.

> For one member of the group the complete experience of belonging has brought a whole new focus to her life... It has enabled her to confront her difficulties in a constructive way. Writing is often a solitary experience and being able to work in a group with discussion and shared points of view has added to the pleasure.

Just like any writing group really.

And now for something completely different...

Four years on from the beginning, I read them some poems from Julia Darling's *Sudden Collapses in Public Places* (2003) last week. They liked, no, we *loved*, the metaphors that tell it like it is – like her body as a house. 'You don't have to explain it' says John with sudden explosive insight. 'When she says she's had to leave her house to all the people working on it and go and live in the extension round the back, that's how you feel.' Then, wistfully, 'I like poetry to rhyme though.'

'Well', I said 'there is one but it's difficult. It's called "Chemotherapy"'. I read it. Tough stuff – for me. Difficult – as the group was quick to point out – for me to read out loud to them about baldness and the misery of it all. Too right it was. The poem wasn't as difficult for me as the reality for them. An example if ever there was one of the great truths: 'Poetry speaks for you as well as to you.' 'Now that', said John, 'is what I call poetry'.

So that's what makes it all worthwhile. It's not always comfortable for me but it's always satisfying and stimulating. I haven't always tried to make contact with people who would never volunteer to come to the group. A couple of years ago I had to start coming in earlier and earlier so that Lol could explain to me why writing wasn't his cup of tea, that he had nothing against me personally, and that he would be willing, before I went off to do the fancy stuff, to tell me his life story, and that of the trade union movement and how actions speak louder than words. I would accept his decision bravely, silently cheering him on.

I listen, I talk. Sometimes I write the stories people tell me. Now that is really relaxing. A way of paying attention, being together.

The shared poem   *Kate D'Lima*

Teaching creative writing in a hospice day centre was at first a daunting prospect. I began by feeling nervous about choosing the wrong subjects to write about but discovered in the first week that one woman had chosen to write a poem to her cancer. I was also surprised by the speed at which participants took ownership of the group and introduced a regular writing feature called 'The Shared Poem', where each group member wrote between two and four lines each and passed it to the next person. Far from being disjointed, these poems had a unity that reflected the cohesive nature of the group.

These workshops were part of a research project with participants interviewed at the end of the ten-week writing courses. The day centre was one of four groups including mental health, drug and alcohol and health practitioners and educators. It was funded by a research bursary from the Arts and Humanities Research Board and the Arts Council of Wales and supervised by the University of Wales, Swansea, as part of my PhD on creative writing and health.

Courses were taught as an art form rather than a therapy, since I am a writer and creative writing tutor. All groups met in their respective health settings and I worked alongside a staff member to ensure adequate support, and the continuation of writing groups after I left. The day centre nurse acted as co-facilitator in the hospice and we all undertook the writing exercises during the two-hour sessions. In the last five weeks of the course, a gradual handover took place so that the group felt confident to continue without me. Additionally, a set of ten lesson plans, writing exercises and course handouts were given to co-facilitators so that the course could be replicated with other groups.

I began with mixed feelings about an Ethics Committee member's concern about emotions produced by creative writing in palliative care. Although a sensitive approach is necessary in any health setting, this view seemed overly paternalistic: we are all emotional beings, especially during illness, and should be allowed to make an informed choice regarding creative pursuits. On the other hand, unburdening the mind of thoughts and memories onto paper can unleash attendant emotions.

In my experience as creative writing tutor to many groups, people usually 'self-limit' and will not read a revealing or emotional piece of work aloud unless they feel confident in themselves and supported within the group. However, it is occasionally possible to be taken by surprise when a piece of writing leads down unexpected paths. Because the course I designed included spontaneous writing exercises to illustrate writing techniques, I began cautiously and made the risk explicit to group members.

As with all groups, ground rules concerning confidentiality, appraisal techniques, ownership of written work and voluntary participation were stressed in the first meeting. Participants were free to withdraw at any point without giving a reason and could choose whether or not to read any piece of writing aloud. During this first session, I also introduced confidence-building exercises such as shared writing activities and we generally got to know each other better.

One very shy member of the group had been writing secretly for a while and had the courage to read one of her poems to us. Another woman read an angry poem that she had written to her cancer. By the third session participants felt confident to laugh or cry within a supportive and trusting environment and, as with all the best writing groups, there was no unmentionable subject. The group was never required to write about illness, but they often chose to. Laughter was the dominant sound, even if the humour was sometimes dark.

The shared poem came about at the suggestion of one participant to write a poem about whatever subject we had been discussing most during our frequent wanderings off task. These poems, later typed and pinned up on the ward, had surprising unity and many group members felt there was a shared consciousness at work amongst us. One poem, written close to Christmas, featured a robin that came to ask for food at the window, and, in one of those rare, magical moments, a real robin came and perched on the windowsill.

The group began with six members but illness meant that only three could be interviewed at the end. The dominant experiences that emerged were, in order of prevalence: increased self-confidence; trust and empathy with others; the unburdening of emotions through self-expression; and a sense of well-being associated with stress relief that accompanied the writing. One participant spoke of using creative writing to control anger and anxiety, which also helped control pain. The day centre nurse was impressed by the confidence, closeness and sheer enjoyment that resulted and she intends to continue the writing group.

These experiences were also in other health groups but one theme was particular to the palliative care group: who we write for. People felt that they wrote first for themselves but in editing their work later they would consider other members of the writing group. In the shared poems, however, they wrote for people on the ward and those who might succeed them. These poems were generally positive and reached out beyond personal experience, as illustrated by the two poems below, each written by four members of the group.

Autumn
At this time of year the gossamer threads
travel on the breeze, over the fields.
I move in time free to express myself,
I build my beautiful web with exact precision.

I watched that big hanging butterfly
at this time of year.
Beautiful red wings and slender body.
As I approached that big beauty
it fell to the ground,
leaving me over surprised;
that big beauty was last year's green life.

As the leaves on the trees
turn from green to the bright golden browns,
some dotted with red, their beauty almost heart stopping,
then all too soon they fall to the ground
to make way for new life.
The night-time comes earlier;
there's a nip in the air;
as families draw closer
at this time of year.

Memories
Memories come back like shooting stars
from the blackness, quick tiny lights.
Momentarily numb, my troubled brain
transforms them into a state of heightened awareness.

Calling me in tone, singing name,
or harsh it is. A sign of love or anger
that goes along until
silence falls and his sound fainted.
It was a flash to remember
my name again, in a singing voice.

As our thoughts evolve, a moment of panic,
for those precious memories belong to a past,
a past that has slipped from our grasp
only to be recalled, then fade in oblivion
until that memory will return, once more.

Care mind in 31 syllables   *Kaichiro Tamba*

Word is double-edged sword.
Some expressions make people happy and some make sad.

People who are in difficult situations such as the end of life due to advanced malig-
nancy do not seem to be happy with logical sentences such as these. 'Abdominal
CT shows thousands of small metastases in your whole liver; these findings predict
the rest of your life is about several months.' 'You may eat if the doctor inserts a
metal stent into your oesophagus, though the procedure has 30 per cent risk of
perforation with serious pain.'

Such people might be healed with illogical lines of words: verse. They may get
more relief if the verse is more personalised. I tried to make 'ultimately' personalised verse which contains their names. The verses shown here have the style of
Japanese traditional poems: *tanka*. Some readers may remember the rather famous
and rather newer style of Japanese traditional poems: *haiku*. Haiku, although of
Japanese origin, has also been used in other languages. It has three lines, usually
containing 5, 7 and 5 unrhymed syllables. Tanka is a longer verse form containing
5, 7, 5, 7 and 7 unrhymed syllables. Names of a patient and his family are not
revealed here, to respect their privacy. The fourth poem, which includes the name
of the town, is an illustration of the idea.

A 55-year-old man was admitted to the hospital for a close examination of metastatic bone tumour with unknown primary. He owned a big pig farm, and loved the creatures very much. I gave him an ice-breaker poem.

YOTSUASHITO
IEBA TOKANAI,
KABA, TANUKI
DAKEDO TENKEI
ICHIBANWA BUTA

Let's cite names of four-footed animals!
Reindeer, hippopotamus, raccoon dog…
But you know what?
The number one God's gift is SWINE!

四つ足と言えば
トナカイ・カバ・タヌキ
だけど天恵一番は豚

His hospitalised life was boring and brought him no information about the primary tumour, but a new lymph node swelling of mediastinum.

After his vertebral metastases worsened, he could not come to my clinic and a home doctor visited his house every two weeks. He loved not only swine but also jazz. We exchanged CDs and he gave me Keith Jarrett's. When I went to Kobe to attend a congress, I sent him another poem.

TEPPANNO
MUKOUNO KABENI
IKABATAA
KISHITUSHITEKIKU
Keith Jarrett

When I came into a Japanese pizza restaurant,
I found your name-like menu on the wall.
'Calamari sautéed with butter'
Then I returned to my room and
listened to Keith Jarrett.

A year later, he was admitted to our hospital because of paraplegia and urinary retention due to the invasion and destruction of lumber spine by malignant cells. He not only owned a pig farm, but cultivated rice. He told me how delicious his rice was. Though I wanted to see him harvesting rice on his field after pain relief, it was already over. He had a gentle family who were devoted to his care. Since it is impossible for me to put all the names of his family in a short poem, I made the third one with his name and those of his most important family member, in other words, his wife.

INAHOTARE
KAKI MINORIYUKU
SATONO AKI
ASUO SHINJITE
SUKINA Jazz KIKU

Rice ears are bending
Persimmons are flushing
The autumn in country is coming
Tomorrow which you are hoping
Sound of Jazz is whispering

Several weeks after discharge, I received a parcel from his wife. There were rice and persimmons in it. The taste of the rice was really delicious, as he had told me. Though the fruit was not completely ripe, the slightly sweet taste of it was sublime to me.

His home-care doctor sent me an email about his serious condition. He had been to the dining-room in a wheelchair for meals with his family every time even though he could eat just a little.

I felt the time he would be drawn up to heaven was coming, and sent the final letter with gratitude. In the letter, I added one more poem which contained the name of the town where he had been living and loving. The name of the town is underlined.

FUROUFUSHINIWA
JAZZGA ICHIBAN
OKOMEMO BUTAMO
KAMINO IKI

Jazz is your elixir of life.
Rice and swine equal to your life
They are works of God supported by your wife.

At his funeral, his daughter told me that the letter arrived just in time before his loss of consciousness. She cried, filled with sorrow, but she was pleased with the last letter.

Four years have passed since I began to make personalised poems for palliative care. I have a 15-year history of making Japanese traditional fixed form verse, haiku and tanka. At first, I made one for a patient and his wife: I could not stop the urge to write a special poem for their china wedding anniversary. Later I realised that making poems for palliative care is not only for patients and their families but also for myself. If the poem had a smell of literature, I would feel healing power on it. I know such sense of smell is derived from my self-satisfaction, though. Do you think it is selfish?

To make double-meaning syllables in poems, I used two techniques: puns and acrostics. Since Japanese has four styles of character and is phonetically simple, we have a small advantage in making poem with puns. However, it is not so difficult to create such poems even in English, if you use acrostics. Each poem shown here has a different role: ice-breaker, say 'forget-you-not', a tribute to him and his wife, applause for his life and his town. Developing such poems is similar to solving a crossword puzzle. Down clues are the individual's names. Across clues are key words from his or her life, job, family, etc.

Many families give me letters, picture postcards they have drawn, or even tanka they have written. I feel those replies have a great power of healing.

Won't you try to make such poetry?

Staying with dying   *Hilary Elfick, with David Head*

In the mid-1990s a series of workshops about poetry and death was run at The Princess Alice Hospice in Esher, Surrey. It was part of an 'Arts and Death' course for staff volunteers and supporters. I led the sessions at the invitation of our newish chaplain, David Head. I am a poet, a broadcaster, and had been a trustee of The Princess Alice for 20 years.

I taught that in poetry about any subject you may record your feelings; you try to do so in a way others will want to read. It is important to avoid getting sucked in to the demands of rhyme and rhythm that you remember from early childhood, contorting the things you want to say into a box which doesn't fit, so often producing doggerel which does not rise to the size and weight of the experience. Instead you try to tell your own personal truth in ways that haven't been used before, ways you yourself may not have tried before, perhaps in words which are very much your own. You trust your experience to be unique.

What makes something poetry is whether it has a life of its own or not; whether it speaks effectively to someone who doesn't know the poet. It helps, of course, if you read contemporary poems. These don't just record experiences we can recognise; carefully chosen, they can give us ideas about how to say what we want to say in new ways that others will appreciate and respect. So an early session was spent looking at such material on the subject of death, dying and bereavement. Among these poems were *Eden Rock* (Causley 1988), *Interrogation* (Mackay Brown 1989) *Spring and Fall* (Manley Hopkins 1956), *The Father* (Olds 1992), *What If This Road* (Pugh 1997).

Poetry can be therapeutic when we read or hear it, and we do have poetry readings in our day hospice, as well as poems displayed about the building. It was for some a completely new experience to discover that contemporary poetry can speak so effectively of familiar things, especially the kinds of things we find hard to express.

Poetry can certainly be as, if not more, therapeutic in the writing. Sometimes we cannot lightly say what we feel, but we may be able to write it. This was certainly my own experience when I began.

By the beginning of the second session, those on the course felt not only that they could indeed 'tell it how it is', but that there were various ways in which they could structure and control it. And we discovered that worrying whether what we write is poetry becomes irrelevant when what we've written takes on a life of its own; once it does that, it automatically becomes a poem.

That truth emerged as we continued with a series of workshops for anyone wanting to try their own hand. I explained that the poet's task is to get under the skin of experience, tackling writing in the context of strong emotion.

We did exercises where people learnt to show, tell, allow others to see for themselves, not spelling out and explaining every detail but letting the rest of the group participate by feeling their way into what the writer had said. They discovered that the others picked up quite quickly the emotion behind the experience; this gave them the confidence to trust that their words were effective without being overstated.

A few became so interested that they asked for further training in the use of a variety of skills – how to use sounds which supported the feel of the emotion, and forms which feel right for the story we want to tell. The earliest English poetry rested effectively on echoes which might appear anywhere in a line, and which depended on repetition of consonants – dragon*fl*ies' *fl*ame – or vowels – the pl*ai*nest of J*a*nes – or even both – my *la*zy *la*dy (skills used constantly in English speech – if sticks and stones…).

There is – and must be – much music in contemporary poetry, but it is a subtler thing than cat-mat rhyming, and so much better suited both to the English language and to the complexity of emotion recorded at times of stress.

Then there's form. The group found that having no discernible form at all can lead to dissatisfaction. But it can be much more subtle than a hymn tune, and when it is, and feels, right, it supports the content of the poem. Broken feelings: broken lines in jerky sound. Pain which goes round in circles: lines or words which repeat throughout the poem, producing sad music. A sense of finish or completeness: a shape on the page which appears ordered, with regular rhythms, or a couple of end-rhymes in the last part of a poem.

This was really how David Head and I began to work more closely together. He became a student at first, but it was not long before we exchanged new poems. He had daily contact with all our patients, including those at home, and began to write what he observed, telling it how it is, avoiding wrapping up tough things in caressing language.

We also explored the limits to writing in the hospice context: the Data Protection Act (the subject of one of his poems), the sensibilities of family members, and the importance of being truthful about our own responses and vulnerabilities.

> *Not for crushing*
> Your flicked-up specs echoed the
> curved wings of the Volvo you idolised.
> The Simon Templar sort,
> zippy, sassy, cool, antique.
>
> I got myself lost in sentences
> tortuous and signpost-less as wartime Norfolk lanes
> trying to explain that it would be
> unprofessional
> if I let you give your car to me.
>
> It sat in the yard of the charity you finally gave it to,
> undrivable, rusting, slumped on its chassis.
> I passed it on my way to work and
> every other day, till you died, I leaned forward to your good ear
> with my hand on the bed-frame
> and said it had beautiful lines.
>
> (David Head)

We put together a poetry collection relating to death, dying and bereavement (Elfick and Head 2004), continuing to collaborate, using each other as bouncing boards for new writing. This does not mean our writing began to mirror each other's; as we progress, our distinct ways of seeing and expressing experience have been enhanced.

If you feel like writing, what I suggest is that you don't worry about rhyme or classic metres. Make sure that your words are true and the sounds do what you want. Let the shape support the message. Tell the story. If you find yourself a good writing partner it will help; you will hear more clearly whether what you are saying is being responded to and understood, as you share poems with each other.

'Writing is a way of saying things I can't say': A qualitative pilot research study   *Gillie Bolton*

My research into therapeutic writing with palliative care and cancer patients (www.gilliebolton.com) began a unique process of enquiring towards the 'heart' of therapeutic writing and its value to patients, who made such comments as: 'I have been able to reach that depth'; 'it became quite purgatorial, therapeutic'. Staff commented that:

> For some it was a pleasant hour but for others it went much deeper. Some found a new talent for story writing, which gave them creative release and improved their self-confidence and esteem. Others discovered the value of diary writing and continued to express their feelings in writing long after the sessions. Others used the time to really tackle some of the harder issues they were facing.

The pilot study began to demonstrate the value of writing to very sick people: the ways it can enable them to understand themselves better; think through issues, memories, feelings and thoughts more clearly and appropriately; accommodate to what is happening to them better; and communicate more effectively with significant others. The focus was on writing processes, rather than creation of finished products.

A research finding was that explorative and expressive writing:

1. enabled patients to explore and begin to discover some of the causes of their anxiety

2. supported them to express and communicate some of these issues, as well as some which they knew about beforehand but found difficult to express and share

3. involved people in a satisfying creative process, taking their mind off present problems, anxiety, and pain, giving a sense of achievement and authority in a valued sphere.

Funded by The Arts Council of England, the research was undertaken at King's College London University, Medicine and the Arts (English Department), and University College London Hospital. Direct patient statements are in quotation marks; interview transcripts and personal written essays by patients and staff are also incorporated.

Experiential expression and exploration

People often don't know what they are troubled by. Some are aware they are unsettled or anxious; others experience physical symptoms. Our minds have a way of storing our most troubling or distressing memories or thoughts inaccessibly, so as not to hinder everyday living. But the material does not go away, causing such problems as sleeplessness, headaches, worsened symptoms, background unexplained anxiety. 'Give sorrow words. The grief that does not speak / Whispers the o'erfraught heart and bids it break' (Shakespeare, *Macbeth*, Act IV, Sc iii). Some people are aware of their troubles, but cannot express them helpfully. The bigger the problem, the more the difficulty in communication, and the more it needs expressing, often repetitively. Friends and relatives can only take so much, and psychotherapeutic time is limited and costly.

Psychotherapy and psychoanalysis give sorrow words as helpfully as possible, and with as little damage to the individual as possible. No one doubts the beneficial effects of the *talking cure*. The *writing cure* can be an adjunct to psychotherapy

(Bolton *et al.* 2004), or used as a relatively cheap and straightforward artistic form of expression and exploration (Bolton *et al.* 2006). As a private, silent form, writing is particularly useful for people who cannot bring themselves to vocalise their troubles, or to communicate directly with another.

What characterises therapeutic writing? How is it different? A particular quality is that it is personal and 'not really for anyone else other than yourself', as one patient put it. Explorative personal writing like this needs to be tentative: 'If it's written only for the self, then it can be un-said', said in different ways, or it can be deleted and the opposite tried instead. Its impermanence is an essential element: process work, not writing for a finished product.

An expression of the otherwise inexpressible seems to be enabled. The quietness of writing, and there being no immediate listener unlike to speech, seems to make it conducive. 'Writing is a way of saying things I can't say. I do it when I'm on my own, and as a way of coping with being down. I know I mustn't give in to being down and give in to the cancer, and writing helps.'

Personal material can be dumped: 'words on a page are one of the dustbin men.' It is generally spontaneous and written 'in a fairly haphazard, unstructured kind of way'. 'I write without pre-censoring what I will say', with 'recklessness, in a moment of madness'.

These very sick, dying or bereaved people said they had a 'mass of jumbled thoughts and feelings'. Writing in this way can help to 'put it in some sort of order'. It gets these 'things which swirl around my head' 'outside' where 'it will be easier to deal with', 'instead of just keeping them like bottled up'.

Many people felt the process 'unburdened' them. One patient said it 'took me some way towards purging it and integrating it into my life'; another: 'once it's outside its easier to deal with'. And 'I do find it easier to talk about it now'. And the very creative process made for pride and enhanced self-respect and confidence: 'I'm proud and stimulated by some of the things I've written'; 'It's something I have done myself. No-one can correct me. It's mine. It doesn't matter if it's right or wrong.' I quote from my notes:

> C said he used the writing to help him to regain a hold on reality. He felt he'd lost the plot in his life, was identifying too closely and muddlingly with other people he knew with cancer. He found it very useful when I suggested that the illness has made him lose the plot of his life, by disrupting it so thoroughly. I suggested he's writing to 'heal his story' (Brody 2003). He found this metaphor very useful.

Another patient wrote:

> Now having been stretched mentally to the outer limits, I've realised because of my terminal position, how we worry, too much, about the future… We can only live, and should become more aware of, the moment, now! That doesn't mean reckless and irresponsible behaviour. It means consider the value and quality of whatever you're doing now.

Fiction or autobiography

Many writers seek to make some sort of sense of their lives. C wrote about the death of his mother, comparing it with his own experience of cancer, and trying to work out the significance of her dying of the same disease while he was so very ill himself.

Some write fiction, such as Master S. Here is the final section of a story about a five-year-old protagonist:

> The other children that he had made friends with on the ward were very friendly and talkative. They knew each other for about a year now, and they were ready to do anything for each other because they had gone through so much together, experienced so many pains together.
>
> The next day the organisers introduced a singer who brings the children some presents. He sings pop music, and he's been on *Top of the Pops*. His songs have been number one. He also does many charity events, concerts, and he loves children. With him he brings copies of his albums with diskmans – one for everyone. And autographed pictures, and photographs and things like that. All the children are really excited when he sings live for them.
>
> He has heard about Ben's sleeping problem and he tells him that everything will be ok. He tells him to listen to his music and that'll help him sleep. He tells him to just think of ideas at night for stories – could be anything – adventure, fantasy, horror – like the story they heard read at night. And he tells him that the ones he wants to remember maybe he can write them in his diary or something the next day. He suggests Ben might write a diary about what's been happening.
>
> Ben is amazed at what the superstar is telling him and he is surprised at how much the guy knows about him and his life.
>
> In the common room after hearing the story all the children and the nurses say goodnight to each other with hugs and kisses and retire to their beds.
>
> As Ben wasn't sleepy he reflected back on the words of the superstar. And he decided to write a diary.
>
> First he wrote about his parents and his family being there for him all the time. He dedicated a number of pages to his kittens for being there no matter what happened, even when he was in trouble.
>
> He wrote about all of his friends, his superstar, all that had happened on the first day. He wrote about the nurses taking care of him well, activities taking place, and what he planned to do ahead.
>
> He writes a couple of lines about the surroundings and the countryside.
>
> He thinks he can cope with it now, and people have comforted him and told him of techniques he can use.
>
> He came back to the present and dreaded the moments when his parents would leave him.
>
> He lifted up his diskman, put the headphones in his ears and slowly closed his eyes.

I quote from my notes:

> Another patient was an extremely polite, serious, charming 14-year-old, whose school work was nearly always scientific. Yet this long story was written on several occasions. His little protagonist is very young, yet he bravely tackles his fear and isolation in the story situation (one similar to the writer's cancer ward). And he is helped by an

authority figure – a pop star. He used his little character's struggles and life successes to say things to himself. A five-year-old can be frightened, and accept such help. Master S can accept it on the five-year-old character's behalf.

Master S was always very definite about his stories. I made an error once in typing because I couldn't read the writing. He very politely told me he must have said it wrong before, but what he *meant* was… He then repeated exactly what he'd written the week before. Yet despite this clarity and certainty, he often used the provisional tense – maybe the character did certain things. Does he live his life in maybe? The pop star is the wise person who knows Ben inside, and can offer wise advice. The pop star knowing about Ben's sleeping problem came quite out of the blue; the story shifted emphasis and importance from then.

This young fiction writer was using his story to hear the strong, wise *authority* figure in his own head: the pop star is his own wise strong self.

These palliative and cancer patients spoke of therapeutic writing as beneficial for exploration and expression of personal thoughts feelings and experiences. Such areas can be difficult to access and painful to communicate; therapeutic writing seemed to ease both. The patients found useful: 1. the processes of writing, and 2. talking about their writing to me, the writing therapist researcher, and to others such as relatives and clinical staff. Engaging in writing similar to the initial stages of literary writing, as well as talking about their writing, provided essential reflection at that most significant stage of their lives.

11. Creating *The Tuesday Group*: A Palliative Care Play

Bobbie Farsides and Sue Eckstein

It is now five years since *The Tuesday Group* was performed on a stormy winter's night in central London. The auditorium was filled to capacity with people of all ages and we had an irresistible urge to stop people on the way in and say, 'why have you come?' The actors were well known but the playwright was not. The theme did not promise an evening of light entertainment. Yet people came and thereby reinforced our view that they wanted to hear what our dying friends had to say to them.

They were many tears shed but also much laughter and as the evening ended, with Ewan McColl's voice drifting over our heads. We felt that, although the project had taken us on a very difficult journey both technically and emotionally, we had given voice and new life to the special but also very ordinary people whose conversations had filled a hospice dayroom many years before.

Bobbie Farsides

I still remember sitting in the shade in my garden in Brighton working my way through the big pile of neatly organised papers. They had arrived the day before in a carefully sealed cardboard box which I opened with a great sense of anticipation. I had been working for some time with my colleague Barbara Monroe on a project looking at communication within European palliative care. A truly interdisciplinary project involving colleagues from nursing, medicine, social work and academia, it was also an international project: we constantly learned from each other, finding points of interesting similarity and difference. We both knew there was an element missing from our work. Certain voices could not be heard and we were now trying to address that omission. Our interest at this stage was purely academic – how could we incorporate within our research the voices of service users? How could we ensure that we gave a good account of the patient perspective on communication in a palliative care setting?

Then Barbara remembered the box: a carefully stored record of hospice patient support group discussions over many years. My job on that sunny afternoon was to see if the box contained data useable for some form of qualitative analysis. It was our last chance because project time was running out. It did not take me long to realise the transcripts were not going to serve the purpose we had hoped. The notes varied depending upon who had written them: some full and reflective accounts of meetings, others sketchy lists. I wondered whether I should put the papers back in the box, but I simply could not do that. By the end of the afternoon, I had followed the group over a period of approximately five years. To say 'the group' is probably misleading; it was of course in the nature of this group that its membership was changing regularly. I had come to know particular characters and had coped with their disappearance from the text, had mere glimpses of personalities whose illness took them away far too quickly, and had 'heard' the thoughts of people long since dead. I had, in some way, learned a great deal.

Over the following weeks, my mind returned to the notes time and again. I had told Barbara of their failings as data but had not yet admitted that I was having a problem with the idea of handing them back unused. I felt very privileged to have been given access, and felt bound by a duty of confidentiality not to chat casually about them, even with informed and sympathetic colleagues. It became clear that it would be wrong to return the notes to a hospice cupboard, but I knew that I would need to be more creative.

It would be wrong to say that my work excludes the possibility of creativity but certainly, as someone with a grounding in philosophy and pretensions towards social science, the opportunities to operate 'outside the box' are not plentiful. Happily, however, I have always been drawn to friends and colleagues who nurture and exercise their creative instincts alongside their professional careers: published poets, accomplished pianists, playwrights and novelists. Maybe that was where I needed to look for a way to bring the notes to life. This is not to say that I had lost the sense of contributing to my larger academic project; indeed it could be seen as an opportunity to enhance that project by embracing novel approaches.

I decided to speak to my colleague Sue Eckstein who had just begun to allow herself the time to develop her love of creative writing. This was a shameless act on my part. I knew Sue well enough to know how to pitch my idea such that it would appear feasible, attractive and, indeed, an offer she could not refuse. I crept up on her with tales of my disappointment in the notes. I tantalised her with the promise of stories from the end of life and reminiscences of lives lived.

'What about a play?' Sue said.

'A play?' I asked, with feigned hesitancy. 'Mmm, an interesting idea, but wouldn't it be a rather big job?'

'No!' said Sue. 'It would only take a couple of weeks if you've got all the raw material.'

At this point, friendship responsibilities intervened. I had hooked her, but had to explain the need to ensure the play was factually accurate, true to life and grounded in an account of the group that emerged from the notes. It might take a bit more than two weeks 'but it'll be fun, Sue. You'll love it. We'll work together'.

I have since wondered if it was this final assurance that most filled Sue with dread. How do people work together to turn a box full of stories into a play with a message with resonance for a number of different audiences? A play that was to be a part, indeed a product, of an academic enterprise, yet at the same time a play that would speak to people facing death and bereavement or caring for those who would attend just such a group.

Sue's appetite having been whetted, we arranged to visit Barbara at the hospice to see what would be required before Sue could have access to the box. Barbara invited her colleague Isobel Bremner, and she agreed to ask the social work team for their blessing. Although participants in the groups had agreed that notes should be taken and used for education or research, this was not a use we felt could have been anticipated and therefore we felt it particularly important that the team was happy. Whilst at the hospice, we took the opportunity to visit the room where the meetings were held and sat for a while, no doubt in the same chairs that had been there for years. For Sue, the notes were still only a promise of inspiration and dramatic material. For me, I visualised some of the participants to whom I had attached some physical characteristics. I heard the gentle chatter and the occasional cry or sob. I liked the sense of being in a room where important work had been done.

On leaving the room, we passed a woman in the corridor with a small boy, and a bundle of things in her arms. Having spent a lot of time with palliative care colleagues, I immediately assumed that this little boy was going to work on a memory box. The afternoon would probably pass in gentle conversation as the social worker helped him create a decorated receptacle within which to collect and store memories of someone he was about to lose. With this in mind, the paraphernalia of sticking and cutting and the, as yet, plain square box took on a whole new meaning. Having children of the same age myself, the poignancy of his bright little face combined with what I assumed to be his planned activity for the afternoon was very powerful. I could still describe him to you.

In a sense, the way he made me feel made me even keener to pursue this project. Not everyone has someone so special to remember them and however good a memory box it would not capture for that child the thoughts, hopes and fears his parent or grandparent might have shared with fellow patients. By writing this play, we might be able to give some people access to the thoughts of their loved ones and in doing so help them to keep the sense of who they were alive. But this play was not going to be written for any one little boy or any particular bereaved husband. Our characters would need to speak on behalf of many individuals and our audience would need to respond to what they said, even if they did not recognise the particular person they had lost. It sounds pretentious, and probably wrong-headed, to say that we would aim at the universal. Maybe what we needed to do was find the universal in the particular.

A week later Barbara called to say that the hospice liked the idea of a play and what is more they wanted to see if there was any way of getting it performed in public as part of their mission to inform and engage the people of London with their work. We were ready to go.

Sue Eckstein

It was only when Bobbie said we would work together that I felt I could possibly agree to become involved. I had had no professional or personal experience of the world of palliative care and the very intimate space occupied by the dying. I felt that, with the blessing of the hospice and Bobbie's involvement, the endeavour would be not only possible but one with which I could not easily refuse to become involved.

I still smile ruefully when I remember with what misguided confidence I guesstimated that the play would be ready by the end of the month. In my defence, I had imagined the notes comprised of dialogue and stories, and that my role would be merely to craft them into a dramatic form. By the time I realised that this was not the case I was too hooked to retract.

Once the notes had been anonymised by the hospice, I read them from beginning to end. Then again much more slowly, noting the themes and preoccupations that recurred over time. These included the 'big themes' of death, the afterlife, pain, desolation and anger but also the more mundane such as shopping tips, the quality of wigs, the insensitivity of husbands or fussing of wives: clichéd but apparent. I then set about creating characters who could embody and bring alive these themes. They had to be types but not caricatures, 'everyman' and 'everywoman' but also individuals and they also had to be true to the characteristic make up of a group at this hospice. I created a life outside the group for each of them and gradually found myself with a new group of friends. A group of friends I knew I was going to lose; nothing I could do would save them.

The hospice catchment area has a well-established black community, so I created George, 73, a Jamaican who came over to Britain on the SS Windrush in 1948 and has lived here ever since, and Josie, a 34-year-old woman of West African origin bringing up her young daughter alone.

I wanted to show that many people living with terminal illness have a dual role: patient and carer; so I created Margaret, a housewife and mother all her life, in her late seventies and married to Jack, also ill with cancer. She has decided not to burden her husband with the knowledge of her cancer.

Then I wanted two women in their forties who would be typical of the sorts of people who might be attracted to a group of this kind: Mary, a paediatric nurse, lives with her husband and 15-year-old son. Rachel, an illustrator, whose husband is a documentary producer, has three young children.

In contrast I needed a character who would be profoundly uncomfortable in a discussion group such as this: Catherine, 60, is single and has no children. She is a retired teacher with no close family or friends to support her.

For many people, terminal illness is just one of many difficult and painful things going on in their lives: 66-year-old Vi had been a school cook before stopping work to look after her husband who had Alzheimer's and who has recently died. Her very difficult daughter and four grandchildren under eight have moved into her one-bedroom flat.

And then Dan is in his early twenties. He is a film and music enthusiast who lives at home with his parents and his pet rat, Nicole.

I decided to structure the play in five acts to follow the group over a series of meetings, admittedly with the Woman's Hour drama slot in mind – but early feedback was that they had 'done cancer'. The play needed to reflect that not everybody would make all five meetings, that some would resist sharing, some would attempt to disrupt, others would take time to make the most of their attendance and see the group as a refuge from their everyday lives:

JOSIE:	Look, if I'd wanted to bleeding well get all miserable, I could've stopped at home and listened to sodding Classic FM. Saved the bloody bus fare.
GEORGE:	No one's getting miserable, Josie love. I tell you, I can look at a grave stone now and it feels like I'm going home.
JOSIE:	Yeah, right!
GEORGE:	OK, given a choice, I'd rather go home to lie on a beach in Jamaica than lie in a hole in the ground off the A22 but seeing as Him up there's not asking me to state a preference, I'll have to settle for the hole in the ground and not complain. Compared to the years I spent driving the number 38 bus and the endless council committee meetings I've sat through, dying seems like a great adventure, Josie girl. You have to go sometime. Now seems as good a time as any.
RACHEL:	Do you think it's better to die in summer or winter?
JOSIE:	I don't bloody believe this! Why can't you talk about something else?
LAURA:	What would you like to talk about, Josie?
JOSIE:	I dunno. Good things. What I'm going to do when I get over this. Me and Natalie's going to move to the country. Gonna buy a big house with a garden and all. And a fish pond. I've always wanted a fish pond with them big carp things in it. Silver and gold ones. Koi – that's what they're called. Koi Carp. And Natalie'll have a pony. She's mad about horses.
CATHERINE:	(*Dryly*) Don't forget to send us a postcard. Nor you, George while we're at it.
GEORGE:	(*Laughing*) Don't you worry. I'll tell you what it's like up there. What the angels are playing on their harps. What questions I'm asked by St Peter at the pearly gates.
VI:	Do you suppose you get to phone a friend?
JOSIE:	You lot are all sick!

The play's mood could not afford to be flatly bleak, either dramatically or in the interests of veracity. There was plenty of humour in the groups and the frequent

laughter when the play was performed did not detract from the underlying tragedies of people's stories:

FLORENCE: I know what you mean, Dan. I used to find that ever so useful
              when Jack was still driving. We could park right outside the
              Co-op and pop in for a bit of a browse and a cup of tea.

VI: Ooh that's such a bleeding awful shop – excuse my French. I
              know they do cheap funerals but I'd rather pay a bit more and go
              somewhere less depressing. I'm thinking of one of those nature
              burials. Where they put you in a cardboard box.

FLORENCE: I think that would make me feel a bit like a pair of shoes.

MARY: You know what Sean said when I brought home a pair of shoes
              last week?

DAN: 'You'll never fit into that box?'

MARY: (*laughing*) You're assuming that he's got a sense of humour. No. He
              said 'why are you buying new shoes?'

JOSIE: And what did you say?

MARY: I said 'because I am alive'.

JOSIE: Good on yer!

CATHERINE: I can only ever think of good replies when it's too late.

JOSIE: Tell me about it! Trevor was over the other day and said he'd put
              the dinner on. I was gob-smacked! If you knew him, you'd be an'
              all. And you know what I said? 'It won't suit you.'

At the completion of each act, Bobbie and I worked together to check that we had
incorporated the key themes that the notes suggested. For example, social isolation
and embarrassment were common themes, and one of the main advantages of the
group was that people felt comfortable to be honest about their feelings and the
realities of their illness, if of course that is what they wanted to do. The play gives
space to Josie to deny her illness completely and ignore her dying. It also allows
Rachel to rant and rail in a way that she cannot afford to do in front of her three
small children and her husband, who seeks constant reassurance that she is all
right:

RACHEL: It's funny, isn't it? The way we all say we're fine when we're not. I
              don't mean you, George, just in general.

LAURA: Why do you think that is?

RACHEL: I've never really thought about it. The other day one of the mums
              at school asked me how I was and I know she was expecting me
              to say 'fine, thanks'. The way you do. And suddenly I really
              wanted to grab her arm and say, 'well, actually, now you ask, just
              about as well as can be bloody expected after eight weeks of
              picking clumps of hair off my pillow and throwing up in a bucket
              while cooking supper for the kids.' But I didn't of course.

| VI: | You should've done. Last time I was in the General, looking forward to a bit of a rest and some peace and quiet, the woman in the next bed asked me what I was in for. Looked set to chat till the cows come home. So I said I was in for a full frontal lobotomy for murdering my entire family and that shut her up pretty quick, I can tell you! |

I introduced Dan in part for his dramatic impact – a young man, an unusual character who bursts in on the group, unsettling many of them.

DAN:	Well, it's like I've got used to having this. And all the perks.
RACHEL:	We are talking about the same thing here? You have come to the right group? It is cancer you're talking about?
DAN:	Yeah. Like there's no pressure to do things, make big decisions. All me mates are, like, signing on, and being hassled by the benefits office or doing crap jobs for shit bosses for the minimum bloody wage and being nagged by their girlfriends to get married and settle down and by their parents to move into their own place. And I don't have to do any of that stuff cos I won't be around.
CATHERINE:	But there are other ways of not succumbing to peer pressure.
DAN:	Yer what?
MARY:	You don't have to die to avoid doing what all your friends are doing.
DAN:	Yeah, well, like I wouldn't have chosen to get cancer, but now I've got it, it feels like – I dunno – an OK option. I can park anywhere I like, you know. Got one of them orange badge things.

I was worried Dan would not ring true with my better-informed hospice colleagues. In fact he worried them because he bore a striking resemblance to someone who had only recently attended the group, even with a name too close to the real person's. Given that we had not been given access to notes taken in recent years to avoid confidentiality and anonymity problems, this was unexpected. We changed some of Dan's distinguishing features and ultimately decided that anyone who knew the young man would care only that he had been sympathetically represented and that his contribution to the group had been acknowledged. Though Dan leaves the group, disgruntled, after the second meeting, he reappears in some sense at the end of the play, in a positive and characteristic manner. He sends the group a tape. His unlikely, but perfect, choice of song is a gift to the group, where even he got something out of the company of a 'bunch of sick old wrinklies'.

12. The Power of Music

Diana Greenman, Frans Meulenberg and Mike White

Music can make contact with deep parts of us, even reaching into people who've lost speech and other mental abilities (Sacks 1985; www.musichaspower.org). Diana gives moving accounts of concerts in hospitals, hospices and day centres. Frans tells how music enabled contact with his mother after her stroke, and of her re-making contact with herself. Mike describes vital involvement in music in intensive care.

Music is the best medicine in the world   *Diana Greenman*

Live music lifts the spirits, touching a chord where traditional medicine cannot reach. Music stimulates a wide range of emotions and has the capacity to tune in to deepest feelings. It has the power to break down preconceptions and barriers thrown up by illness, disability and age. It fulfils not just physical needs but psychological and social needs.

Music in Hospitals is a charity whose aim is to bring the joy and therapeutic benefits of high quality live music to adults and children with all kinds of illness and disability in hospitals, hospices, daycare centres, special schools, nursing and residential homes.

I will never forget my experience in an enormous empty hospital ward where patients of all ages were ushered in, many in wheelchairs, about 30 in total. Jean, who had cancer, took my attention. Slumped in her wheelchair, she was obviously distressed and in pain. A saxophonist, flautist and pianist were performing. I noticed Jean, still slumped, start to tap in time. Then she raised her head a little and I could clearly see the joy on her face. It was difficult for her to applaud, but she tried. By the end of the concert she was sitting bolt upright with a beaming smile, waving a flag in time to 'Land of Hope and Glory'! Live music may not provide miracle cures but this was proof that it certainly helps patients forget their immediate worries and helps reduce pain.

A patient's daughter remarked:

> Mum was feeling much better that day and you sang for a long while at her bedside. Afterwards we talked about you both and your 'giving of music' in this way. That was the last time we shared quality time together, as she died the following day. Somehow your musical visit has taken on a special meaning as it was something she really enjoyed and the last time of sharing companionship together. We thank you for sharing your music in this way.

Mary coped for years with the agonies and crippling effects of rheumatoid arthritis. She never let the pain get the better of her; then cancer was diagnosed. Mary, who always tried to stand straight with her head held high, was admitted into a hospice where no further treatment was available. On her second day, after a live concert, she said, 'When I woke this morning I thought, I can't face another day. Then I had a bath and felt a little better. Then I was invited to the concert. It was so beautiful I was glad to be alive.'

One girl in particular thoroughly enjoyed a children's hospice concert. The musicians were told later her sister had died the night before. Amidst the pain, she found a moment of happiness by which to remember her sister.

When you think of a live concert, you may imagine performers on a stage playing to an audience seated in rows, quietly listening and watching. Every Music in Hospitals concert is performed by professional musicians carefully selected for high standards of musicianship, communication skills and breadth of repertoire. These essential skills enable them to relate to each audience member whatever their age, illness or disability. Small groups of musicians walk around wards, dayrooms or stand at the patients' bedsides performing, making eye contact, holding hands, exchanging anecdotes or explaining their instruments: all the time sensitively encouraging each individual member of their audience to join in. The joy and laughter can be infectious during a live performance. Only a live performance can be adjusted according to the mood of the moment. This interaction and participation can help adults and children find different ways to come to terms with their illness.

Studies show how patients receiving treatment are naturally anxious and worried about life-limiting illness, and their future. It is believed that, if stress levels are reduced, such as by live performance, patients are able to make the most of the limited time. Being non-verbal and non-threatening, live music frequently provides a catharsis for emotional release for patients, families and staff. Patients are often described as opening up after a live concert. Innermost feelings are shared, assisting clinicians to understand patients' anxieties and fears, as well as revealing personalities. Alleviating depression and anxiety can give physical benefit; nausea from the effects of chemotherapy can be reduced, and pain relieved. The reduction of anxiety and depression can assist the body's immune system. Music has been shown to increase endorphin levels, helping the body make its own anaesthetic and enhance the immune system (Staricoff 2004).

Nurses were astonished to see the heart rate of a child attached to a heart monitor begin to return to normal as she listened to 'Twinkle Twinkle Little Star' sung by her bedside. A lower heartbeat creates less physical tension and stress, calms the mind and thereby can help the body to heal itself. 'My illness makes me feel trapped, but the music made me feel as free as the birds flying outside', said one patient.

Imagine a grey day, pressing down heavily: low clouds, low faces, low energy, low hearts. Then, like a great burst of spring sunshine and abundant new energy, a small group of musicians enter the room. Dazzling, sparkling, wafting perfumes, moving, thinking! Sometimes just joining the low mood for a moment, helping tears flow. Then lifting morale again, lighter than it was before. The energy, colours, sounds, the lightness stays for hours, even days afterwards; everyone, patients, family and staff, feels so much better.

> I regret not having a camera handy to send you the wonderful expressions on faces. It was lovely to see patients become more relaxed. These very special live concerts breathe life!

Voices   *Frans Meulenberg*

When I was a child, I used to hear unknown voices on the gramophone. They were singing a duet with my mother who was in the kitchen, or in the bathroom or on the allotment. Most of the time, I could not understand her. She was singing phonetic arias: understandable for a farmer's daughter, the youngest of 12 children. 'Being heard', she often said, 'is sometimes more important than being understood. Remember that.' On other occasions: 'When you are singing, there is nothing more to say.'

Many years later she showed me a scrapbook full of newspaper and magazine cuttings about her favourite singer, Kathleen Ferrier, whose career progressed from teaching to world stardom, the announcement of her cancer, and finally her death. Ferrier looked a bit like my mother. In the photographs, I always saw her dressed in rather prim suits, made of a rough fabric. Frivolity was unheard of in those days. Her hairstyle was not easy to maintain: unruly ashy-blonde hair, roughened by the salty sea wind. No, she was certainly no beauty, with her lanky, rugged figure and prominent cheekbones. A simple girl.

Since my father became a pensioner, the couple had their breakfast at about eight o'clock. For the past ten years, this had taken place in silence, with the local paper next to their plates. The world outside rolled by like a silent film. The man took a cautious sip of his hot coffee. Somewhat annoyed, he looked at his wife, who suddenly said loudly: '…puppet show…are you coming?… John…help me…'. Her right hand slowly slipped towards the edge of the table. The glass of milk was the first to fall, followed by the cutlery and the plate. Cherry jam splashed like blood onto the light-coloured floorboards. The stare in her eyes was like dirty glass, '…nobody…slice of bread…'. Her body drooped slightly, just for a moment, but then buckled over. As she fell, she pulled the tablecloth with her.

The young doctor called the ambulance. 'Brain haemorrhage.' A routine job. The hand of an unknown man offered comfort, mouthing 'Everything will be alright, my dear.' She heard nothing. Her thin hair was sticky against her forehead.

In the accident and emergency unit, she scribbled something on a form with her almost paralysed hand. Fortunately, it was cool in intensive care. She did not notice it. Fear scorches the senses. 'If you want to phone anyone, sir, the telephone is over there', a nurse said to the man. He was glad to be able at least to do something, even though he did not know what to say to anybody.

Two hours later, I arrived at the hospital. 'Son...' Mother was crying because she could not remember my Christian name. I told her about the train journey and smiled at her. 'They gave her the newest drug straight away', whispered father. Infuriated, five minutes later I was sitting in front of the neurologist. 'My mother must immediately be taken out of the trial. What on earth induced you to allow someone who is so terrified to sign anything?' Silence. 'What do you mean – informed consent? Where is your sense of decency? Sir, I repeat, where is your sense of decency?' In the meantime, the form with the scribbles on it fluttered in 16 shreds into the overflowing waste paper basket.

Months later.

Here in the hospital ward, the heat is becoming stifling. Even the sunflowers are fading in the summer heat. I dab away the beads of sweat – gathered like a sticking veil on her forehead – and on her pumping, almost naked body. She wears an over-sized nightgown, tied up with gauze bandage.

Hospital togs.

'Are you still frightened?' I ask.

She nods.

I put my hand on her neck.

Then I embrace her.

A sigh escapes from her body.

The stroke happened three months ago. Fate has two faces. A stroke unmasks a person. For years, the 'normal' face had apparently concealed something else, something primitive with its own individual will: an asymmetric face with one seemingly up-turned corner of the mouth and smooth forehead with slightly drooping eyebrows. She listens as I read to her or tell her what is going on outside. She forgets most things. Especially what happened yesterday. But, does that matter?

Her death is announced now: blocked arteries in the neck, inoperable. One eyelid droops limply like a rolled-down shutter. How much do a few grams of death weigh?

'Do you still listen to Kathleen Ferrier?'

'To whom?' she mumbles.

I repeat the name.

She wants to, but cannot remember. Her two-faced head shakes a negative answer. She can hardly speak any more, she can only lisp a little with the feeble mouthing of someone who is paralysed.

I help her into the wheelchair and walk with her through the crypts of the hospital. In the basement, it is quiet and cool. I take a discman out of my bag. I put the earphones on her head and let her listen to Brahms' Alto Rhapsody, as sung by

Kathleen Ferrier. She does not react until some ten minutes later, when the voices of the choir surge above the string instruments like a swallow casually leans on even the heaviest squalls.

My mother cries. She laughs too. Emotion is like rolled gold as she remembers. Her memory may well be erased, but not the voice of Kathleen Ferrier.

Do you do Queen?   *Mike White*

Over the last three years the Centre for Arts and Humanities in Healthcare and Medicine (Durham University) has been helping mentor the progress of a discrete arts service that brings live music to the intensive care units (ICUs) of two Tyneside hospitals. This is arts in health, yes, but also arts in extremis, connecting with people in crisis. Both the principles and process under which this work is done could also be applicable to the use of music in palliative care.

I would like to describe a typical session that I observed being carried out by Tabitha, a cellist, and Margaret, a jazz singer – not a likely duo, but they have developed an extraordinary musical rapport in the course of this work.

On arriving at the ICU, we are greeted by the unit's nurse manager. She by now seems quite relaxed in having the musicians' regular 'recovery service' brought into the unit. She tells me how one of the nurses has been really excited by this project and is writing about the therapeutic uses of music as part of his degree course in critical care nursing.

This is the time of changing work shifts in the ICU. Today is less busy than usual. Present are seven nurses, four doctors, a domestic and four patients only one of whom is conscious. Tabitha unpacks her cello and uses an orthopaedic stool as a makeshift music stand. Margaret stands in the middle of the floor. 'Start me off, she says, 'what should I sing?' I suggest 'something by Frankie, but mellow'. And she's away singing a cappella *It's One for My Baby (and One More for the Road)*.

Then Tabitha plays two Bach airs, Margaret joining her on the second one, popularly known as the Hamlet cigar tune. (Somewhat ironic I realise later, given the north east has the highest cancer rates in England. This hospital is also in a district with just about the worst coronary rate in the country.) They sing and play at a level just above room noise. And, in the pauses between tunes, the chamber music of intensive care asserts itself like subdued Stockhausen – a constant hiss of gas cylinders, the occasional monitor bleep, and the clinical babble of staff quietly conferring. Everything here is as it should be – intense.

But the mood becomes more relaxed. The conscious female patient blinks recognition at the end of each number. Staff are preparing to move her to the High Dependency Unit next door. Tabitha tells me that at their last session all six beds were occupied. One old guy clapped feebly at the end of each piece, later confessing, 'You don't know the good that's done me. See, I'm a musician too.' A heartfelt response as this is not a place for sentiment. At their very first session the musicians were asked by a family to play last requests for a dying relative.

Margaret encourages the staff to make their own requests. So we get 'La Vie en Rose' and a medley from *The Sound of Music*. Two relatives come in to attend an unconscious elderly man in a corner bed, while Tabitha is playing an Irish melody.

The nurse manager enquires if they'd like the music to stop as they're clearly upset. No, they say, but ask if it could be more upbeat. Tabitha obliges. The musicians are constantly judging the appropriateness of what they are doing, responsive to the medical teamwork and trauma going on around them. Every bit of this 'performance' is in a very real sense on the edge.

Visiting hours begin. A last song from Margaret, 'Shall I do *Every Time We Say Goodbye?*' Her mouth opens, then she checks herself, abashed. 'No, definitely not…*Wonderful World*', and she's off again.

Afterwards during tea break in the staff room, Margaret says last week a young male patient asked her to 'do some Queen'. 'The only one I could think of was *We Will Rock You.*' 'Better than *Another One Bites the Dust*', quips a male nurse, evincing the kind of humour you need to retain the sanity required of the job. And I imagine that, her singing 'you got blood on yer face, yer big disgrace…we will, we will rock you', transforming a macho anthem into a lullaby.

How do you put a value on work like this? Some ICU staff have anecdotally noted a reduction in blood pressure in coma patients that has coincided with these music sessions. One might speculate – and indeed the staff do – on the power of music to reach into the deep and dislocated consciousness of such patients, expressing tender care and human connection where no conventional treatment can go.

This is an area, I believe, where hospital arts and palliative care could develop an interesting exchange of research and practice. But attempting to research this will require great sensitivity. It is probably the most extreme circumstances you could place the arts in, short of a war zone. I am awed by the pluck of these musicians in taking on work as challenging as this. It goes to the very core of both the healing arts and the patient experience.

13. Writing through Bereavement

River Wolton, Haifa Al Sanousi, Amy Kuebelbeck,
Judy Clinton and Robert Hamberger

Bereavement is a rollercoaster ride of emotion. Events and feelings need re-experiencing over and over, as meanings and some sort of understanding and acceptance emerge. Art is a way of undertaking this positively, without exhausting friends and relatives who can only listen so much. 'The meaning of life is connected, inextricably, to the meaning of death: mourning is a romance in reverse, and if you love you grieve and there are no exceptions' (Lynch 1998, p.29). River, Haifa, Amy, Judy and Robert here show how writing eased their suffering, helped them to continue living and increased their understanding.

Death and poetry: How writing helps us say the unsayable
River Wolton

> *Death is the mother of beauty*
> > *Wallace Stevens (2001, p.83)*

Death opened the door and shoved a pen and paper in my hand. I was a reluctant writer, an unlikely poet. In 1986, when I was 22, my mother was diagnosed with ovarian cancer. We investigated alternative treatments but the nature of her illness and her faith in the medical profession meant that she consistently chose chemotherapy, even when palliative care was offered. It was too late for her, but the world of complementary health changed my life. I read about Jo Spence, the feminist photographer who documented her cancer in unflinching self-portraits, and who recommended creativity and co-counselling as tools for self-awareness and healing. Before my mother died I completed a co-counselling course, started seeing an art therapist and keeping a dream journal. Through sheer despair I started to write, first in personal journals, later in poems.

While my mother was dying, I acted with deceptive maturity, drove her to hospital, cooked and shopped, organised her care. But I was being swept away. Everything was played out on a backdrop of silence – never an emotionally literate family, we went along with my mother's unspoken rule: she was going to get better, to speak of anything else was betrayal. After two years of illness, she died at home, mid-way through a course of chemotherapy, dragging herself on hands and knees to vomit in the toilet, refusing to see the GP. I never saw my mother cry and her dying was no exception. She brimmed with anger. I felt she could not forgive me for witnessing her vulnerability. That last afternoon she stared out of the window with pure rage in her eyes.

Her death tore me up. I dreamt she sat up from her deathbed, blazing: 'How dare you write me off!' I could not tolerate the fact of her death, coming as it did on a bedrock of non-communication, a relationship that had always been distant. But what floored me was the guilt – which at the time I could not recognise – guilt that I had not kept her alive, guilt for my anger, guilt for the specific failure of having been out of the house when she died (in desperation I had called a friend and we were up the road smoking cigarettes). As well as the guilt I felt shattered by the physical proximity of death: closeness to her dying body (I massaged her emaciated head and swollen feet), seeing her newly dead, touching the marble-cold corpse at the undertaker's.

Therapy and co-counselling provided an outlet for immediate grief. However, while the catharsis of co-counselling helped, it sometimes left me empty, feeling that I could not really communicate what was happening inside. In therapy, the inevitable mother-transference left me silent and sullen for months at a time, unable to make real 'contact'. Writing filled the gap. My journals of the time record vivid dreams:

> 8 January 1990. I'm in an underground room, with brick sides, ledges along the walls. The middle is raised so that you can just about walk around it in a narrow gangway. There's a man with a machine that can blast through rock and earth. The machine has a skull on the front. On the ledges are dead bodies, still clothed and fleshy; putrid but not skeletons. They wear old-fashioned clothes and armour. He says they've been there since a battle in the English Civil War. He prods one of the bodies, it's fat and wobbly, but I know it's rotten inside.

I started going to a women's writing class and a friend gave me *Writing Down The Bones* by Natalie Goldberg (1986). This book was a revelation; Goldberg's fresh and fearless writing lit me up. It was deeply exciting to move the pen across the page, to be given permission to write from immediate experience, to be momentarily freed from the shackles of the inner critic.

How did writing help? First, it took the unbearable edge of experience out of my hands and set it apart from me. It created a writing 'self' that provided a continuity of being that I did not experience in my daily life. Like many people who are drawn to express themselves creatively, I had a fractured and embryonic sense of self. I did not experience what Winnicott (1962) and later Epstein (2001) describe as 'going on being'. 'If a young child has too much to deal with…she is forced into a reactive mode that removes her from her own experience, forcing her to cope prematurely with the needs of another', thus interrupting 'the flow of authentic self' (Epstein 2001, p.30). In writing I was grappling to mark out a territory safe enough to exist within; once this was established it helped me to communicate with the outside world.

Second, writing opened doors both to my unconscious and to a wider, less self-oriented consciousness – the 'wild mind' (Goldberg 1991). In my own writing practice and in my work with groups, the magic of reflective writing lies in the surprises. When people write into their fears, when they topple through the constraints of their current self-image, they contact the bare skin of reality in a way that is both profoundly personal and universal.

Try this: Write a letter to someone you have not seen for a long time – someone who has died, someone you are estranged from or have lost contact with. Start with 'Dear…' Write for ten minutes without stopping. Don't worry about spelling, 'proper' sentences or finding the 'right' word. It's OK to repeat yourself, write the worst junk in the universe, and to stop making sense. When time is up, breathe in and out and read it aloud to yourself.

You may write something unexpected. The more you are able to relax and keep the 'what's the point of this?' and 'is it any good?' thoughts at bay, the more you may surprise yourself. Painful feelings may arise, that's absolutely OK. You could write for another ten minutes on the feelings that come up. Describe them in detail, the memory alleys they take you down. Feel free to follow the mind's pathways. There's no right or wrong way to do this.

My father (25 years older than my mother: 88 when she died) began a new lease of life after her death. He began to visit me regularly (in my co-counselling communal lesbian households), went on holiday, started painting again and basked in the company of his children and grandchildren. My awareness of mortality had begun around the age of seven when it dawned on me that he was an old man and might die soon. This awareness ran through my childhood like a granite seam, my younger brother and I were bullied for having an old dad, and it became a source of shame. My mother's attitude didn't help – she openly resented him, his slowness and lack of energy. He was, in fact, remarkably healthy, and having outlived my mother (and two previous wives) seemed immortal, surviving a stroke, pneumonia and several infections, living to the age of 99. His continuing existence reawakened and heightened my life-long anxiety. As he became increasingly frail and confused, I obsessed over how and when his death might happen, whether each visit was the last, if the phone would ring in the night. He continued to survive medical predictions, hanging on with stoicism, humour, and an appetite for the love and attention of his family. Born into the Edwardian upper-middle class, in his final years he experienced a level of physical care, intimacy and companionship that had been absent in the rest of his life. But I had many moments of longing for it to be over, of murderous impatience coupled with insatiable guilt that we hadn't ever known each other at all.

As his death came closer, I found some stillness with it; the writing (and the support of my lover at the time) helping me to slow down and witness events as they unfolded. As with my mother, I was not physically present at his death.

Strangely and ironically, a friend took the message that he was very ill but forgot to pass it on. However, I was able to find some reconciliation with having missed the event that I had anticipated for so long. What helped was that my brother and I spent several hours with my father's body, and with the consent of my other siblings I photographed his corpse and the room that he died in – an idea borrowed from friend and photo-therapist Rosy Martin (1995). Having these photos has enabled me to remember and write about his death in much more detail than my mother's. Even though his death was profoundly shocking, the shock did not freeze me in its grip; it clenched and then let go. The following year I was commissioned to write and perform *Beyond Words* for a local literature festival: a journey through our relationship – my coming out, his old age and confusion, our struggles to accept each other, our quiet moments of mutual understanding. It was accompanied by slides of us, and a sound-track of his reminiscences. I found myself moving towards the idea of creating something beautiful out of mortality, a sense of acceptance and celebration rather than defeat. There have been many more poems since then.

> *6 June 2000 (from* The Underground Orchestra, *2005)*
> In the end, the body stayed all day.
> Although we phoned three times
> the surgery failed to understand
> it was a death certificate we wanted.
>
> By then, perhaps, we spoke a different language,
> words of after-death, in rooms
> still filled with the moisture
> of his final laboured breaths.
>
> It was absurdly bright,
> the residue of childhood summers.
> London languid in a milky heat,
> yellow midday sharpening the shadows,
> and the drawn blind rising, falling
> in the open window's mouth.
>
> We floated in a confluence of light,
> under the eye of his grandfather's yacht –
> an oil painting half the room's width –
> that he'd rigged and re-rigged in his final months,
> imploring us to mind the boom,
> to hoist the spinnaker, the jib.
>
> We waited. On the desk a recent letter
> from the Harbour Master, Famagusta, Cyprus
> in dark-blue fountain pen: Dear Sir,
> Regret we have no record of your boat.

Try this: How do we say goodbye? Imagine a busy departure terminal at an airport or train station. Think yourself into the setting – the sounds, sights, smells, noises. Describe three different partings that are taking place. What are people saying and doing? What is your way of saying goodbye?

Sometimes when we know or work with people who are experiencing intense grief or fear at a life-threatening diagnosis, or despair at losing a loved one, we think it's better to smooth it over, to take their minds off it. In my experience, writing (if it's sensitively handled and as long as there's not too much distress bound up in the act of writing itself) can externalise the pain and provide the writer with some ground to stand on, so that the immediate identity of the individual has respite from being utterly and completely bound up in the sense of endless pain. Writing also validates the uniqueness of the individual experience: 'I am here feeling this and no one else can say it like I can.' If this kind of writing is shared in a group, particularly where it is not negatively commented on or deconstructed, it has a dual effect: each person's life is validated and the diversity of the group is honoured. Participants are always amazed at how many different tangents are taken – and none of them wrong! It's a powerful demonstration of how we can co-exist safely and respectfully with the maximum plurality.

Try this: Write your own epitaph. How would you like to be remembered? Write a list of words or phrases – complimentary, rude, flippant or celebratory. How would you like them displayed – on a headstone, a billboard, a website?

Funeral fashion parade: What would you like to be seen dead in? Describe your ultimate coffin accessories – a ball dress, a hula hoop, an all-over body tattoo?

In working with the dying and the bereaved, we confront our own mortality again and again. Through reflective writing we can find 'safe enough' ways to explore our feelings towards our own death and find slender moments of equanimity with our fleeting and ephemeral nature.

> However certain I feel about the necessity of my existence, the only certainty I face is that this seemingly necessary being will perish. This heart will cease pumping blood, these lungs will cease drawing air, these neurons will cease firing in my brain. My body will rot or be consumed by fire, and within a matter of years I will linger on by the slenderest of threads as a memory in the fading minds of those who once knew me. (Batchelor 2004, p.14)

The novelist Philip Pullman (2000) makes Death into invisible characters who accompany the people to whom they belong. With great kindness to ourselves, we can gently turn our focus; how do we imagine our death will be, how do we approach it – with terror, curiosity, relief?

What do I need to die well? Writing Practice May 2004
I need brushed cotton sheets and another 30 years of silent sitting. I need my mother and father to hold my hand, stroke my head and promise me my death will not be like theirs. I want to crack open like a pale-blue robin's egg. I want to go savouring each raw breath with my love in my arms. I need more of the moments – like tiny glass splinters snagged in a carpet – moments when I can let death be itself and not paint it with monstrous teeth and me running away in the fastest silver running-shoes. Please save me from that gulf when I begin to miss the body, the bluntness of bones, love in the dark, air on the skin. Don't let me hang on at the last minute to the sound of a waterfall or the sharp midnight of lavender.

Try this: Find a comfortable, undisturbed space to write in. Write for 10, 15 minutes or more without stopping. Some starting points: A letter to Death; What do you need to die well?; What do you love most about life?

Arny Mindell (1989) quotes a 30-year-old man dying of AIDS: 'Everyone is pregnant with death. Everyone needs it. Near death, we all have the same chance. We all have the chance to become our total selves.' Whether near our own death or that of others, death opens doors. We may be utterly unwilling to bring our attention to it, we may step in with blindness and resistance in every step, but if met with creativity and the crazy sanity of the moving pen, unexpected jewels can arise.

Thanks to Dhammagita for the following writing exercises: Write your own epitaph. What would you like to be seen dead in and how do you say goodbye?

Death and Departure of the Sea   *Haifa Al Sanousi*

After my mother's death I cried every day for many weeks, but now I can look back at the precious time I did have with her and remember the happy times, and how wonderful she made me feel. I can use my memories of her to help me through life and, in that way, she will always be with me.

My mum came from the old Kuwait, carrying with her the ocean breeze, ancestral root, and filled with integrity and purity. She was a moral dictionary that was difficult to find. She greeted us farewell and left us as quietly as she came to this world.

Inspired by and dedicated to my deceased mother, my story collection entitled *Departure of the Sea* is often engaged in the reminiscence of the earlier period in which my mother lived. The title story, "Departure of the Sea," describes the many virtues of earlier times as seen through an old woman's recollection of her life. On her deathbed, Fiddah, the main character, recalls a series of bittersweet episodes from her youth. Her old house was nothing fancy but it provided a shelter of love and warmth. The sister of a young girl who always escaped housework to play with other children and of another child who was too mentally disabled to take care of herself, Fiddah develops a strong sense of responsibility to others early. As much as she wanted to play with other children, she never refused her mother's order to do housework because she empathized with her mother's plight.

"I was wise despite my youth. I did want to play with Nurah and her friends, but I pitied my mother who was continuously fulfilling her endless responsibilities. I felt it was necessary to help her with the burdens of the house."

The reward for being an obedient child was that Fiddah received repeated praise and honor, and was blessed by God with having a nice family when she grew up. At the end of the story, the elderly Fiddah dies surrounded by loving children and grandchildren. Like the sea that bordered Kuwait and provided its lifelines, Fiddah symbolizes the noble people and ethics of the past. She is the literary incarnation of my mother who died and left an empty place in my heart. Here is a part of *Departure of the Sea*.

The surrounding walls just about suffocated me. Sharply, the odor of paint penetrated my nose. How I detested the odor of paint! I was used to the smell of houses built with mortar and the breeze of the sea. But such had vanished.

O, where were the mortared houses? Where had my mother's face gone? That was another thing that had disappeared, without a trace.

Where had my father's face gone? Where was his pleasant voice chanting the Koran each dawn? Where was the sweetness of the calls for prayer that used to shake the walls of our home?

Where was my father's voice that woke us up every morning?

"Wake up, girls. It's time for prayer. Prayer is better than sleep."

Then my mother came repeating:

"Time for prayer. Hissah, Fiddah, Nurah. Wake up and pray."

Hissah and I jumped up out of the bed to clean ourselves and pray, while Nurah still wrestled with her slumber.

My mother continued to nag until Nurah got up.

Where were those days? Gone already?

Yes. It appeared that they were gone and I would be leaving soon to live in another world, a world I had no clue of!

Time had left its traces on my body. Days drew wrinkles on my face. That was the judgment of destiny, which could never be reversed.

I looked at the ceiling of this room now. I looked out at a sky that I could barely see. My voice, submerged inside, was whispering religious expressions; these had never left me, not even for a single day. (O God, I pray for a gentle end.) That was a phrase whose spirit I inhaled in every corner of our old house.

While my tongue repeated it quietly, I felt as if I was breathing in the air of our house.

I was walking between the rooms. I saw the faces of my mother, father, and the faces of my sisters. I became a witness of the time that had gone.

I became a weak body carrying the features and memories of something called the sea. And was the sea that I saw years ago the same as the one my parents knew? No, no. I don't think so.

I felt a sudden shiver when the nurse opened the door of my room abruptly. I saw her carrying in her hands a container which had needles, alcohol, and other things whose names I hadn't the slightest idea of. She injected a needle into the vein of my right hand in order to withdraw a sample of my blood.

She then inserted into me another device.

I didn't protest. I never did. I didn't object at all. I surrendered to my fate completely.

I accepted this reality even though it was a bitter one. What was the use of protest? I endured the pain even as it hurt. I tried not to scream because I was used to suppressing my screams. Destiny. One should not fight one's destiny.

Here is the last moment, the moment of my mum's death where I imagined that she had explained it to me.

The time had come. Now was the time to depart. I felt weaker and weaker. The faces of my father, mother, sister Hissah, my former husband, and others had come back to me. The house built with mortar returned. The mosque's prayer started to be chanted: (God is the greatest. God is the greatest. God is the greatest. I witness no gods but God.)

I took my last breath and felt strangled.

I saw a bundle of light, heading toward me, taking away my vision. My tongue grew very heavy…

My mother remains alive in the depth of my heart and whenever she comes to my mind I say "I hope you are resting in peace with the care of Allah, I will never ever forget you as long as I live."

Waiting with Gabriel   *Amy Kuebelbeck*

I knew for three-and-a-half months before my son was born that he would die. That doesn't give away the ending, but only the beginning.

A prenatal ultrasound revealed that our son had an incurable heart condition. Despite some wrenchingly aggressive surgical options, no one could give our son a good heart. So we set out to give him a good, although brief, life. What followed was an extraordinary journey of grief, joy and love as we waited with Gabriel. During that gift of time, we prepared for his birth, prepared for his death, and embraced his life.

Gabriel lived for nine months before he was born and for two-and-a-half peaceful hours afterward. We had written in our birth plan that we wanted his life to be free of pain and filled with love. And it was. During his gentle transition from life to death, he was cradled by my husband and me, surrounded by a roomful of people who love him. As we inscribed on his gravestone, he knew only love.

I now look back on that time with Gabriel – before and after his birth – as one of the most profound, meaningful experiences I've ever been privileged to have. Elisabeth Kübler-Ross once said:

> Our present Western society is not willing to experience death, in the sense that it is hidden by a conspiracy of silence. The sudden and unexplained death of a baby is very tragic, yet it is not regarded as something to be sad over, especially if the baby has never lived. As a consequence, parents are often not given permission by family or friends to mourn the death of their baby, and they are very often left alone in an apparently unsympathetic world, not knowing how to feel and not knowing how to cope. (Kübler-Ross 1986 [video])

Fortunately, we are now seeing a significant cultural shift in which parents are starting to be given permission to mourn the death of their baby. Driven by persistent efforts beginning in the 1970s by bereaved parents and organizations such as National SHARE Pregnancy and Infant Loss Support Inc. in the US and SANDS (Stillbirth and Neonatal Death Society) in the UK, hospital practices and societal attitudes regarding miscarriage, stillbirth and neonatal death are gradually changing.

A newer challenge is that, as prenatal testing becomes increasingly routine, more parents are learning devastating news before their babies are born. We are now in a brave new world where the ability to diagnose fatal problems prenatally has raced ahead of the ability to care for these families.

In a compassionate and practical response, a few hospitals and hospices around the world are starting perinatal hospice programs for families who wish to continue their pregnancies with babies who likely will die before, during, or after birth. Under the conventional hospice model, services do not begin until the baby is born or is discharged from the hospital, which is of little help when a baby has a life expectancy of hours or even minutes. A perinatal hospice approach, in contrast, is intended to support families from the time of diagnosis, when their grief journey begins. Perinatal hospice honors the hospice principle of neither hastening nor prolonging death, and it fits beautifully with this well-known statement from Dame Cicely Saunders, pioneer of the modern hospice movement: "You matter to the last moment of your life. We will do all we can not only to help you die peacefully, but also to live until you die."

Some may question why parents would continue a pregnancy following a terminal prenatal diagnosis. If the baby is going to die anyway, what's the point? Why draw it out and bring grief upon yourselves? Why not just get "closure?"

We looked at it differently. If our baby was going to die anyway, then why not embrace what little time he would have? Why not protect him and use that gift of time to create some memories and give him – and ourselves – the gift of a peaceful, natural death?

Cutting a pregnancy short is not a shortcut around grief. Grief is a natural and healthy response to the death of a baby, and allowing parents to experience their child's life and death helps them later in their journey through grief. Parents who continue a pregnancy also may receive much greater understanding and support in their grief from family and friends, who otherwise might dismiss a terminally ill but unseen baby as simply a forgettable accident of nature.

After Gabriel died, however, it seemed that what had happened was so remarkable that I couldn't bear to forget any of it. I quickly filled a journal, and then I tucked it safely away with Gabriel's mementos – his soft cotton clothing, his plastic hospital bracelet – and thought I was done. I never intended to share the story publicly. Eventually I came to think that perhaps my story wasn't meant only for me. I hoped that our story might offer a gentle example of one way to approach a pregnancy like this, and that it might be a companion along someone else's journey.

I have been humbled and gratified to receive beautiful letters from parents who wrote that our story helped them to say hello and goodbye to their own baby. Some have said my book (Kuebelbeck 2003) gave them a map to follow in otherwise uncharted and frightening territory. Others shared my book with their own circle of family and friends, to help others understand the magnitude of their loss.

Some say they can't imagine continuing a pregnancy if the baby is not expected to live. I hope that by telling our story it will help people imagine.

As a parent, I can think of no greater tribute to my own son.

Writing: A lifeline through grief   *Judy Clinton*

At this time three years ago, my son Robbie, aged 22, had embarked on a horrendous seven weeks of acute alcohol abuse which took him to his death on 4 June 2001. Robbie had been damaged at birth by a faulty forceps delivery and had never been able to come to terms with his resultant disabilities. Alcohol gave him temporary relief from the inner pain but eventually the drink itself took hold of him and he was lost.

Seven weeks before he died he came to my door. He was on leave for two weeks and didn't know what to do with himself. He told me that he had taken out a loan and that he was 'going away'. I asked, 'Where to?' He said, 'I don't know, just away somewhere.' Quite unexpectedly I became ice-cold and the words came into my head, 'You're not going to make it.' Robbie had always had problems but it had never entered my consciousness that he would die. He was too much of a fighter – *we* were too much fighters. It was a premonition that day of what was to come, but over the next weeks I fought that truth.

From then on Robbie's behaviour became increasingly extreme; my answering machine was constantly full of messages from people who had seen him drunk, unconscious or doing something outrageous or from him himself, drunk and talking anxiety-filled nonsense. I had the feeling he had got on a fast train and could not get off.

During this time I suffered most terribly and at times feared for my own sanity. There was no reaching this son of mine, he was hell-bent on destruction and I was rendered powerless, as were his friends and others who loved him. I began to write, continuing my daily journal and writing poems.

Then came the day, ten days before he died, when I met him in town 'by accident'. This was our farewell; the poem describes it although it does not say that I found myself saying, from the deepest part of myself, 'I don't want to lose you, but if you have to go, you have to go.' I had given my son permission to die. The strange light that poured from his eyes told me that his soul had responded.

My son
'What are you doing?' I asked my son
As he leant against the wall
In May-time sun, in the city
That Thursday morning early
'I'm drinking, Mum,' he said
I saw the rashes on his so thin legs
His haggard looking face
I saw him going away from me
I had no power to stop him
'At a deeper level, I mean,' I said
He looked me in the eye
'I don't know, Mum,' and he began to cry
Yet we knew some purpose there
He looked at me with eyes so strange
With a light I'd never seen
He did not want me
I had no answers
To the hell he was living through
So I turned and walked away from him
A humbled, tiny child

Ten days later he was dead, choking on bags of dog excrement that he stuffed into his mouth when police came to pick him up as he scoured bins in his mind-distorted state.

Again I was taken by surprise, when I saw him in the mortuary.

On seeing your body
Thank you, I said
Over and over
Unbidden, unexpected

I stood in awe of your dead beauty

What strength in your face
What accomplishment

You always were unpredictable

That evening I felt that he had been released.

The night he died
The moon shines full tonight
Pure, clear, beautiful
He will not see it or any moon again
Not with human eyes that is
But dancing somewhere amongst the stars
Goes free my son
Free now, his journey done
His body gone
His spirit shining
Pure, clear, beautiful
Not fettered any more
By the body that he loathed

Then began my grieving process, intermingled with such strong feelings of his continuing existence, but now in a different form. Poems again charted my experience.

My son lives after all
My son lives
He has not died after all
His body is gone
That I know
But hush, still my heart
And he is there
Not dead at all
Even more alive
Than he was then
This is not memory
Images from the past
But life-giving energy
In the now
This is his love
That never died

There was one point, on the day of the inquest, when I briefly wanted to die too.

Oblivion feels attractive now
Blatant loss
Loss I say
A hole
So deep within me
That I fear I will disappear
Never to come out again
Fearing it yet almost wanting it too
The effort to stay at the edges
Too much
Too tiring
Oblivion feels attractive now

But hope kept shining through as well as the misery of loss.

Permission to live again
The other night you came to me
Unrequested
I was on the border of wake and sleep
You said most emphatically
Forcefully even
'I want you to be happy'
My tears fell at that unfelt possibility
But today I noticed I laughed
Wholly, with all of me
Like I used to once
Perhaps
You have given me permission to live again
As I once gave you to die

Through the inevitable peaks and troughs of acute grief, I began to find a way of relating to my son which felt acceptable to me. As more time passed so I began to see Robbie, our lives as mother and son, and his loss as part of a much bigger, spiritual experience and so this poem in the grief series came to a point of rest.

You are so silent now
You are so silent now
No sound of your voice or
Feet crashing down the stairs
None of your constant movement
Your comings and goings
Your door-bell pressing
The phone ringing
I only have memory of you like that now
But somewhere within me
The essential you lives
In the silence
In the deepest me
In my love

The grieving goes on. Perhaps it always will at more and more subtle levels, but now it is within a bigger context and that makes it bearable and usable. Writing the poems helped me at the time of writing and they remain with me as a record of where I have travelled. It was my lifeline.

Grieving before death   *Robert Hamberger*

A man my age
I watch a man my age with his mother
chat across restaurant cutlery
and wonder how it might be
if you could speak again, recover.
He hands her one photo after another.
She stays so polite it's hard to see
who's pleasing who in their careful meal. Three
years after your words have gone I discover
I miss your voice. You'd never talk
about the big things, how it felt for you.
I never asked. Could we speak
at last like equals, as if we're due
to unfold our stories, break
our silence, hear the words, believe they're true?

I decided some time ago that I wouldn't wait until my mother's death to write 'bereavement' poems about her, because there are poems about our relationship now that demand to be written.

I'm struggling with the fact that physically my mother is here – beautifully, heartbreakingly here – palpably in the present. I can hold her hand, talk to her, kiss her, try and reach her, and sometimes her smile hints that I might have succeeded, even fleetingly. But the elusiveness she showed in our relationship before her illness – her strong working-class taciturn quality – has returned in a different way. Now she can't speak, say any words back to me, and in an odd unresolved sense I'm still trying to 'reach' her.

Although watching someone deteriorate with Alzheimer's has been called a living bereavement, it seems to me that two essential elements of bereavement are the physical absence of the loved one, their disappearance, and the survivor's continuation without them. During a long illness there can be no sense of 'closure' for the parties involved. The struggle is partly due to the paradox that many of the loved one's important characteristics are lost, but the loved one remains. So the relationship continues unresolved in the present: still open to the possibility of change.

14. A Legacy of Understanding

Monica Suswin

It is well to give when asked, but it is better to give unasked, through understanding.
Gibran (1974, p.27)

My engagement with this explorative and expressive writing about the death of my father and the slow decline of my mother has taken many months, but it has given me an unexpected legacy of understanding. I have discovered an excitement in the unfolding power of the writing itself to guide me on a healing journey I never even expected, as it took on its own momentum. I wrote about my father's last hour and it became a useful text for teaching; writing about my mother brought me and my sister closer together. In our relationships writing can help us to relate more fully to the other people in our lives, as I found with my sister, who wrote to me: *Isn't it strange sibs last for life.* This chapter charts this lengthy writing process and includes recorded interviews and extracts from my journals. My mother died very peacefully in January 2007.

My mother in a nursing home

On my mother's eighty-sixth birthday, I went into the nursing home with a huge bunch of garish beginning-to-wilt carnations: all I could get on the Tuesday after Easter Monday. It is the coming to terms of my mother *not dying* which has been difficult with the refrain *my mother is never going to die* running through my head as every year we reach one more birthday.

> 2 March 2000, extract from unsent letter to my mother
> …your eightieth birthday looming…for your sake I hope and pray you die in your sleep, still knowing who you are, who we are and the day of the week.

Mother's vascular cerebral dementia took its hold well before my father's death the following year in 2001. After the funeral, I brought her home thinking we would manage to look after her for six months and take our time over the inevitability of a nursing home. I lasted six weeks.

For the last five years the Catholic nuns and lay staff have looked after her. There is always a lively and welcoming atmosphere in the home with staff going about their duties. Mother's corridor has its own small lounge; her bedroom has lovely views onto the walled garden. My sister, who has other family commitments and lives several hours away, visits regularly. We are in constant contact.

We are fortunate mother has never shown any distress, only ever smiled. The staff have never ceased to tell me how content she is; once one of her carers, Veronica, approached me to say: 'Even though I only see your mother once a week I know it's me she smiles at – her smile lights up the room. She lights up my day.' Today the smile is weak, her body crumpled in the armchair, her hands clenched into fists, her blouse stained with drink and dribble, but I too am in no doubt she recognises me. It is some years since she spoke; she watches me, attentively waiting for me to make mouth shapes, which she is eager to copy.

> 13 January 2004 – She is tucked tightly beneath the pink cotton interlocked woven blanket. I am wearing a lime-green neck warmer – a woollen tube scarf. I lift the bottom hem, stretch it out and up over my face and unexpectedly mouth: Peep-O, Peep-O. She simpers in delight. One more time. Peep-O Peep-O. And one more time…

Sometimes I think I have no emotions left, yet leaving today on her birthday the familiar pang of sadness at parting pierced me once again. My mother's hold on her life is extraordinary. She had been ill that week, but as she has done so many times before, she bounces back. 'I've seen so many "ready to go" and come back', says the Principal Sister. The general medical practitioner (GP), responsible for all the residents, has been visiting weekly for the past three years. She says: 'It's not primarily the medical intervention which prolongs life; if anything the medical care is less than in other homes, but the nursing care at your mother's home is very different.' When I question Sister on the longevity of many of the residents, she looks at me knowingly: 'We give them good care and lots of love.'

I suspect I have done my grieving in increments ever since the day when I first knew something was amiss. In August 1997 I telephoned to say what time we would be arriving the following day for our visit. Mother became very flustered, expecting us that day. Did it start then when I realised she was beginning to lose it? Or was it some years later as I followed her into the lavatory? I took a deep breath and knew I was going to have to wipe her bottom for the first time.

At the nursing home, it is common practice for the majority of the residents to be padded up. I soon learned all about the different sizes and thicknesses of incontinence pads. But it is wrong to think they are entering a babyhood state. This is not like dealing with your own child, however much at times the parent may begin to feel like your baby. I felt this particularly when I wrapped mother up in a big towel after the shower and talcum powdered her feet. Babies grow up. People at the end of their lives are meant to die.

26 July 2002 – I have been sitting with you for 40 minutes. You must let me go, I say. Her fingers tighten around mine. Our fingers are locked together, her arthritic bent index finger hooked into my palm. I prise my fingers out of hers.

It is rare that staff might have known residents when they were independent adults. There was an occasion when I came in to meet a cousin and found mother sitting in her chair, eye shadow and lip-stick worn more vividly than she would ever have applied it herself, and big shiny ear-rings clipped onto her ear-lobes. It is true she may well have enjoyed the attention lavished on her by a carer who also may have had fun relating to her, but my immediate thought was: *She's not a plaything, she's not like a doll to dress up.*

Stage by stage, I have relinquished feeling responsible for my mother, so that in time she has come to belong to her carers more than to us. In her helpless state, she certainly does not belong to herself. A sense of meaning has begun to elude me since mother's day consists of being moved from bed to armchair and back again, and her brain activity is so reduced that a simple instruction like lift your arm can not be followed. Sister says: 'This is when it becomes more difficult for the family to keep up the visiting and some relatives give up completely.'

On mother's eighty-third birthday Ellie, the eldest grandchild, in her mid-twenties, steeled herself for a visit but was in the end pleasantly amused. She slit open the envelopes and handed her grandma the cards. As mother ate some grapes, she put the seeds into a discarded envelope on her lap! Nevertheless this is Ellie's view three years later:

> It is very sad seeing grandma. I don't agree with looking after elderly people in a way that their last years are dragged out like this. I've been expecting grandma to die for years; I don't like to see grandma ending her life like this. It's not how I remember her when I was a child.

> 22 January 2003 – I am in the attic; on a rafter is the navy blue straw hat with an artificial emerald flower on its brim. She wore it at Prize Giving at school. She was definitely the prettiest mother.

And from one year later:

> This will be the last time I feed you. I cannot cope with projectile vomit. It went everywhere. I leapt up, shot into the corridor. The staff came quickly. I went and laid clean clothes out on your bed.

Yet does this dedication to caring for the elderly really prolong their lives beyond what feels fitting? 'We do not have a say over someone else's life', says Sister, who does not think modern medicine keeps people alive. My mother has been on aspirin for years to reduce the chance of a stroke or heart attack; she lost the sight in one eye on becoming erratic taking her medicines in 1999. Treatment already in place is difficult to change and it has been unthinkable in all discussions about her medication to consider stopping the aspirin as the consequences are most likely to be distressing. The GP explains: 'It may well be withdrawn towards the end of someone's life, but so often you do not know when the end is.' There is no doubt in my mind that aspirin in these circumstances does prolong my mother's life when the quality of her life could well be questioned as I watch her deteriorate week by week. However, I have come to accept that my mother will die in her own time, not mine, and within the current social climate.

It was not so long ago that flu was the old person's friend. However, since 1998 it has been recommended that all people aged 75 years and over to be immunised against influenza. Every autumn most residents are given a flu injection. 'The family gives us the direction', says Sister. NHS policy has now dropped the age to 65 and encourages GPs to support the Department of Health's influenza programme by offering financial incentives. It is considered good practice to give the flu jab to 'at risk' groups, particularly in long stay residential homes, to prevent the rapid spread of infection causing outbreaks with high morbidity and mortality. 'This spares many elderly people from suffering the illness as well as a possible hospital admission', says the GP.

> 24 April 2004 – Your mother is sitting outside under the parasol, I'm told. The sun is very bright and it only takes me a split-second to know something is odd. Her eyes are open staring upwards, her mouth strangely open and tight. Her head fixed at an angle. I fetch the staff nurse: 'She was fine when we brought her out.' Our Nursing Sister comes rushing downstairs: 'Now I'm glad you've seen it. A little transient ischaemic attack (TIA). She gave me a shock the other day. Look she's coming back. There you are there she is.'

This is not a textbook description of TIA as understood by the medical profession, according to the GP. She says it is not clear what is happening during these episodes of glazed eyes, low pulse, clammy skin and vomiting, but the carers certainly know what they mean.

Sister's approach for people in the last stages of life embraces a spiritual healing: 'To me your mother is perfect', she says, 'she must have suffered knowing she was helpless, but she has reached a state of total acceptance of her dependence on others.' I intuit that perhaps my mother has wanted to be looked after; it may well have nurtured some part of her in a way that she craved and never got in her life. What I do know is that she was born one year after a sister died from peritonitis; and she grew up in full knowledge that she replaced this little girl who was the apple of her daddy's eye. Although she too was a very pretty girl, did she also carry a sense of not being allowed to die right through to this long and protracted end? I think so.

> 17 November 2005 – You are allowed to die. I have taken your handbag, your gold bracelet, your gold necklace which was your daddy's pocket watch chain and you have worn that since he died, and now I have taken your teeth. All that is left is your body.
> Mother is asleep. Her face looks like a death mask. She opens her eyes – her one good eye is bright with life and her skin pinkens as she wakes up. She smiles but for the first time I am not sure she recognizes me.

'There is not much recognition during the first 20 minutes of my visit', says my sister, 'when I don't see her I feel guilty that I can't do more but I am grateful she is looked after, and whilst she is alive I do not have to say goodbye.' She also accepts the whole situation as it is, more like the yogic acceptance of the present: 'I don't have your responses. If you look at our life-styles, our emotional make-up, you are so very different from me.' Here is a typical example:

Dialogue with my sister.

ME:	I think it's time to remove the television from mother's room.
MY SISTER:	No. It gives her something to look at, keeps her alert. I think she still has some visual fascination for movement or people.
ME:	There is quite enough television throughout the day in the lounge. Surely at bed-time she can rest in her own world, or if it's still light look out through the window at the trees, the clouds in the sky. This constant stimulus is irrelevant.
MY SISTER:	That's your opinion. I believe she appreciates the fleeting images of the TV more than the unchanging view from her window by the attention she shows to the screen.
ME:	But don't you think I've got a point when she is in her own room?
MY SISTER:	No. You make it sound as if she is being deprived of peace and quiet and being stopped the pleasure of peaceful gazing outside the window. She'll drift into her own world with or without the TV on. She likes the telly.

This is what her carers also believe, noting how she watches the moving pictures. I think much of the time she's mesmerised and when I come in and see a news report of one of the world's tragic events, or yet another 'entertainment' depicting violent scenes, I find myself minding that she is being pulled into a world which she has long left behind. In fact the Nursing Sister, who always listens to my views, agrees with me and encourages staff not to switch the television on throughout the whole day but finds her wishes are not always carried out: 'We want a pleasant atmosphere, soft music, the kind of programmes residents might have enjoyed in their own homes. It's one of the issues I address often in meetings.'

After several variations of that dialogue about television, I have finally accepted my sister will never understand my perspective, and we have got on better. This long drawn out last stage of our mother's life has thrown us into much more contact than we might otherwise have had, and over five years has tested our relationship to the hilt as we have many fundamental disagreements.

Now the latest issue is mother losing weight, not taking in her blended food. Sister assures us that, if she refuses a main meal, Complan is given to maintain her strength: 'Foods and fluids are a necessity to life, to withdraw them is the most cruel thing to do to a human being.' Yet replacing one kind of food for a fortified liquid nourishment is surely not withdrawing food. I wonder, if I could agree with my sister, whether I would be within my rights to argue the case for not providing Complan. 'No', says the Legal Officer from Help the Aged,

> this is very shaky ground. The law doesn't allow a relative to decide something of that magnitude. A court would need to make a declaration as to whether withdrawing life sustaining nourishment is in the best interests of the individual. It is very difficult to assess the nature and quality of life for someone who lacks the mental capacity to make such a decision; it is also very difficult to judge whether a life is being prolonged or not.

Mother has not fed herself independently for a long time now. Is it a sign to be respected if she herself no longer wants her food? Am I wrong to think that if a person can no longer feed themselves then there may come a stage, apart from times of serious illness, that this is against what feels right. When my mother's hands are no longer the instrument to put food into her own mouth should someone else do it for her? Is my view cruel? A counsellor friend who has been a hospital social worker gives this advice: 'It is important to offer food appropriately but not force it and for this routine to be continued.'

'There is a need to maintain a quality of life', the GP explains: 'You can do this better with calories and vitamins from Complan. There is even pleasure sometimes in feeding and an element of comfort is kept at a basic level, oral hygiene is important and sore mouths are prevented.'

Away from the nursing home I know I feel differently. I wonder if it is instinctive to feed another person who is unable to feed themselves. My sister certainly thinks so: 'When I see mother I want to feed her, it is a natural loving thing to do. It is my process of relating to her and gradually she becomes more responsive to me, and for the hours I'm with her I feel I improve the quality of her life.'

This is the long slow bereavement of losing someone while they are still alive. Thirty years ago when I witnessed my grandparents dying, the crossing of that threshold appeared more straightforward. I remember my grandmother as a wizened old lady lying, but quite alert, in a bed far too big for her also in a Catholic nursing home. I was in my twenties, visiting: 'Darling', she said and pointed to the glass of medicine on the side-table, 'just pour that into the plant pot'. Of course I did. 'Enough is Enough', she used to say, and my father often quoted her and I expect I will too.

Mother never faced her own mortality. When she and my father were still in the family house, I used to take her for walks along the promenade. We'd sit on a bench, looking at the gulls flying over the waves: 'What will happen to me?' she asked one day. 'We'll look after you', I said. And we have.

> 04 October 2004 – Mother is in the nursing home. That is her home. Near me. She is near my home.
>   Why will she not go to her real home?
>   Why does she not know it is time to go home – time to leave?
>   Mother – it is time to leave home.

Learning through example: My father's last hours – 15 January 2001

My father's death came suddenly after a tense Christmas visit in 2000; he was visibly strained with looking after my mother and on leaving our house made a decision to stop his medication. We can only speculate on his intentions but the result was hospitalisation, a stroke and death by mid-January.

As my father lay dying in a hospital side-ward after a stroke, my mother, sister and I were by his bedside. His speech had gone and he was almost completely paralysed, but he could move his right arm and so through raising his hand up or down we knew he could hear us and respond meaningfully.

I feel privileged to have had that time with him. If I had not watched a young nurse who allowed herself to show love for her patient, a dying man, a stranger, then I don't think I would have quite known how to show love towards my own father, and had such an intense experience. I learned how to be with him on that last day from her exemplary care as she fed him at mid-day:

15 January 2001 – She feeds him a few spoonfuls of semolina. She looks lovingly into his eyes, calling him by his first name. His eyes open wide. I am taken by surprise at this contact of the young nurse feeding him, and then washing his mouth with such love and care. He is very responsive and alert.

3.00pm – I have just had an hour by myself with father. I sat by the bedside. He clearly wanted to hold my hand; his head on the pillow, lying on the side, just looking at me. We had an hour of intense looking at each other, and with much raising of our eyebrows we communicated. His breathing was very rapid and I tried to breathe with him. The vibrations were too fast for me. It was very physical and primal, like birth… (Suswin 2002, p.5)

When his breathing started to rack and became noisy, he was given a nebuliser to take the moisture out of the breath and within ten minutes he fell asleep. An hour later he died.

My writings on the final hours of my father's life were read to students on an Access to Nursing course, on the caring role of the nurse within the general debate on the role of nurses and healthcare assistants. The students came from a variety of different backgrounds and different first languages; many were already working as healthcare assistants. Sally Tolputt, their lecturer in communication studies, found: 'It was a perfect way of demonstrating the power of the personal story in bringing a subject to life: the students' responses show that they felt engaged and moved.' Here are some:

It was very interesting – the daughter silently listening and watching the treatment given to the father.

The personal story was very interesting as it showed the daughter…noting how her father responded to the nurse and the tender way in which care was offered.

I did not know I can communicate with my eyes with a sick person.

There are certain times in nursing when no procedure will make it better; only caring will help.

I felt it was very true, how we reach out to each other on so many different levels, when there is no other way, and it showed a very caring way a nurse would act to a patient…

I think he had a nice treat in the hospital before he died.

This last sentiment perhaps was not quite as my father would have expressed it! The memory of that last hour with him in January 2001 is hugely significant to me. As he lay dying, I believe we experienced a rare flow of love between us – it was a healing moment in the context of our whole relationship with many difficult memories of our differences.

The realisation that this short piece of writing works on a number of levels is satisfying: it demonstrates true nursing care; it shows that learning can take place through observation, and that a real-life story enlivened a lecture. It shows that when we allow ourselves to be touched by the essential qualities of human contact the real learning takes place. My immediate reaction to the extract being used for teaching was: what would father think? It only took me a few seconds to agree, but I carry a sense of responsibility in maybe transgressing his privacy.

I trust that in writing about his dying I have respected above all the importance of this last act of life and its sacred quality. My father was not a religious man and neither did he show his feelings easily: it is an enormous comfort that the end of his life was marked with love and care

Conclusion

Writing honestly out of our feelings and beliefs requires trust, a love of the truth, and an enormous respect for following where the writing may go without a vested interest in results. If we trust this process our consciousness expands so we begin to feel more fully ourselves. Writing about my parents has given me a sense of completeness about my relationship with them. Although during my adult relating there were many gaps in communication which left me unsatisfied, here I have found how to express the love for my father in his last hour; a way of channelling my feelings and reactions about my mother's long stay in a nursing home; and through the contact with my sister a meeting in the middle ground of agreement. All this gives me that sense of rest with the family into which I was born.

I have to admit that my initial impetus in writing about my mother was only to explore my own view by challenging caring practices currently in place which puzzled me. I gave lip service to my sister's views which I included. However, it was necessary to get her permission. This I anticipated would prove difficult. As children we were very close; as adults we have grown apart.

The draft I sent my sister exposed our differences. An intense exchange of emails allowed each of us to state our case, point by point. I revised with close attention to her responses and really began to want to reflect her particular voice, her thinking; it made for better writing. She thanked me, and we ended up collaborating on the finer details. She still pointed out she does not share my sentiments and wants to distance herself from this writing.

Through conducting a number of interviews, I have been able to question the values in how we look after the very elderly in the last phase of their lives in nursing homes; this has brought me right up against the real world. The email communication between my sister and myself provided a medium to bridge a rift unlikely through conversation. I believe we worked through something together through the power of writing. In many ways the writing brings its own gifts unasked.

Note

New legislation addressing the highly complex matters concerning directives for the care of the mentally incapacitated continues to be drawn up under the new Mental Capacity Act (2005). A new more comprehensive power of attorney, to be called a lasting power of attorney, may well address decisions regarding welfare and medical treatment. The present enduring power of attorney only deals with property and financial affairs.

15. Reading to Help Practitioners and Patients

Ted Bowman and Rogan Wolf

A book must be the axe which smashes the frozen sea within us.
Franz Kafka (in Astley 2002)

Poetry should be part of every modern hospital... It's a powerful force, which can help us through the darkest times. I would like to see more poets in residence, more poetry books in waiting rooms, more poems on the walls, more training in creative writing for doctors, and more poems printed on primary care leaflets... [It] offers comfort and inspiration to all of us. Poetry can save lives!
Julia Darling (in Darling and Fuller 2005, p.13)

Books, magazines, papers offer us one of our most available art forms. Expressed in our everyday communicating medium – words – literature can be picked up and put down at will, borrowed free from libraries or friends, bought cheaply. And we can learn so much from literature.

Writers are generous with their experience: it is the stuff of literature, whether fiction, poetry, plays, autobiography or biography. Authors share the insight and understanding they've gained in their own lives, ensuring 'nobody can be ignorant of the world, and nobody may say that he is innocent of what it's all about' (Sartre 1950, p.14). Literature is powerfully educative of our minds, emotions and spirits.

Michael Rosen's Sad Book, for example, is a gift, reaching out from the depth of his own tragic loss of a son to others who might suffer untimely bereavement (Rosen and Blake 2004). Ann Kelley's *The Burying Beetle* (2005), also written from deep personal experience, concerning a child with a fragile hold on life, is a story of hope. Dermatologist Anne MacLeod (2002, 2004) has written two novels about life in the face of injury, adversity and bereavement. Andrew Greig's poetry about nearly dying, and the difference that made to his experience of the wonder of living, shares with his readers not only the pain and fear, but, more vitally, the intensity of finding himself still alive (2006).

Staying Alive (Astley 2002) justifiably became Britain's most popular poetry book within a fortnight of publication. Along with its companion volume *Being Alive* (Astley 2004), it offers 'poems that touch the heart, stir the mind, and fire the spirit'. These anthologies are lifelines: open them at random and a poem will leap off the page and wrap warm arms around you, or offer wise counsel. Poetry can not only seriously affect your heart, but also seriously damage sadness and nightmares; it can help you say hello to a sliver of joy even in a time of adversity or bleakness. Reading a poem at a funeral 'aloud, or hearing it read, may seem to open the wound but the intensity of that openly collective experience brings everyone closer as the poem's words speak for all' (Astley 2003, p.9). How could anyone describe grief and bereavement more achingly than: 'The stars are not wanted now: put out every one; Pack up the moon and dismantle the sun' (Larkin in Astley 2003, p.9). *The Long Pale Corridor* (Benson and Falk 1996) is a collection of bereavement poems.

The Poetry Cure, co-edited by Julia Darling, who died of cancer shortly after publication, can help people find their own words for their own troubles (Darling and Fuller 2005). A close friend undergoing chemotherapy found it altered her perception, gave her a new vocabulary and a sense of support. She, like the writers of these poems, suffered less in private silence. She thought about her own poems, even if she lacked the energy to write. We laughed as I greeted her when she called, with: 'I know I'm supposed to say how's your cancer?, rather than 'How are you? in an underlined voice' (How to behave with the ill, Darling and Fuller 2005, p.16).

Finally, Cecil Helman's *Suburban Shaman* (2006) is electric shock therapy for what medicine and healthcare can and should be. A human and humane memoir, I think Franz Kafka would have put it on his list, when he said: 'One should only read books that bite and sting one. If the book we are reading does not wake us up with a blow to the head, what's the point in reading?' (Astley 2002, epigram).

Ted and Rogan give their experience of the value of reading poetry and prose.

Caring and helping with literary resources   *Ted Bowman*

> *When I finally recovered the will to read [I] searched around me for any book, essay or sentence that might speak directly to the hole I was in… In that deep trough…I needed to read some story that paralleled, at whatever distance, my unfolding bafflement – some honest report from a similar war…*
>
> *Price (1994, pp.180–181)*

A daughter assists her father as he goes to the toilet. Picture her facing her father as they emerge from the bathroom, walking hand in hand. Galway Kinnell tells the story in *Parkinson's Disease*.

> She is leading her old father into the future
> as far as they can go, and she is walking
> him back into her childhood, where she stood
> in bare feet on the toes of his shoes
> and they foxtrotted on this same rug.
>
> (Kinnell 1994, p.43)

Families and professionals often describe such persons like this old man as child-like. This can be demeaning, robbing someone of dignity and station. Kinnell's poem invites the reader to distinguish between childlike *and* flashbacks of child-hood experiences. Nurses, particularly, get involved with people in caring acts that may contain memories of earlier times. He also reminds all helpers who observe such moments that their time may come also when he adds: 'I watch them closely: she could be teaching him / the last steps that one day she may teach me' (Kinnell 1994, p.45). Observe carefully, the poet seems to be saying.

Poems like this can be used with family members, following them with questions such as: 'What are you now doing as a caregiver that your parents did with you?' This might invite helpful information about the family system, whether problematic or positive in childhood. It can also be an opportunity to 'reframe' challenging and burdensome actions. To transform the move from bathroom to bedroom from chore to a foxtrot can help lighten the load.

Consider using a Billy Collins poem, eloquent in reframing a situation unlikely to change. Collins used a metaphor of a neighbour's dog that would not stop barking: 'They must switch him on, on their way out' (2001, p.3). The writer turns on a Beethoven symphony full blast to cover the sound of the barking dog. Even though the muffled sound still can be heard, reframing occurs:

> …now I can see him sitting in the orchestra,
> his head raised confidently as if Beethoven
> has included a part for barking dog.
> …sitting there in the oboe section barking.

I used this playful poem with hospice workers recently. After reading it, they wrote about situations that were challenging for them that were also unlikely to change. Then, they each chose one challenge to explore reframing so that they could move away from anger and blame of others. Family members have also found the poem helpful in facing an inevitable or near death. A change in attitude might allow them to enjoy the moments they have left, focusing there, rather than on the moments they will never have.

A woman dying with cancer, after reading such poetry, sent a prayer-poem, *Teach Me How to Die*, by Ted Loder, that had profound meaning for her:

> Teach me the ways of courage past bravado,
> That whether death comes gently or harshly,
> Be brief in coming, or lingering,
> I will be able to face it…
>
> Teach me to be graceful in the present
> As even now my horizons shrink…
>   (Loder 2000, pp.153–155)

Later she shared one of her own poems, written at the cancer centre writing program for patients and families. Her poem, *I Never Would Have Thought*, shows she was able to practice a similar prayer.

> Cancer taught me
> to live in the moment:

radical blessing.
Stacks of card
visible and outward
signs of love.

It took cancer
for me to know.
       (Zabel 2003, p.6)

Zabel's selection of the prayer-poem and her later writing could serve to invite
people to explore insights and learnings that have been meaningful, in spite of
losses. A question might be: 'What have you learned that you would not have
learned if you had never been diagnosed with cancer?' Or 'If you could give advice
to someone beginning to face what you have faced, what advice would you offer?'
Such questions not only reframe experiences but can also provide ways to be altru-
istic. Many persons with cancer and other challenging conditions believe that they
have little to offer; they have become 'dependent'. Questions like these invite them
to be wounded healers by sharing wisdom and insight gained from undesired
conditions.

People often find it helpful to write about their cancer, sometimes directing
their words to the cancer.

This is to inform you
that despite reckless and relentless
division and multiplication
of your militant cells,
you will never win.
          (Barrineau 1991, p.15)

Writing in this way can move the 'enemy', even the loss, outside oneself so that it
can be addressed. After reading, patients or family might be asked, 'Have you ever
talked to the cancer? If you have, what did you say? If you haven't, I bet there are
things you would like to say to it. Let's try it.' They may think you a bit strange.
But, in the act of inviting stories and words, you give a kind of permission for
facing what Miriam Greenspan called the dark emotions.

Others find it helpful simply to tell the story. Alan Shapiro wrote a memoir of
his sister's dying. In it, he seemed to clarify for himself and his readers one of the
many dilemmas of end-of-life care:

however much we suffered as we watched my sister die, we didn't merely suffer. There
was joy, too, or something like joy, in the suffering itself. Joy in the self-forgetfulness
that came with tending Beth, with grieving for her, and in caring so tenderly for each
other as we grieved…joy, in other words, in an intimacy whose very rarity added
sadness to the joy. (Shapiro 1997, p.5)

Writing about confusing feelings and realities can enable the writer to gain a bit of
mastery over something that at times can seem overwhelming and out of control.
Shapiro wrote also of the strange experience of leaving the bedside of his dying
sister and going to a grocery store. He had been so absorbed in the dying that he
naïvely presumed everyone else would somehow know also. To his surprise, they
shopped as if nothing significant was happening just down the road. Writing (or

reading or telling stories) can help make sense of such paradoxes. 'How is your story different or similar than Shapiro's account?' 'How would you describe your situation?' Whether written or not, just to say it aloud can be powerful.

Each of these writers highlights the importance of words for coping. The old adage if it is unmentionable it is unmanageable leaps from their sentences. Their own care begins with finding words, even for the unspeakable.

Reynolds Price's words above emphasised that in their deep trough patients and families need to give voice to their story. Finding aspects of their story in a poem, illness narrative, fiction or music encourage or reflect that voice. 'Seriously ill people are wounded not just in body but in voice', wrote medical ethicist Arthur Frank (1995, p.xii). 'They need to become storytellers in order to recover the voices that illness and its treatment often take away. The voice speaks the mind and expresses the spirit...' (p.xii). The same could be said for nurses and other carers.

Grieving people frequently cite poetry, stories of loss, and inspirational writings as important resources. Price and Frank have described a quest for words that can be a source of information, comfort, insight, challenge or companionship while grieving. In spite of this common practice, more often than not, nurses and other palliative care providers draw primarily on their medical, psychological or theological training and sources, failing to use the insights of poets and other writers to guide their work. Some even fail to inquire about readings the grieving or bereft person may be using as a resource. Ask: 'What readings or stories do you draw on to help with your illness?'

Here are only a few examples of ways to use or draw upon literary tools in the care of the dying. Add to these examples. Pursue other books and workshops about the subject. Most importantly, aid patients and families in giving voice to their story.

What can a poem say about dying (that we don't already know)?   *Rogan Wolf*

> *It's extremely moving – all the more so for being completely unsentimental and continually sharp-eyed. It doesn't flinch and it manages to combine the anger of grief with a sense of something more stoical – accepting the inevitable I suppose... I think it would work very powerfully in performance.*
>
> *Andrew Motion (UK Poet Laureate)*

> *Beautiful and exquisitely moving... Everyone who reads it will get to know the young mother whose life and death it celebrates, and most will also relive – as I did – our own griefs for loved ones lost... I wept each time I read it. It's a lovely poem...*
>
> *Debjani Chatterjee (poet)*

The poem *A Light Summer Dying* tells the true story of how a young woman I knew died of cancer, leaving behind her husband and two small sons. A good half of it was written as a kind of diary at the time and she knew I was writing it. I actually read her the first excerpt. She took comfort from the thought that her sons would be able to read about her death later in their lives.

I have read the poem to the following groups: social work staff and students (twice), student nurses on a bereavement option (once), teachers involved in nurse training (once), a group of poets and others interested in things literary, including the local vicar (once), a similar group but this time including practising hospice nurses and their chaplain (once). From me each reading has been an experience of high intensity. Afterwards I have always felt, 'this is what the poem is for, doing this; this is what poetry is for, doing this; this is what I am for, doing this'.

That intensity lay partly of course in the words and the story they tell, but partly too in the electric charge they seem to create in the room. On each occasion, reader and listeners have gone through something quite cathartic together and in doing so have formed a circle of shared experience that needs careful and sensitive handling. We have needed to find ways of easing down together, before separating.

One has to ask, why has a poem that simply tells the story of just another death proved so powerful? The inescapable answer is that, even among professionals who work with the dying, society's taboo and our natural escape mechanisms remain at work, encouraging detachment and abstraction. The poem challenges that detachment, and succeeds in its purpose insofar as it makes the experience of the dying woman, her family and her community, real, present and poignant.

Perhaps my biggest test so far has been reading it to hospice nurses and a chaplain. If I had been moved to write it at least partly because this was my first close encounter with death, how would experienced staff react to it, who work carefully and sensitively with dying people every day? Would they find it merely presumptuous, self-indulgent? On the contrary, their feedback was perhaps the strongest and most positive of all. They said it made real, vivid and human an experience that their daily exposure to death too easily objectified; it somehow released and sensitised them to the value, meaning and largeness of what they do and the life-defining significance of what their patients are living through. Here is an excerpt:

...this evening at home
his eyes are staring and fixed
ringed with dark
and the one-year-old is yelling.

It's bedtime
the essential blanket
still in the wash.
He gets too little sleep

and now is shrill and can't settle
darting here and there on the edge
of one clenched thought after another
none of them central or complete.

Today the doctors have given him
a sick note for three weeks
but his quota for sickness on full pay
is nearly exhausted.

A gladioli from the garden has been snapped off.
'I'll take that for her!' he exclaims

and leaps for a newspaper to wrap it up.
'She's leaving me,' he says.
For the past few days she's been too tired
to take him in,

to help him carry the weight,
contain the pressure,
to attend to his accounts
of the day's doings and concerns

his feelings and experience.
She hasn't been able to hold him anymore.
No connection. She isn't there.
Her blue eyes keep wandering

to a picture on the wall
of a massive rock the sun bombards all day,
a domed church just visible on the top
tiny on a scorched cliff-edge.

'I realise now how much more
support she's given me
than ever I gave her,' he says.
'And how does that

leave you feeling?'
I ask, expecting guilt.
'I dread losing her,' he says.

Once the children are in bed
he goes as usual
to spend the last hours of the day
alone with her

in her hospital room.
Upstairs,
two small boys
sleeping through their trouble.

Downstairs, a forgotten gladioli stem
wrapped in the day's dead news…

Poetry on show in healthcare   *Rogan Wolf*

*Poems for the Waiting Room is an inspired scheme…I've been delighted to be part
of it.*

Andrew Motion (UK Poet Laureate)

*I think this is a wonderful project giving people something meaningful and personal
to consider, in what can be an anxious place.*

Rt Hon. Tessa Jowell (UK Minister for Culture, Media and Sport)

Poems for the Waiting Room offers collections of 145 A4 poem-posters for display in healthcare settings for only a postage charge. Hospices, hospitals, health centres and community centres, have displayed the poems in all sorts of ways: in frames in groups of four or five; enlarged to A3 and framed individually; in ring-binder files on the waiting room table for browsing. I have heard of more than one example of poems being displayed in staff lavatories, which I think is a wonderful idea! Or how about changed regularly in a display cabinet or a new one each week on the screen saver?

What's the gain? I love the idea of poetry escaping the specialist bookshop shelves and getting out there. Poem-posters can help to make the waiting room more personal and human: for all of us, at some point. In a waiting room we find ourselves in the middle of quite a long pause, often a very difficult one. A good poem that speaks to us can be welcome and rich company, bringing community to the room and to those long moments.

We have heard already from large numbers of patients, visitors and staff how much the poems are valued – by hospices as well as the other varied settings – and we have undertaken a small initial evaluation. And often the posters have acted to encourage people to contribute their own writing for display.

Poet Laureate Andrew Motion launched the 2005 collection, opening up a new dimension. It consists of 45 poems written in non-English languages, each with its English translation. Thirty-five languages are represented, including Arabic, Bengali, Farsi, Hindi, Kurdish, Mandarin, Punjabi, Turkish, Urdu and Vietnamese. We have called the collection 'Poems in Praise of Diversity'. It teaches something simple very powerfully. It makes new and necessary connections.

Other plans include audio versions, and to explore some ideas for different forms for display. We are also now looking for commercial sponsorship.

Two organisations with similar titles make poems available to healthcare settings. The other one, Poems in the Waiting Room, offers A4 brochures containing fresh collection of poems that come out regularly. Patients are free to take the brochures home with them (www.pitwr.pwp.blueyonder.co.uk).

16. Artists: Survivors

Tim Jeeves, Mitzi Blennerhassett and Michele Angelo Petrone

Involvement in an art (professionally, in art therapy, with a writer-in-residence, or alone) can really help people in a great range of ways, as the rest of *Dying, Bereavement and the Healing Arts* demonstrates. Tim, Mitzi and Michele describe their experience.

On catharsis   *Tim Jeeves*

Nothing ever leaves us.

It may be transferred onto something else, it is often ignored, and occasionally it becomes integrated into our consciousness, but once an emotional state is experienced we can never disentangle ourselves from it, we can never become the person we were before.

This is time passing.

Some things are too horrible to look at face on.

Some things are too painful to return to.

And that fear to look at them shapes our actions; we throw ourselves into work, we abandon ourselves to alcohol, we lose ourselves in shopping. We do anything we can to avoid re-experiencing that which has hurt us.

But this limits our experience of life.

We cannot filter out the negative by focusing only on that we see as positive, for the one contains the other.

The pain of heartache and the joy of being in love stem from the same root. To refuse to ever feel heartache again means to deny the chance for further love.

And vice versa.

But if we believe that facing that pain benefits us, if we go some way to absorbing it and make it a positive part of who we are, if we can expand our view of the world so that pain exists within it, then our appreciation of the beauty of life becomes more profound.

Maybe even more truthful.

Art allows a safe revisiting of that place of revulsion.

It has been compared to a rollercoaster ride.

We ride a rollercoaster in order to be terrified, and yet none of us would willingly step on a rollercoaster knowing it to be unsafe.

This is the contradiction of tragedy that Aristotle first explained, and, even though art has gained a much broader definition than the simplification he wrote of, such a sentiment still holds true.

Whether witness or artist, something within art must communicate with us, or it has no meaning.

In December 2003 the fifth anniversary of the completion of my treatment for cancer was marked by a performance in Euroart Studio's Gallery in Tottenham.

The Last Days of Mourning lasted six days, over which time I wrote 1825 memories of the time I was ill on the walls of the gallery. This number of recollections was chosen since it corresponded to the total days in remission on the final day of the performance.

My reasons for making the piece were varied.

The most obvious, a celebration of five years of remission, a milestone commemorating the magical date that had seemed so impossibly distant when I first finished my treatment. Alongside this, I wanted to make a tribute to those who had been with me on the ward and who weren't alive to celebrate their own five years without treatment.

And it was a challenge to myself.

Whilst I had always tried to be accepting about my illness, whilst I had tried to integrate it into myself, I knew that in all likelihood this would now be the only opportunity to spend so much time immersing myself in the memories from this hugely formative period in my life.

I knew I was going to complete the work; it was too important for failure to be a possibility.

But the piece was a challenge to see how far into myself I was willing to delve, a provocation, a dare.

As the six days passed, my overriding sentiment was that I was being weak, that I was not reliving the times I was writing about enough.

I only cried once.

Standing on the small mezzanine, looking out across the room, over the heads of the people reading what I had shared, one thought on the opposite wall stood out amongst a mix of memories.

'I remember when Nicky died.'

Maybe I didn't lose myself in the past as much as I could; but now, nearly a year later, I know I could never have lost myself as much as I desired.

I had naïve hopes that this piece would release me from the significance that the time I had cancer has in my life. I allowed myself to think that this would normalise cancer completely for me.

In the weeks after the performance I had to cope with the disappointment that this was not the case.

No work of art, nothing in life, can remove something so utterly.

As I have already stated, time passes down a one-way street.

But art, writing, music, even simply allowing painful memories to wash over us as we gaze at a scene of beauty; all this allows us to revisit painful times whilst knowing that the seatbelt is secure around us, rigorous safety checks have been passed, and we are going to walk away from the memory intact.

Some part of the meaning and significance of art comes from its insubstantiality, its ability to facilitate an understanding of the world's own lack of substance outside of that which we inject into it.

Catharsis is expression to a (imagined) listener who understands.

Therapeutic eruptions   *Mitzi Blennerhassett*

I never set out to write poetry, or to use writing as a therapy. The poems were born because my experience of cancer treatment in 1990 left me in deep mental conflict.

False reassurances had lulled me into a false sense of security, allowing the diagnosis (carcinoma of the anal canal) and brutal delivery to achieve maximum impact. I was told the side effects of treatment would be nausea, sickness, diarrhoea and wind. Nobody mentioned pain. Well-meant but mind-blowing paternalism (endless smiles, false reassurances, conflicting information) wiped away my trust. Apparently 'caring' attitudes contrasted dramatically with shockingly painful events and prolonged, acute pain, creating enormous conflict, completing the recipe for turmoil.

Afterwards, I suffered years of daily playback. Unable to sleep, I started jotting things down to try to make sense of them and in expressing my feelings I slipped inadvertently into 'poetry' mode. It is only now, as I write this, that I have a comprehensive understanding of just why I had to write.

My marriage had broken down long before the diagnosis and it is important to recognise, but not disproportionately, how much this could have contributed to my state of mind. After a week of simultaneous chemotherapy and radiotherapy, I drove 90 miles daily for three weeks' radiotherapy. I had great difficulty sleeping and eating, while increasing pain left me banging my head on the wall. I was told I would be 'a bit ill' and sent home (I could not lift a glass of water) had another two weeks' radiotherapy and finally went into hospital again for radioactive wire implants.

Admission to a cancer hospital had been overwhelming as I became aware of the hundreds of patients. The difficulties for staff working in such a place also burdened me acutely. Some of my poems reflect how I suffered for them too!

Death row?
Sixteen beds, but isolation
Heaving wards of shell-shocked faces
Overwhelmed by all the sadness
By the scale of desolation
By the role that staff must play

Chemotherapy lamppost pumping
In rude health, apart from cancer

Sit upon the bed, not in it
Just a vain and futile gesture
But it's something I can do
I'm the one who's going to beat it
I'm not ill. I'm not like you!
But they're dying all around me
Did they think the same way, too?

Simultaneous radiotherapy
And a wheelchair now appears
(Though I'm capable of walking)
Challenge, and permission's granted
But the seed is deeply planted
Now confirmed: my deepest fears

It's quite clear, what they're expecting
It's quite clear what is assumed
Shockingly, yet just routinely
Everybody thinks I'm doomed

My questions were answered, but rarely to my satisfaction: plenty of smiles, but mounting discrepancies. As my body deteriorated, persistent questioning seemed to signal an 'inability to cope', rather than a 'need to know'. The cancer had spread to lymph nodes in my groin, but there was no discussion about the seriousness of my situation. Everything was minimalised.

The first two days and nights were spent listening to a dying patient trying to cough. In an eight-bedded bay of a 16-bed ward, I experienced the sights and sounds of other patients' suffering in addition to my own. It was an alien place of death, yet staff smiled as if it were a holiday camp.

Charnel house?
Days and nights of unsought sharing
Rasping, gasping on display
Oxygen cylinders, rushing and clanking
Relatives' vigil: time to pray

Curtains closed for the conclusion
Starkly, in the new-born day
While the daily buzz continues
Stands the (briefly) empty bed
All around, the buzz continues
And nothing is said
Nothing is said

I had asked friends and family not to visit me but I hadn't realised how lonely I would feel. I could hear nurses laughing and chatting at their station, but no one came to talk to me. I even became envious of patients having their temperatures taken! At the same time, I did not exactly invite support. 'I'm fine!' ('Miss Independent') – an enigma, wanting credit, not 'protection', yet so needing a hand in mine. And I had to be seen to be coping in order to get information, so it was difficult to admit to my needs.

I thought I might die there, in that first week. Within the first two days I imagined what that would be like, the effects on my family, and came to terms with it. But nobody knew about this, because nobody talked to me.

Preconceptions, misconceptions
Pain and nausea, diarrhoea
Now I come to terms with dying
Conquering the final fear
But there's no one here to listen
No one who has learned to 'hear'

Even when they find me crying
(Picturing the ones left grieving
That's what needs the healing balm:
Mothers should protect their children
Buffer them, not cause them harm)

No one uses the right questions
They see only fear of cancer
(I am made of sterner stuff!)
Even though they're really trying,
Kindliness is not enough

At the end of treatment, I emerged with a survivor's gratitude, but a teenager's resentment – and all the guilt this jumble of feelings engendered. It was two years before I felt strong enough to leave my husband. Meanwhile, the conflict and need for truth reached extreme levels with my impending move and uncertainty about my prognosis. Would it be fair to my son to take him with me?

The poems began erupting at 3am night after night, pouring out as if written by someone else. I had never written poetry before. I wrote with tears pouring down my face. They were simply expressions of frustration, of need for answers and acknowledgement. How could such excellent 'surface' care have allowed such mental and physical suffering? How could they send me home to be so ill, without support, to pain that left me suicidal? Why didn't they talk to one another? Why didn't anyone acknowledge the side effects that could happen and ensure relief was in place? Why couldn't they see what a heroine I was – and credit me? How could I feel like this, when all I should be feeling was gratitude…?

The poems relieved my feelings and later helped other patients to cry. I hoped they would perhaps be used in medical education one day. But my early attempts to improve services for future patients had met with huge defensiveness, so I shut them away. Now, medical schools are using them and I offer therapeutic writing workshops for health professionals, patients and carers. A book on these lines is forthcoming through Radcliffe Press, and a CD (Vinegar and Brown Paper; obtainable from myself). And, yes, the poems still allow me to cry.

Painter Michele Angelo Petrone explains how the writing of a dream, and the essential reflection which the writing occasioned, helped him in a situation which anyone would find almost unbearable. Written immediately after the dream, and while still in the struggle of an illness and hospital experience, it has not been redrafted. The writing is vivid, drawing the reader into the unreal experience, alongside the writer.

The Tattooed Intruder   *Michele Angelo Petrone*

'Shit!' Startled in my sleep. Towering above me, beside my bed, was this tattooed stranger. Menacing crude indigo tattoos on his scrawny-yellowed skin. Not pictorial, but almost as if self-inflicted, drunken inked scratchings, piercings, mainly on his neck. I remembered particularly this large square, amongst others, over his Adam's apple, his voice box. Who was he? What was he doing standing over me? I don't know him. He scares me.

I awake. It's the middle of the night. It's 4am. I call for a urine bottle. I'm on a fluid chart so all my pee has to be measured and my last one is full. It gives me a chance to wake fully, pull out my notebook to not forget this nightmare and write it down. How could I forget it? But like a dream startled in the night, this was the one I wanted to have forgotten about in the morning.

I know who he is. He is my cancer. The tattooed intruder. He has no name. Only a description. Yet he is a part of me that I don't recognise. That is what brings tears to my eyes. In the calm darkness. In the stillness of the night emerges death. I want to think it is only a shadow, a sign, a symbol, a possibility. Not a fact this time. But it is a possibility I am aware of. A possibility I want to deny. Another throat cracked, teeth clenched, sick stomach, body shuddering tear swells in my eyes. Blurring my vision.

I continue to write in this emotional haze, through this painful sea that threatens to drown me. Yet I have this sleepwalking drive to ink the tattoo here on this paper. Unthought, uncorrected, just scrawled as it is, gripped in my tracks. Word for word, moment for moment, tear beat, heart shudder. This is no premonition. No dream to be forgotten in the morning. This is what is happening.

As my senses are fully taking in, I'm in the dimly lit corner of a four-bedded ward. The sound of the 24-hour constant fungal extractor is the measure of my silence. I remember I am tethered, to a LCD flashing chemo pump beside my bed by the triple alumen Hickman line that protrudes out from a gash in my chest, still only two days sore and the black dissolving stitches still visible. The red electronic display flashing in three descending lines, like those of a mobile phone on charge. Only it is a sign of me being charged day and night by the cisplatin chemotherapy drug and accompanying saline solution. Charging through my body. 0.50mls per hour and 0.48mls hour respectively. What is that 0.02mls difference, flush? Who knows. 0.02mls dash of healing.

I have nausea on the tip of my throat, standing at the entrance of my gut. And a constant ache round my temples. It is not as bad as times before. But it is a sickness I did not feel three days ago, before my treatment started. This is not my bedroom of three days ago neither. I know it is now my home. Three different institution patterned curtains partition me from three other beds and the outside ward. Behind me on my left, someone else is also awake. He frightens me also. I know his name. But we haven't spoken. His white patchy skin, scrawny skeleton, cowered bent forth stance from which hangs his pyjamas stalk me. Telltale signs of future possible side effect of my impending transplant. Graft versus host disease. Common enough here as people talk about it in the corridors, by the nurses in it's abbreviated terms GVHD. One of the many acronyms…HGL (Hodgkin's Lymphoma – my disease), NHGL (Non-Hodgkin's), AML (acute myeloid leukaemia).

GVHD. That haunts me. Because that is not real for me yet, and may not be. But it haunts me because of its possibility, because of my decision. Because of a frightening possible side effect of my decision. A decision to go ahead with this bone marrow transplant from my Italian cousin. She is a perfect match. But she is not my bone marrow. And so there is a chance that her bone marrow once transplanted into my body, through now a relatively simple procedure of a blood transfusion after enforced growth through injections, and harvesting through transfusion, may reject my body. They say it can be chemically, medically controlled. But I can see his skin has been rejected. He looks half ghost, the patches of pigment less, bloodless, lifeless, what do I call it, engulfing his body.

I didn't realise until yesterday morning that the boy in the other window is also suffering this. Latex gloves cover his raw skinless hands. His girlfriend explained that he now has GVDH in his liver and is in daycare receiving the drug to combat this. And he is still smiling. No let up since 1998 for him, except for one holiday, a cruise, to find out after he had relapsed again with NHGL. His bed is empty but is always here for him. His bag keeps watch beside it, a constant reminder that a bed awaits for when he is more ill. Everyday he returns for five minutes, ten minutes, half an hour. A quick hello. 'I'm going home', he says cheerfully. 'Just waiting for my blood test.' And off he goes with his girlfriend, who bears a t-shirt with 'treat me like a princess' on it. She smiles too, disbelieving of his constant outward cheerful demeanour that hides a myriad of constant disappointments and hardships.

Here you can't but be confronted by future side effects, sickness, decisions, enforced, unknown, unwanted, even agreed to. I'm still one of the well ones. I still have my hair, my short goatee stubble, my slight tan from my recent Italian holiday. I pass open doors with people, bald, ashen, gaunt, slumped in chairs, silent, alone, waiting for it all to be over. Room after room. Surrounded not by personally picked paraphernalia of homely delights. No individual swathes of taste, neither Habitat nor Ikea, neither Harrods nor World of Leather. But hospital property, polystyrene ceiling tiles, miles of tasteless curtain track, the obligatory visitors chair by every metal institutional bed. The fan, the blood pressure pump stand. The oxygen mask and the green tubes. The anglepoise lamp. The bed number, the room number, the ward number, the floor number. The alarm switches, the fluorescent light switches. The sickness bowls. The definitely not bedroom carpeted lino floors. The alcohol wipes. The functional sinks. The weighing scales and the sharps only bins. The communal telly, the hospital clock. The smoke alarm and telltale security, safety indicators. Left, right, up, down and all around. And yet it feels safe.

I want to go to sleep now. I want to go to the loo but I remember that my loo is the plastic bottle with its ml counters up its side. A fan swathes some coolish air on my face, a somewhat short relief from the constant fresh less heated environment. I may need a cool drink too. It's a hassle. My tethered lead doesn't allow my free movement. A metre or two to the left or right of the bed. I could unplug for a moment or two, wheel my five unoiled screeching castors around to waken my other room companion. The only one asleep, too sick to be awake. I'm reminded of an Antoine de Saint-Exupéry quote that the beauty of the desert is that it conceals a well. Oh where is that fucking well?

Afterword

It was cathartic to write this down… I wrote it as if recalling a dream/nightmare literally on the ward at 4am, just after waking and it helped me gather my feelings and emotions, my fears and my concerns, where I was and how I was. It is really hard to be able to express your feelings in the hospital environment and even though the dream was startling, frightening, it helped me place myself, express myself to myself and that was such a release.

The truth is – it is frightening; and one does feel the impact of being in an institutionalised environment, not at home, with no privacy, control and that is hard. Although it was also hard to write it up too… But it was the eye of the storm and I was able to take through issues on board, particularly the impact of the other patients – as they were suffering serious side effects of the transplant that is proposed for me. And then that became the basis of my questions, which I probably wouldn't have asked about, with my consultant, and that gave me in turn more answers that have given me more confidence about the treatment. Funny how these things work.

17. Professionals: Artists

Steve Seagull, Tim Metcalf, Oliver Samuel,
Kieran Walsh and Christopher Johns

Medical, healthcare and therapeutic professionals caring for very sick, dying or
bereaved people carry heavy burdens. Many, such as these authors, create art to
help them understand and come to terms with issues and feelings, thoughts and
fears. A critical reflective use of art can also help to increase empathy with patients
and other colleagues, as well as professional self-understanding.

Steve Seagull

In the dog ended hours of the day
I am troubled sometimes
by the memory
of my personal dead.
Where is the penny
I should pay
Charon for you all?
Where is the purse
to keep so much money?
Your dead eyes watch me as I
prepare you for your long sleep
in forgetfulness of me.
Sometimes I have been
reluctant to touch you
fearful that your
silent body will leak
its memories into my life,
muddy the waters of
my own being
with your longing
for existence.

With passing time
you all left me
washed away in the waters
of innumerable showers
and the concerns
of new working days.
Yet each of you,
like streams feeding a river
flow in me
somewhere, unseen.
I remember perhaps
a name
a smile
a harsh word
or a humour.
Sometimes
sometimes
I need to forget
I work amongst
the dead and dying.
Sometimes
I need to know
I am alive
that i still breath.
Sometimes I need
to feel the wind on my skin
the heat of the sun
the cold light of the moon.
Sometimes i need to make
fires in the open air
and howl into
the night
cry out to the hours
I exist
I am alive
I am alive.

The kookaburra and the snake   *Tim Metcalf*

I have often wondered how I came to be a doctor. Certainly my parents thought medicine a laudable career, but my parallel work in poetry suggests it was the language of biology that held the necessary fascination. At six years old I was found with the school's entire collection of biology books, overdue and under my bed. I flirted with literature all the way through my education, publishing such edifying poems as *Head or Tail/ Pass or Fail?* in the medical school magazine, and risking Professor Attwood's wrath by reading T'ang poetry instead of pathology.

Ultimately I graduated, and such fascinating words as paraneoplastic and phospholipotransferase no longer exerted the charm necessary to protect me from the reality of clinical work. There can be no denying the pressures, the emotional intensity and the long hours of my early life as a solitary doctor in remote Australia. Poetry was crucial to helping me lay those disturbing years to rest.

> Thunder over the lake…
> thus the superior man
> understands the transitory
> in the light of the eternity of the end
>
> (Hexagram 54 from *I Ching*, tenth century B.C., in Brower undated, p.30)

Poetry is but one facet of human creative expression. I recall lengthy inner deliberations on this vital question in my early twenties: why I eventually determined to focus upon poetry to the exclusion of others, even to the destruction of my medical career, I cannot be sure. My mother, a teacher-librarian, was an almost pathological reader who could consume three detective novels a day, and my father was a prominent engineer: entertaining quotes from poems were part of the family vernacular. I also discovered, through reading those T'ang poets, that nature and the eternal were what mattered, that money could be an illusory form of wealth, and that if I wanted to be a poet I should do it before I was old.

When I was young, I dropped a brick on my foot. I yelped with pain, but to my surprise found myself laughing instead of crying. Life at medical school, and later at the work I came to call the 'painface', dropped a few more bricks – dissection, surgery, interviewing the psychotic and the dying – and I was one of those who responded with that jet-black humour notorious amongst medical students.

All that laughter now seems as reflexive as that elicited by the brick: it was neither sophisticated, nor for the civilised public. It was a natural response to painful situations. The often confronting experiences of an intern in rural Australia soon restrained this type of humour. An example that stays in my mind was heading on to the wards with my two hours of barely recalled palliative care training. I was extremely nervous, almost too shy to speak with the terminally ill. What on earth could be worth saying? Would I slip out with some terribly inappropriate joke?

Being thrown in the deep end certainly taught me quickly about people. Though the urge was powerful, I was far too busy to express myself in a satisfying poetry. It was over many years that I refined and unified the conflicting laughter and anxiety of that first year as a doctor into a technically adequate poem.

> *Too busy for life*
> At first I was angry with her.
> She had wasted the time set aside
> for us to discuss euthanasia
> by deciding to stay alive.
>
> I lectured myself and grinned:
> I'd have coffee and cake at my leisure.
> Life was busy, but with time today to kill,
> I could hasten my death with pleasure.
>
> (Metcalf 2002a, p.59)

In 1985 thoughtful and organised pain management and a broader conception of palliative care was certainly being developed in the bush. At the same time, each senior doctor had developed his own style. One surgeon would never tell patients what they had or if they were to die; another would. An intern had to know each GP and each specialist's preferences, or risk the wrath that could be incurred by crossing passionately held and staunchly defended religious, moral, social or intellectual boundaries. For the country doctor at that time was a person of considerable importance to the community, someone who bore a number of onerous responsibilities, and someone whose ability to study and then to decide what was right for the health of the people was trusted implicitly.

As a lowly member of the hospital staff I could inconspicuously keep my head down, fill in the paperwork, and listen, should I have the time and the energy, to those patients who wanted to talk. I privately admired a fellow intern who played his guitar for the rehabilitation ward. As I was overworked and isolated within the structure of the hospital, I mostly had time to talk to myself, and to make occasional scribbles of proto-poetry on pieces of paper. Along with the piece from the *I Ching* reproduced above, I had this poem from the eleventh century B.C. *Tao Cheng* on my door to read as I went to work each day, because I found them both intellectually soothing:

Of all the elements, the Sage should take water as his preceptor.
Water is yielding but all-conquering. Water extinguishes Fire,
or, finding itself likely to be defeated, escapes as steam and reforms.
Water washes away soft Earth, or, when confronted by rocks, seeks a way round.
Water corrodes Iron till it crumbles to dust; it saturates the atmosphere
so that Wind dies. Water gives way to obstacles with deceptive humility,
for no power can prevent it following its destined course to the sea.
Water conquers by yielding; it never attacks but always wins the last battle.
The Sage who makes himself as Water is distinguished for his humility;
he embraces passivity, acts from non-action and conquers the world.

(From *Tao Cheng*, eleventh century B.C., in Brower undated, p.14)

As often as possible I drove away from the hospital and into the wonderful open countryside for air fresh off the southern ocean and vigorous exercise. It was certainly an advantage to work in a small hospital close enough to the coast for the pager to work!

Stages of dying (after Elisabeth Kübler-Ross)

Denial

In anatomy class
we cut textbook lines
into the dull clay of our body.
We shook dismembered hands,
and bragged of cricket with arms and balls
for a joke.
We washed the formalin from our hands
for the next two days.

Shock

A pregnant girl collapsed.
The scalpel cut quick and deep.
Her grey belly peeled apart.

The monitors ticked:
a mechanical requiem.
White gloves pulled out the baby
cold and dead like the streets
I wandered half that night.

Guilt

As an intern
I was anxious, and obedient.
To cure at all costs
was the boss' creed.
I had no time for the old woman
we made betray her faith.
Soon after the transfusion
she died of cancer.

Anger

Some drunken bastard
hit this woman with his car.
Her young breasts quivered
each time we thumped her chest.
Over half an hour
her face, burned alive,
set cold, branding for life
the mind of her child.

Sorrow

Was it happy, his final memory?
This poor bloke, purple-faced
and next in line for death?
I was naive, yesterday,
regarding his broken heart.
Today it wouldn't go anymore.
Tonight I was drunk.
There were tears, briefly.

Acceptance

I went to see an elder on his beach up north.
He didn't say much.
There was this sky-blue dreaming;
the ocean its lucent mirror,
flawless like an egg.
I heard he died around sunset.
That night a warm breeze blew
the soothing tune of the sea.

(Metcalf 2001, pp.14–16)

I think I completed my medical apprenticeship in death in the remote Northern
Territory in 1986, when I was posted as a flying doctor to Groote Eylandt. On the
island, 700 kilometres from the nearest specialist, palliative care involved signing
the prescription so the nurse could take morphine from the only drug cupboard to

someone lying under a tree on the beach a few hundred metres down the hill from the clinic. For my Aboriginal patients, surrounded by their people, overshadowed by vast tropical sunsets night after night, genuine peace seemed possible.

For a second-year doctor, helping out with the pain relief was an easy way to care, but of course I knew it was not real caring, that my actions stood on the utmost periphery, and that it really was only an apprenticeship. My prescription in this sense was my pain relief. A slow but thorough learner, I was busy trying to come to terms with the intellectual consequences of a dysfunctional individuality and a pressurised consumerist secularity. Reading the entire *Golden Bough*, and selected Freud, Jung, and contemporary feminism, whilst working with a tribal people served to greatly sharpen my questions to society.

The Aboriginal Dreamtime, so far as I could comprehend it, had the beautiful quality of being absolutely self-contained. It seemed to me an internally complete worldview by which many doubts, including time, and therefore death itself, could be annulled, and in which the uncertainty and angst of white healthcare workers over proper palliative care was not so much forgiven as never a question that arose. To work with people who had no use for a linear time and its accreted capitalist imperatives was one of the most profound experiences of my life.

The poor health of Aboriginal Australia, too often the result of disruption of its numerous cultures, has not been dragged from its abject 'third-world' in the 20 years since I experienced it first hand. White Australia has steadily improved its physical health over this same period, but arguably deteriorated psychologically. Now all of us have vast epidemics of depression and obesity to cope with. We can expect palliation to expand out from its 'traditional' base of pain relief in cancer to embrace the new intractable health problems.

To heal
Setting out to climb the hill,
land and sky
cut a clean horizon.

Planting your staff, the line dissembles
into individual stones,
the pulse of blood in your ears.

Reaching the top, the range is revealed.
The kookaburra laughs.
A snake slithers on ahead.
                    (Metcalf 2002, p.62)

Healing reminds me of bush-walking up the mountains of Australia's Great Dividing Range. Here the snakes are real and everyday (though the poem equally recalls the snake cult that was absorbed by that of Aesculapius, millennia past) and the summit seems vague, somewhere in the trees, and not yet the top I was aiming for. The kookaburra is a modern addition to our poetic iconography. Its call, justly likened to sinister or mocking laughter, insists the pain will come, soon enough: that we never really heal. The kookaburra is a ruthless predator of young snakes, and with its savage beak stakes out its territory of death.

Step by step my understanding, and consequently, I believe, my acceptance and my ability to truly care, improves. This journey is as arduous for me as it is for the healthcare profession as a whole. Laughter and tears help us deal with it, but palliative care will increase in importance, and in difficulty, with the projected rise in chronic illness worldwide. As caring is not widely understood as economically rational, I cannot imagine it devoid of that least expensive and lowest technology of today's arts: poetry (Metcalf 2006).

It is all in the bones   *Oliver Samuel*

As physicians, we attend and try to help patients cope with their illnesses and distress. Sometimes we succeed and the patients feel better. But most of what doctors do has only very occasionally anything to do with altering the duration of life itself. Ours is seldom the place either to prolong or (heaven forbid) to shorten the duration of an individual's continuing existence. We serve as attendants and comforters, but don't have much to do with determining how long an illness will actually last. That is determined by complex factors far beyond the reach of a mere medic. This is all in marked contrast with the popular image of medical prescience – how often do we hear that 'the doctors gave him only six months to live' or similar definite limits, which the patient has either rigidly followed or, more likely, magically managed to defeat.

I first learned about the power of the mind over such matters from my grandpa, who used to tell such wondrous stories about his childhood in Australia way back. About how the Aborigines could make an enemy die by just pointing at them with the sacred bones. They knew that continued existence was about the spirit and the will to live, without which survival would be impossible. And pointing the bones was powerful magic enough to steal that vital sap.

Grandpa was Australian through and through. He had been born in Melbourne and, despite a lifetime that took him all over the world, two things really mattered, his family and his love of cricket. In his later years, he and Granny readily agreed to leave their home in Sydney and take a flat to be near us in London. It was, after all only a short bus-ride to Lords. They were both in their eighties and neither was well. But that hardly limited their interest in what was going on. And Grandpa was really excited by the prospect of the being able, for the first time in his life, to watch a Test Match at Lords. Australia was on a roll and he had tickets.

But in the preceding winter months, he had become sick and breathless and was found to have myeloid leukaemia – in an era when there was precious little that could be done about it. Gradually the illness sapped his strength and, despite repeated transfusions, he found it hard to walk more than a few paces.

He was a stoic and never talked about his problems and still made up wonderful wild stories and gave us sweets whenever we went round to visit. But he was clearly now housebound and it was only springtime. The cricket season hadn't even started yet.

This was an era when television had just opened up. A set was wildly expensive and had a tiny six-inch screen encased in a large elaborate mahogany piece of furniture. My mother decided that this might offer a useful solution to Grandpa's immobility, but the equipment was simply not available to hire. But she was not inclined to allow such matters to pass. So she chatted up the manager of the electrical department at the grandest of department stores and explained to him about Grandpa. He told her that, although hiring a set was impossible, she could purchase it on a month's trial. If she paid for the installation of the aerial and delivery and then asked to have the set removed before the month was up, there would be no further charge.

So with careful timing the magic of television entered our family with just one week to go before the Lord's Test. Grandpa didn't seem all that interested as we crowded into his bedroom to gaze wondrously at the little grey screen. He looked sort of pale and serene and spent most of his time dozing even when we three crowded in to his bedroom to tell him about school and all that was happening – and, since we were there, to watch a few magic moments on the screen before Granny gave us some milk and biscuits and packed us off home.

But then the match started and Grandpa was totally awake, explaining about the subtleties of the game and his many memories and scenes that he had seen in the past. Australia was batting and at last Don Bradman, Grandpa's hero, came in to face the bowling. The first ball came hurtling down across the tiny grainy little screen and Grandpa raised his index finger and said 'He's out!' My Mum said 'He can't be. He's only just come in.' But Grandpa had closed his eyes and gone to sleep. And of course he was right; Bradman was out for a duck. And next day we were told we couldn't go round to the flat and visit as Grandpa wasn't there any more.

But what would have happened if Bradman had played one of his famous innings and scored a century? Grandpa would have watched every stroke and then confidently looked forward to the Test at the Oval? Of course he would!

Afterword

You will know that childhood memories come in snippets and the space between these is often filled by other peoples memories of the same events, and all these become reinforced in the re-telling. I wrote what is, I suppose, from our family's mythology. I am unsure how much of my grandfather's death I remember myself and how much was about what was later retold by my mother and other family members. But I have never discussed this story with my brothers, who will have their own angles on what 'really' went on. So writing it down was one more way of conserving my ever fainter memories of my much loved Grandpa, along with those of the caring concern of my mother and the lengths to which she went for him.

The piano   *Kieran Walsh*

'But doctor, the worst bit about it is that I can't play the piano anymore.' He was very small and frail and was sitting in his pyjamas beside the bed. And his hands were ruined by osteoarthritis. As I examined them I remembered textbooks from my medical student days describing osteoarthritis as a mild disease or just a bit of wear and tear. But I was never completely convinced: if osteoarthritis of the knee is caused by wear and tear then why is one knee often affected and the other one fine? They have both done an equal amount of mileage. And this man's hands seemed to defy the textbooks once again. I had taken a history and examined him and then done what we geriatricians call a functional assessment – a wonderful term. We always did a functional assessment as part of the integrated care pathway for inpatients. When I had exhausted all possible questions about doing up buttons and putting keys into locks, I started on about Velcro fasteners and knives and forks with enormous handles. Then he started talking about playing the piano.

'I know that playing the piano isn't very important', he said, 'and I know that there's nothing you can do but it would be nice. Most people don't know that I used to be able to play – they probably think it's sitting in the corner as decoration. But I did meet up with some old friends last year and they asked me did I still play. We were in Normandy at the D-day celebrations. But I couldn't of course. And the funny thing was I couldn't play either the last time I was there – all the pianos were mined.'

Afterword

I wrote this story about eight years after I heard it. I worked as a specialist registrar in the care of older people for about six years and most of the people that I looked after were old men and women sitting in their pyjamas beside their bed. Only after a few years did I realise that their uniform was an effective way of dehumanising them. The only way to tell them apart was by their illness and so doctors found nothing unusual about calling a person 'the chronic arthritic' in bed 8. And this is an example of the polite names that elderly patients were called. All members of staff laughed when patients were called GOMERs (get out of my emergency room) and dements and Gerries (geriatric patients).

Some months later when I met patients in the clinic wearing their civvies, I had great difficulty recognising them. The story also reminded me of how we as doctors look at functional assessment purely from the point of view of what we feel patients should be doing and not from the point of view of what they want to do. Some old people just want to be able to care for themselves and do simple tasks like go shopping. Others want to drive a car or maybe an aeroplane. And there's no reason why they shouldn't – Senator John Glenn was able to fly the space-shuttle at the age of 78. But we treat them in a 'one size fits all' manner. When they protest we infantilicise them by saying 'Oh you really don't want to do that.' We treat them like children and not like modern children either – more like children from the Victorian era.

Too often a functional assessment involves the doctor asking the patient what the doctor thinks the patient should be able to do and then watching him to do it. Then the physiotherapist does the same thing and finally the occupational therapist. Some old people who live in bungalows are not allowed home until they have shown the staff that they are able to walk up and down stairs.

But more than anything else I remember the old pianist's strong sense of irony. Old people have been around a long time and it is rarely a surprise for them to see things turn in circles. And with these seemingly innocuous weapons of irony and gentle humour they can cut through red tape that wants to keep them on the straight and narrow of integrated care pathways. I left this one-time piano-playing soldier with a strong sense of who he was and what he wanted and a faint sense of my own ridiculousness.

Song for hospice   *Christopher Johns*

In the soft light of the evening I pause. I remember a word spoken, or her smile, or a reluctant tear that fell with apology upon my worn sleeve. I pick up my pen and allow myself to dwell in the past experience to capture something of its essence. Something of the mystery of being with the other as she or he journeys like a silver stream finding its own way toward death. The mystery of hospice that I gather up in the cool evening.

I am an artist seeking expression to reveal and honour the mystery of hospice. As I write I find myself retracing the journey and lose myself along the way. Tomorrow, when I return I find myself again, more mindful, more sensitive of the moment unfolding as we pick up the threads of our lives.

Writing stories acts to challenge the taken for granted, the complacency, the habitual blindness that narrows the view and limits possibility. To dwell in hospice must always be an adventure, for it is a momentous journey for those patient and families with whom we work alongside; whether we be nurse, therapist, doctor, chaplain or whoever. We may have had similar journeys but this one is unique and must always be viewed from a posture of not-knowing and deep compassion. Otherwise we may miss the point. Reflection and art is life giving…soul food if you like, to nourish the journey, to pierce but not fragment the mystery. It is finding the rhythm of hospice and flowing with it, finding the right steps when we falter for the ground is strewn with boulders, emerging through the chaos into a place of meaning and stillness.

The gateway to our art is following the heart to the deep well of compassion that stirs the imagination. Through dialogue with our experiencing we create images that reflect an intuitive seeing and knowing of the whole.

As Tufnell and Crickmay say (2004, p.119), 'an image forms a bridge between what is inside us and what is outside – it brings us more fully into a felt relationship with the world'.

Mary-Ann

Last autumn I planted daffodil bulbs in my newly cultivated peace garden. Now, in early March, green shoots push skyward from the clinging clay soil. I wonder at the strength of these apparently frail stems pushing through in their quest to fulfil their destiny. Green; the colour of the Buddha Amogasiddhi, who represents fearlessness, pushing against the odds. Green is the heart chakra, presenting the brave-heart, when filled with a deep passion we find the mental fight to persevere. The image of the daffodil stems deepens my compassion and motivation to ease suffering as I drive to the hospice.

> Winter slides and bursts new colour
> to break open the winter grey,
> so green stems push hard against the dark clay

urged by genetic force
to fulfil their yellow headed splendour
to grace the spring time.

At the hospice, Melissa, a staff nurse, pulls me aside and says that Mary-Ann is keen to see me.

I ask why.

'I told her you are a complementary therapist and she is keen to meet you.'

'Tell me about her.'

'She's a 'young' 52-year-old who has a malignant melanoma that has spread throughout her body. She has a swollen left calf that might be a DVT.'

'Things are not good for her?'

'No…she's here to help sort out her persistent pain.'

I go to see her but her bed is empty. Melissa apologises, 'Sorry I forgot to say she's in the bathroom…she's having real problems with her bowels.'

As I hover I gaze onto the garden through the ward windows. A wry smile in recognition of the green shoots bursting through the soil. Mary-Ann emerges on the arm of Cathy, one of the care assistants. She is tall and very pale with long blond grey hair cascading about her. She says 'Chris?' I smile and introduce myself to this vibrant and inviting woman. Back on her bed she gathers her depleted breath. She shows me her swollen calf and says she keeps massaging it! She shows me the malignant melanoma lumps that have grown back on her back and shoulders. Strange pale lumps. I have an urge to touch one to know it better.

She says 'I am not bothering having them removed again as they will only grow again.' No sense of resignation in her voice. I sit on her bed and we talk though the different therapies I can offer.

She smiles 'I would like the Therapeutic Touch.'

Her partner and daughter are with her. Ron, her partner, is happy to go for a smoke. Jasmin, her daughter, says her goodbyes. 'I'm tired from my bathroom exertion and must rest in bed although I can turn?'

She asks it as a question, anxious not to be a trouble. I want her to relax and say I will work from the front. I commence therapeutic touch by holding my left hand on her alma mater chakra and my right hand on her brow chakra and guide her to relax by becoming mindful of her breathing.

nature unties the binds
release in such a place
allows us to be free again…

I whisper 'Breathe in through your heart and visualise the colour green… breath in love and courage. And with each out-breath let go of fear.'

Her energy field is hot. I whisper 'Visualise a cool blue waterfall cascading over you…cooling you.'

She whispers back 'I see it…the blue is beautiful.'

After 20 minutes I cease. My hands are hot and tingly. Mary-Ann exclaims at the heat of my hands.

'I have a chest infection…that's why I was so hot…I feel much cooler now.'

She is very relaxed yet her knee hurts a little. I wonder if the energy has got blocked above the swelling, so I work further on moving the energy beyond the swollen calf.

Afterwards she says 'I felt transported into another dimension... I can't really explain it.'

I know from experience that therapeutic touch has this effect. Working with complementary therapies creates such sacred moments.

I feel such a strong connection with this brave woman. I imagine she is like the green daffodil stems struggling to burst free of the dark ground of cancer, to find the light and realise her destiny. Fighting cancer requires great courage so as I hold her hand I visualise Amogasiddhi, the green Buddha, infusing her with fearlessness to face her uncertain future.

Three weeks later the daffodil green stems bow with beautiful yellow heads. The bed aglow with vibrant colour. Destiny fulfilled.

At the hospice Mary Ann has been readmitted. She is dying.

Yesterday she got married to Ron at the hospice. Today she sits in her wedding gown, radiant. 'I don't want to take it off.' Such a contrast – in one room Gerard dies and in another room Mary-Ann gets married. Such is the essence of hospice.

I move into the garden and pick a daffodil and give it to Mary-Ann, 'A flower for your wedding.' She smiles and thanks me. She declines my offer of therapeutic touch 'That treatment you gave me was a blessing... I feel at peace now.'

Like the green stems, she has struggled through the dark clay to fulfil her destiny. She shines like the daffodil in her yellow radiance, a surge of energy to lift the gloom.

> There is a way of mending what is undone
> unpicking what is too tight
> soothing what is numb...

> Two days later Mary-Ann has died.
> Her body lies so pale.
> Some flowers lay on the pillow by her head.
> Like the daffodils, she bloomed and now faded away,
> to rest again in the dark clay,
> until another season.

> And in the softness of the fading day
> when daffodils dance and sway with drooping heads
> in rhythm to the cool evening breeze
> the moon in last quarter
> so you too sway
> and fade away into another space
> your pollen but a trace upon my soul.

> In the revealing of the story lines
> in the sorting through the truths
> in the hope that we can make good.

18. Spiritual and Artistic Care: Memorial Services

Mark Cobb and Giles Legood

Spiritual care is vital for the bereaved and those at the end of life. Bringing under-standing, acceptance and greater peace, it can also lessen anxiety. Haifa Al Sanousi shows this from a Muslim perspective in Chapter 13. For a Buddhist perspective please see www.buddhisthospice.org.uk, Lewin (2005) and Rinpoche (1992). Involvement in the arts is often spiritual, so religious practices use many of the arts such as music, painting, sculpture, architecture, drama, literature. Mark Cobb (2001, 2005) and Giles Legood (Legood and Markham 2003) offer wisdom from long experience as chaplains.

Spiritual and artistic care   *Mark Cobb*

Dying is a process through which the organic impulse of life is slowed to a halt, the inspired body is stilled and all that signifies a human being is dissipated. In living towards this absence and silence we face the impermanence of our material exis-tence and the finality of loss. And yet the significance and glory of being human is intimately related to our brevity: we are mortal creatures who experience and express hope in the transcendent and infinite. This irrepressible urge to respond to the paradox of existence is a stance of both defiance and belief that humanity is more than its bounded fragile flesh. Spirituality and art both remind us of the incomplete and unfinished ways in which we understand ourselves, and our world, and point us to a more expansive vision of being human. In some religions the fullest sense of this reality is referred to as God, and the author Jeanette Winterson, in reflecting upon her own beliefs, considers that:

> If the religions agree on anything it's that God is not containable and finite, and that what we know is always very partial and biased. So I am looking for something outside of all that. Part of our challenge and our glory is to live in that largeness. (in Bakewell 2005, p.234)

The experience of dying and the ways in which we care for the dying can suppress the human spirit and diminish anything beyond the concrete reality of illness. Contemplating the transcendent is a common exercise of the spiritual quest and the artistic pursuit: both are grounded in the limits and possibilities of human existence, and both inspire an awareness and discovery of unfamiliar depths and heights within and beyond the immediate. Whilst art can be created or observed without spiritual intention or purpose it is difficult to imagine that the spiritual could be expressed without some form of art.

One of the challenges for people coping with illness, facing dying and living with loss is how to relate to and make sense of these new realities. This suggests a need to explore beliefs, assess values, reshape meaning, and find a way of being in a transitory and finite life. Inevitably this requires a space to attend to experience, to reflect upon our temporal character, and to contemplate the enigmatic nature of humanity that lies beyond direct intellectual comprehension (Cottingham 2005). Faith provides one form of a 'space between' external reality and ourselves in which the abstract, reflective and spiritual dimensions of human experience can be enriched, nurtured and given free play.

This is the space that seems to lie at the heart of religion and art, a creative place open to intuition, revelation, paradox and mystery. Yet this can also be the place of silence, where people move beyond symbols, metaphors, images and sounds, and find fuller meaning in letting go (Jacobs 1998).

Art is a natural 'language' of spirituality which in the world's major faiths find distinctive cultural forms and grammar. In religion art can be a means of expressing a spiritual worldview and it can also be understood as reflecting or revealing something of the nature of God. Therefore art can help us make sense of ourselves and our beliefs through buildings, music, sculpture, poetry, dance, drama. Some of the major traditions are aniconic, notably Judaism and Islam; others make use of a representational images and iconography, such as statues of Hindu deities and the Eastern Orthodox tradition of scared icons. Whatever their form, many artistic expressions of the spiritual are not dependent upon the traditions in which they were originally created. Art has integrity and ambiguity that means people can engage with it and respond to it outside its original context.

Dying is, for many, a profoundly intimate and solitary experience which finds an echo in the solitude and personal intensity of the creative artistic process and the spiritual quest. Art can recall us to the suffering of the diseased body, the lived experience of being a patient, the despair and hope of the carer. At the same time art can open up new ways of knowing what it means to live, remind us of our sameness and interdependence, overcome isolation, and renew a shared commitment to human worth and dignity. This human impulse to search for and express such notions as meaning, beauty and love can be both creative and transforming, inspiring hope and prompting faith.

Sacred space – Locus iste

Locus iste a Deo factus est is the opening line of a short motet set to music by Bruckner for the dedication of a chapel expressing the manifestation of God's invisible grace: *This place was made by God.*

Most hospices and hospitals have chapels, which are the most evident and familiar form of sacred space in palliative care. Chapels often exist cheek by jowl among spaces for such as clinics, chemotherapy suites, day centres and inpatient facilities. Sacred space is unique among them: it is free from clinical activity and the procession of medical professionals, there is no drugs' trolley or nursing station, and hymn books and religious texts take the place of medical notes and formularies. This is the space for people of hope and despair, the searchers and the puzzled, the contemplatives and the pilgrims; those thankful for life's blessings and those whose hearts have been broken with grief, and the ones who live a vocation to care for the dying and bereaved. Sacred space is where the messy truths of the human condition encounter not blood tests, surgery or medication but silence and prayer, symbols and music, scripture and sacraments, and expressions of the spiritual in architectural shape and form.

A sacred space provides sanctuary in the midst of managed care and scheduled treatment, a gathering place for people to tell their stories and to remember the collective stories of others, a space to assemble for liturgy and worship, an environment of stillness for reflection and contemplation, and a source of inspiration and peace. 'Space is shaped into place by the meaning people discover within it' (Kavanagh 1982, p.14). Sacred space therefore can become a significant place when it is more than an end in itself but is the setting for revelation and vision. This is the place which can hold the ambiguities and mysteries of being human alongside glimpses and hints of the holy. It is space of encounter and presence, a reminder of the Other, in which the spiritual reality of human experience is reflected and concentrated.

Sacred spaces embody spiritual meanings and give tangible form to an invisible reality. But these are not auditoriums for an audience, or exhibitions for spectators, but creative spaces open to imaginative forms and inhabited by storytellers, poets, musicians and other artists. It was in such a place that I met once a week with a group of patients from a day unit who attended a short religious service in a hospice chapel. The chapel was not purpose built, it was not a space of beauty or aesthetic impact, and it contained few art forms. But they gathered there expecting that this would become a place of meaning through listening to the stories of their faith community, recounting their own stories and praying to God. Leaving behind the activity and social hum of the day unit we would arrive in the chapel and begin the service by lighting a candle and entering into a stillness and a silence. Over the course of 20 minutes a recorded piece of music was played, a passage from the Bible was read, people were encouraged to reflect upon it for themselves and share with others what it meant to them, and these meanings and the stories that accompanied them were then offered to God in prayer.

Each week they inhabited the chapel and became participants in a creative process that opened up a space for exploring the human and the sacred. The happening was enriched and stimulated by the artistic work of others (music, prayers, images, stories), and this often provided an opening into some aspect of the human relationship to the holy. The room and minimal structure of the event held open space for the indeterminacy of the spiritual search and the creative response. The people brought into the space their beliefs and hopes about who they were and who they would become in living with a life-limiting condition. They left behind no evidence of creativity in either artefacts or recorded forms, rather they returned to the day unit enhanced, stimulated and inspired by shared stories, meanings and prayer.

Modifying an environment into sacred space requires an artistic and spiritual architecture that provides a shelter for the sacred aspects of humanity and yet remains open to the play of the spirit. The significance and value of sacred space in palliative care is easily neglected in resource limited services, but beyond their immediate practical use these are places that can locate hope and our belonging within the vastness of the universe. Without being located our existence has no evident point of reference from which to make sense of life's journey towards death. Margaret Wertheim considers that without this meaning we are left with existential anarchy:

> With no place more special than any other, there is no place ultimately to aim for – no goal, no destination, no end. The cosmological principle that once rescued us from the gutter of the universe has left us, in the final analysis, with *no place to go*. (Wertheim 1999, pp.185–186)

Music – Mozart's Clarinet Concerto

Doreen had finished her living but her body had not yet ceased functioning. Respite from this apparently wearisome situation came in the task of organising her funeral, for which she wanted a chaplain's assistance. She was at her most animated and incisive when discussing the possible hymns and music for the service she would only attend in body. And so we spent time together talking about music, singing hymns, listening to recordings and rehearsing her funeral, much to the disquiet of her family. This was a practical task, and a way of caring for those who would be bereft of Doreen, but it also provided a way for Doreen to face her mortality and explore her beliefs about death. Music was for Doreen a source of inspiration, an expression of the deepest personal meaning and a means of connecting with her sense of the sacred. This inseparability of music and spirituality is well observed, and the composer James MacMillan considers that:

> More than the other arts music seems to get into the crevices of the human-divine experience. Music has the power to look into the abyss as well as to the transcendent heights. It can spark the most severe and conflicting extremes of feeling and it is in these dark and dingy places where the soul is probably closest to its source where it has its relationship with God, that music can spark life that has long lain dormant. (MacMillan 2003, p.36)

The abyss was familiar to Doreen for it felt to her like the place she had often been driven to by the dehumanising and soul-destroying effects of cancer and its treatment. In her bleakest times Doreen could be hard to reach and communicate with; she felt empty and could be unaware of her external world. Her apparent boredom with dying disguised her fear of death and an uncertainty of what her life had been about. Trying to make sense of this was a fearful idea for Doreen as she could not see how to avoid the dark and silent place of the abyss. She had not anticipated that this could be a place of creativity and inspiration, initially as an act of protest, and then in a resolve to be true to herself and to let go into the beauty and hope that music meant to her.

The sound of hymns sung by a voluminous Welsh male-voice choir, German Lieder performed by Janet Baker, and various concertos for wind instruments by Mozart were the sounds of Doreen engaging with her death. The music was also a language of the sacred through which she made sense of her life and in which she believed her life would be completed. Doreen could not abide detailed doctrine or religious requirements of observance and practice, her music could not be reduced to philosophical assent and it represented an intangible space of beauty and holiness which had been a life-long inspiration and consolation. As she became more ill the music she loved became the intangible reality which she knew would endure in the midst of her dissolution. Music is real but not in physical terms except for the instance of the performance. It is therefore free from many of the restraints of other art forms and this is why it is often considered the most direct and penetrating because it does not rely on an intermediary tangible object.

The affinity between music and the sacred for Doreen was self-evident, and she was disappointed that her family and friends did not share much of her enthusiasm for the recordings she treasured. Music took Doreen beyond the bounds of her illness, her words and her mortality, and gave her a glimpse of something more complete and whole. She had listened to the recordings for many years and knew them in detail, and yet they remained a source of emotional consolation and spiritual refreshment. Music was therefore dependable and whilst it seemed to her beyond all suffering it also had a profound relationship to her innermost experiences. Listening to the music that Doreen played was an important way of getting to know her intellectually and spiritually and it gave her a way of sharing what was inexpressible. Perhaps as importantly it was a way of affirming and reminding us that she was more than a cancer patient and that she understood her dying within a more spacious worldview than healthcare.

Doreen died at her home and her funeral took place in her local church. The congregation realised from the chosen hymns that they were the substitute for a Welsh choir, but the other music she wanted came from her own recordings. It was a service that reflected much of what life had meant to Doreen and the clear belief she had that death ended all the constraints and limitations that so frustrated her. Janet Baker's rich lyrical voice both expressed the sadness of loss and something of the reconciliation with death that Doreen found in Mahler's setting of Friedrich Rückert's poems. Finally all our spirits were lifted as her coffin was born out of church accompanied by the rondo allegro final movement from Mozart's Clarinet Concerto, full of beauty, human spirit and hope, and one of his last completed works.

Liturgy – Go forth upon your journey...

The poet's eye, in a fine frenzy rolling,
Doth glance from heaven to earth, from earth to heaven,
And as imagination bodies forth
The forms of things unknown, the poet's pen
Turns them into shapes, and gives to airy nothing
A local habitation and a name

William Shakespeare (A Midsummer Night's Dream, Act V, Scene i, 12–17)

Shakespeare's Theseus reminds us that words catch thoughts, fix ideas and represent a reality either imagined or actual. Words are beautiful and dangerous objects of language and symbols of thought. Through words we name, express, imagine, influence, pray and so forth. In spiritual care a powerful way of using words is in the form of liturgy, which provides a structured order of actions, music, words and silence which enables people to share in ritual and worship.

Liturgy serves many functions but in relationship to palliative care it can be of particular value in a number of ways. First, liturgy incorporates people and overcomes isolation. In palliative care it can be a way of connecting those whose worlds often contract with the progression of their illness to the wider community of faith. Second, liturgy provides a way of engaging with the realties of life and of holding the glories and tragedies of the human experience before God. Third, it provides a way of remembering, both for individuals and for communities. In remembering we bring the past into the present and bear witness to its importance. In facing death and in living with loss, remembering affirms the value of life and binds us into a shared memory. In short, liturgy can help connect people, places, memories and meaning, and its role can be a useful counterbalance to the social organisation of death, dying and bereavement which often remains detached from communities and securely institutionalised.

Dan was a successful entrepreneur and an active member of his local church. His faith and the support of his faith community meant that Dan and his family believed without any doubt that he would be cured of his cancer. Despite the gradual deterioration of his condition through the spread of the disease Dan remained positive and hopeful, describing his life as a ship on a rough sea that had sustained damage but was still on course and riding through the waves. He reluctantly accepted an admission to his local hospice a few weeks before he died.

Dan requested regular visits, asking me to say prayers of healing and to sustain his belief in a cure. It was not long, however, before I was helping Dan and his family prepare for his death. The tradition of his local church was for more informal worship and extemporary prayer, but to the painful contradictions and physical disintegration that Dan was experiencing I offered liturgy primarily in the form of a Eucharistic rite. The Eucharist in the Christian faith tradition is a ritual remembering and thanksgiving for the redemption of the world through Christ, who is believed to be sacramentally present in the bread and wine which are shared. The liturgy is rich in meaning and symbolism; it is inherently conservative in its nature and retains a shape and order that connects it with the earliest historical forms. This continuity and familiarity ensure the reliability of liturgy and enables people to develop their capacity to participate in it. Incorporating the past into the present is a characteristic of tradition, a

> routine which is intrinsically meaningful, rather than merely empty habit for habit's sake. Time and space are not the contentless dimensions they become with the development of modernity but are contextually implicated in the nature of lived activities… Ritual often has a compulsive aspect to it, but it is also deeply comforting, for it infuses a given set of practices with a sacramental quality. (Giddens 1990, p.105)

For Dan and his family the Eucharistic liturgy became a way for them to share in a meaningful act of faith that reflected the physical reality of Dan's condition and the spiritual reality of their hope of heaven. Liturgy was able to contain this ambivalence and to place it within a wider context of human destiny. The words and symbols of the liturgy have a capacity to connect with and inspire people to make sense of the chaos and confusion that may accompany dying by integrating these experiences and naming their reality. In particular, liturgy can play a powerful role in supporting people through transitions most notably in the form of rites of passage.

The last Eucharist that Dan shared was the day before he died. He and his family knew his death was imminent and so the liturgy, which remembers the last meal that Jesus had with his friends, was heavy with allegorical meaning. It was a difficult emotional experience but the rhythm and pattern of the liturgy enabled us to move through it. It was evident that Dan was approaching the boundary between life and death and the metaphors and symbols of the liturgy gave his family a means of acknowledging this whilst affirming the hope of faith. The liturgy when celebrated in a church concludes with a dismissal, 'Go in the peace of Christ', omitted for a person in bed. It felt appropriate to Dan and his family to end with: 'Go forth upon thy journey, Christian soul. Go from this world. Go in the name of God' (from John Henry Newman's poem *The Dream of Gerontius* (Newman 1986), better known set to music by Edward Elgar).

Conclusion

Death concludes life and the possibility of human creation. This journey towards an ending therefore invites, if not demands, a creative response of lament, celebration and hope addressed to the silence and absence of death. This impulse may be without logic but it affirms the fragile nature of existence and strives to reflect the intimations of a larger reality to which we are sensitive. The writer Ben Okri considers that art 'is but a sign and a prayer to the greater glory and sublimity of our secret estate. It is a celebration of our terrestrial intelligence, our spiritual yearning, and the irrepressibility of our mischief and joy' (1997, p.20). George Steiner goes further and argues that, 'Without the arts, the human psyche would stand naked in the face of personal extinction. Wherein would lie the logic of madness and despair' (2001, p.215).

Memorial services   *Giles Legood*

Memorial services, using words, music and other creative media, can aid the healing processes of bereavement. The putting together and carrying out of memorial services can benefit family, friends, healthcare professionals, and indeed anyone connected to the deceased. Planning for such services can be an important act for any people who are thinking through what they would like to happen after their own death. Written by a Christian practitioner, this chapter assumes no specific religious stance.

Memorials – A human need

The need to mark the death of another human being is no modern phenomenon. The first known funeral was the act of burying a person in the floor of a cave in the early Stone Age, some 30,000 years ago. Burying someone is most usually an artistic act, given that it most often involves some ceremony. Even where ceremony is absent, the simplicity or silence which might accompany a burial is done for a reason and speaks volumes by absence. The idea of marking the point of burial of a deceased person also has a significant history. In Malta, for example, there are 2000-year-old stone structures which represent memorials to the deceased. Headstones have great artistic possibilities: very elaborate and unique, perhaps with sculptures, carrying messages from the bereaved or verses of poetry or sacred texts, as in the case of Victorian valhalla, or simple and uniform, as in the case of Commonwealth War graves.

The need to mark the death of a loved one with physical artistry has, therefore, a long history and is found in a host of differing cultures. Some are maybe classically 'religious' where structured, formal liturgies of a religious institution may be followed; others may be 'spiritual' and syncretistic where the ceremony draws upon a variety of religious beliefs from various traditions for its expression. Finally, others may be secular and utilise a rich variety of non-religious or spiritual poems, prose and music.

Most memorial services are held in a religious building rather than a crematorium chapel, which tend to be small or impersonal. A person might have had a funeral at one end of the country but have friends miles away, so a service could be held there. Those who give their body to medical education and research might have a memorial service instead of a funeral.

Truth is what works in dealing with grief and thanksgiving for a life. People often link truth and beauty in expressing something to which words cannot do justice. In such a way, art has an important part to play in dealing with our human emotion or grief and thanksgiving. Rarely do memorial services meet a need if they are held too long after death (say, more than three months). If the memorial service is unduly delayed, it may not meet the grieving congregation's needs so helpfully, and will have less impact. The readings, prayers, music and eulogies should all reflect that the mourners' grief has moved on.

Healing through memorialisation

One of the gifts memorial services bring is that they allow for more creative input that most funerals. Funerals are held soon after death when human emotions are at their rawest and most painful. Memorial services, most commonly held a few weeks after a death, allow time for greater reflection and participation. Words cannot adequately convey all we feel and want to express about any human situation, let alone the intense feeling of grief: other, often artistic expressions need to be made.

Memorial services meet a human need and help in the bereavement process; therefore there is no 'right' way to plan and hold them. Nevertheless the experiences of others, and talking about what they found helpful, will be important to consider when planning a memorial service for a loved one. The time of day ought to be considered as, for instance, a service held mid-morning on a bright spring day may have a different feel from a service held late afternoon in winter. Just as the time of the service will help set the tone of the memorial so too will the physical setting. A service held in the open air, on top of a mountain, will be different in style to one held in a mediaeval church or in the hall of a community centre. Architecture, like art and music, can give expression to things we cannot put into words. Thought can be given to decorating with flowers (perhaps the departed's favourite) and a large photograph of the person who is being remembered may be displayed. There is much scope for artistic expression in many different ways in a memorial service. As well as photography and the artistic use of the natural world (through flowers, or other objects from nature) painted works of art can be very powerful and expressive. Coloured cloths or balloons can also be used to convey a sense of celebration of a life, if this is to be the dominant theme of the service.

Services invariably contain music and readings. The choosing of such material may be healing, allowing the bereaved, busy with practical things, to slow down and think about human, personal things concerning the departed. And it is a chance to work with others also grieving. Planning a memorial service collaboratively brings countless people together, perhaps creatively discussing with joy and relief. A favourite piece of music or artwork can be therapeutic both for the person facing a terminal diagnosis and for their family and friends in discussion with them. Some, facing a terminal diagnosis, find it healing to plan their own memorial service or funeral with others. Such work can also help the sick person's family face the reality of what is shortly to come.

Choices about the music to be played on arrival and departure can be crucial in setting the tone. Perhaps there are family or friends who are singers or musicians and would like to be involved and perform. Perhaps some music written by the departed, even, could be included. Similarly choices of readings – poetry or prose – can include favourite texts of the departed or work written by them. Perhaps something could be written especially for the occasion. Religious or artistic literary texts can be used and one need not be at the exclusion of the other.

A memorial service may bring together people who might never otherwise meet. Different parts of a person's life are brought together: skilful writing of eulogies, addresses or sermons is needed. At the wake or party which may be held after a memorial service, people who have known and loved the departed may meet together to talk about him or her for perhaps the only time. Recognising that the departed was many things to many people is vital if the memorial service eulogy is to meet some of the needs of all those attending.

Any religious content of a memorial service or gathering should be appropriate to the faith of the departed and those attending, and be used with integrity. Hymns or songs are a good way of participating and contributing to the farewell. The sensitive use of prayers can also be important because through saying 'Amen' at the end of each of these, individual members of the congregation have a chance to make the prayer and its sentiments their own. The Aramaic word 'Amen' simply means 'so be it' and therefore people of a religious faith, or of none, might feel able to assent to a particular prayer or sentiment in this way. The word is not exclusively Christian and is also used by Jews.

Different services will have different emphasises and each service may have a number of themes: clarity about these is useful. Memorial services might, for instance: give thanks for a life; give an opportunity for the bereaved to express their grief, pause to think of human mortality, commend the deceased to God, say farewell. A service paper can itself be very creative and healing, and convey the theme(s). It can act as a memento mori, and a keepsake for further reflection of the day and the person commemorated.

A memorial service must be appropriate for those who construct it, and for the departed. Just as there is no such thing as the right way to grieve, neither is there any right way to remember. Some find it helpful to talk to others about the deceased while others prefer to keep silent. While some find listening to sad songs unhelpful, others find they bring comfort and peace. Whatever remembering is done, and whatever memorialisation, it should be real and helpful to those involved and not done simply as a result of pressure or for the sake of doing what is seen as right. Facing death, either our own or that of others, can be a constructive part of life. Work around memorial services with a range of creative art forms can bring healing and peace even in the depth of bereavement.

19. The Art of Care

Yvonne Yi-Wood Mak, Ann Williams,
Corine Koppenol, Sinead Donnelly

Palliative care is the 'opportunity to walk with strangers through their most precious and trying times'.

> *Frances Cordes (palliative care nurse, written during reflective writing session)*

Care can be an art in itself, particularly care of people at extremities of suffering. These authors, all health professionals, offer their own experience. The writing of each text was itself a deeply reflective process for each author.

Am I a physician or a patient?   *Yvonne Yi-Wood Mak*

After my cancer treatment, I returned to work as a hospice physician. As I entered the ward, I felt perplexed and asked myself, 'Am I a physician or am I a patient?' Then a little voice whispered, 'You are a person – you care as a whole person.'

> *Mak (2006a)*

Being a palliative care physician is rewarding, as my patients have taught me much about the essence of living (Mak 2006b). Being a qualitative researcher has trained my whole brain, to be not only systematic and analytical but also reflective and intuitive. But becoming a cancer patient has transformed my whole being and I like the 'me' that I am now (Mak 2006a). Palliative care has promoted my professional and also personal self-development. Similarly, my illness experiences have been an awakening and have also enhanced the way I care and comfort others. The art of palliative care can promote authentic living; personal lived experiences can enrich the art of care. I share my personal journey as a physician, researcher, relative and patient to illustrate this reciprocal cycle of professional and personal refinement.

The art of palliative care

Pioneers in palliative care (Mount 1995; Saunders 1978; Saunders *et al.* 2004) have emphasised the importance of whole person or holistic care, not only addressing the patients' physical but also their social, psychological and spiritual concerns (Heyse-Moore 1996; Kearney 1996). Palliative care is person-centred, attending to the patient's whole being and also their significant others, events and objects that construct the self. Clinical decision-making is ethically sound, taking into account the different frames of reference of the patient, relatives and the multidisciplinary team. It focuses on life stories, the meaning of suffering and ways to facilitate transcendence and healing. Healing, the restoration to wholeness, refers to psycho-spiritual empowerment in the presence of a disintegrating physical body due to a life-threatening disease. Thus psycho-spiritual care is an important aspect of palliative care.

The art of palliative care entails learning to 'be' rather than 'do' (Storey and Knight 1997). Providing empathic presence does not only refer to paying total attention to our patients, sitting down and staying with them, holding and not abandoning them, but also providing a safe place to contain their suffering, to feel secure to confess without being condemned. The process of being respected, listened to and understood is therapeutic. 'Being' also entails an attitude of care where caregivers can create a holding environment and establish a spiritual connectedness with their patients: 'Thank you! That's just what I need. That's what we all need – that loving presence' (Mak 2006b).

Empathy is not difficult as long as caregivers learn to really listen. Instead of, 'I know how you feel', questions such as, 'What causes you most suffering?' 'How does that make you feel?' and 'What do you really, really want?' convey the message that they are not just interested in physical symptoms.

Focusing solely on medical interventions does not relieve suffering, nor does it promote healing. Suffering is multidimensional and unique for each patient. Rather than taking a medical history, patients need the opportunity to talk according to their own agenda. Immersing oneself in the patients' metaphors can provide powerful images of suffering which also serve as useful cues to their genuine needs.

Caregivers need to understand patients' personhood: body, mind and spirit; individual lived past, present and perceived future; personality and hopes, secrets and desires; routines, roles and rights within their political and cultural contexts, and their meaning of existence in relation to the world, events and relationships (Cassell 1982).

Compassion is an essential virtue (Giblin 2002). Not only do caregivers acknowledge patients' suffering but they are committed and willing to accompany them in their suffering. Tears convey deep compassion, which patients appreciate.

Goal-setting has to be flexible, yet realistic, often requiring much creativity and attention to detail. Caregivers promote self-worth by helping patients let go of their old self, including the need for control and independence, and foster hope by enabling a search for renewed meaning. Although their reality cannot be changed, the perception of it can be reframed positively. They are helped to let go of the physical, focusing on what they still have and on psycho-spiritual aspects. Despite disintegrating bodies and exhausted minds, spiritual dimensions can be empowered to restore a sense of wholeness (Mak 2006b).

Being a physician and researcher

The hospice environment promotes personal growth. Many colleagues have been mentors with individual gifts of presence, empathy, patience, gentleness, compassion and comfort. They have a healthy attitude to living and dying and a creative mind in facing challenges. Patients also play a role as great teachers on the meaning of life – appreciation of relationships, the need for forgiveness and reconciliation, the wisdom of surrendering in order to reach transcendence and healing. Their courage has allowed me to face death in a non-threatening way, as I am not the one in the deathbed. Even their anger, rigid personalities and regrets have been lessons for me; at times I feel guilty that somehow their failures are for my benefit and not theirs.

As I began caring for these vulnerable patients, my own vulnerabilities surfaced: of inadequacy of being unable to 'control' suffering, avoidance tactics and helplessness. I became aware of why I acted and reacted in certain ways. Was I treating my patient or myself? I too began to connect with my personhood. Self-exploration revealed many hidden wounds: negative thoughts, unresolved grief, traumatic events and relationship problems. Self-awareness is the key to healing and I had to heal my wounds before I could heal others.

My healing process was most intensive as a researcher (Mak 2001). My research journal recorded patients' subjective experience, values and beliefs; I also reflected on the spiritual, existential and philosophical aspects of my own personhood. Reflective writing (Bolton 2005) allowed me to express my feelings and thoughts honestly: this transcribed personal journal became a mirror of 'me'. The process of recording, rereading and reflecting provided a channel through which I could address my inner world objectively and constructively.

Palliative care has taught me many lessons: the value of subjective experience and experiential leaning; the meaning of suffering, flexibility, the myth of control; letting go of the need for always having answers; 'being' instead of doing; the need for connectedness and trusting my intuition. I thank my patients who 'in their vulnerability…became my greatest teachers on the meaning of suffering' (Mak 2001).

Being a relative

Becoming a relative of cancer patients was the beginning of a transition between being a physician and a patient. I was not dying but my suffering was much more intense than that of a physician. I could empathise with relatives' suffering, the physical, social and emotional burdens, but feel unconfident in how to care: the pain in witnessing my loved ones suffering; guilt and regrets coupled with fears of anticipatory loss; dilemmas in decision-making and the burdens of bearing the consequences if decisions turned out to be wrong (Mak 2006b).

Clinical decision-making became more complex but holistic as I understood more clearly the relative's frame of reference. I began to embrace death experientially rather than intellectually. I surrendered to the brevity of life, its insecurities and uncertainties. I learned to let go of my losses, parts of my old self and situations holding me from moving forward. I reset roles and priorities. I cherished my moments with loved ones. I re-evaluated my values, learning to trust beyond human understanding (Mak 2006b). Paradoxically, by embracing death I began to experience an authentic way of living.

Becoming a cancer patient

When I was diagnosed with cancer, somehow I was prepared. I had learnt about suffering from patients, research and relatives. I created my individualised holding environment of family, friends, colleagues; email, prayers, precious memories; books, films, music, lyrics and verses.

Valuable lessons can be learned from daily life experiences. I kept a diary as a means of expressive therapy, unloading negative thoughts and feelings, recording emails, precious moments and other positive thoughts to help reframe my mind. As I edited my diary, my chaos became more structured, as if I was reconstructing my life with a new hope, and my life of 'mess' actually had meaning. Writing created a self-aware stillness of my inner world during which I became more sensitive to the outside world.

> As no one can ever fully understand another, change yourself and not others… Do not victimise yourself but let go of self-pity… Do not hold onto anger or it will hold onto you… If you forgive, your burdens will fly away… Do not dwell on negative thoughts, feelings and situations; acknowledge them and then let them go… Feelings are unreliable and can distort reality… We do not live to suffer but we suffer in order to learn to live… Cancer is not the end but a beginning… (Mak 2006a)

As I returned to be a palliative care physician, I was perplexed as to who I was. I felt vulnerable connecting with patients as it was no longer 'they' the patients and 'I' the physician but 'we' as mortals who were sharing the same journey and ultimate destination.

My illness experience has qualified me as a 'wounded healer'. I've gained empathy, and share their needs: for intimacy, connectedness, care and respect; to rely on a far greater being with total control; to surrender and trust beyond human understanding; the urgency to sort out unfinished businesses, and to mend past hurts and say thank you.

Paradoxically, embracing death has made me truly alive. Though I often feel vulnerable, I focus on living. Occasionally, I share my experiences with patients, but ensure that my sharing is to empower rather than for my own ventilation. Several patients have noted the therapeutic effects of reflective writing and have transcended through their suffering.

Learning the art of palliative care

Medical knowledge, skills and competence alone do not make good doctors, unless we also have the right attitude of mind and the commitment to care and to learn.

I have found creative writing, reflective practice and experiential learning useful tools for refining and enhancing the art of care. Experiential learning can be more powerful and real than acquiring knowledge through intellectual means. Reflecting on daily encounters with our patients through writing and sharing can facilitate deeper self-awareness. Our palliative care team has used reflective practice as a learning tool for professional and personal self-development when dealing with complicated cases. In addition, the use of music, lyrics, films and literature helps to complement the caregivers' creativity.

I cannot practise medicine without integrating my lessons of life into it and I cannot live life without denying death. So I go to work as a whole person; and I care for my patients as they also care for me. That is the beauty of holistic care…

When worlds collide: Personal life experiences in the professional arena   *Ann Williams*

In the late summer of 2003 I became a grandmother. My grandson died a cot death aged eight weeks and two days. For several months, whilst trying to pick up both the professional and personal threads of my life, I used reflection as a means of managing my emotions. However, merely reflecting did not offer me enough and I decided to present an account of the experience at a Medical Humanities conference. I needed to share my story with others.

Once the first paralysing shock of being told that he had died had subsided, I experienced the feeling that the world was off balance. Twice before, in my professional life, I had driven to the home of a family where a baby had died for no apparent reason. Cot death belonged to my professional world, and this was when I knew that my worlds had collided.

In the following weeks I made notes and jottings – they cannot be dignified with terms like writing or accounts. At that time I was unable to do more than record my feelings. Mostly they were written when the emotion of the situation became too much to bear and provided an outlet or safety valve. I needed to write my feelings before I lost them, but I could not do anything more. Reflection came much later and these jottings gave me the tools with which to work through the reflective process.

The reflection on Luke's death from both a personal and a professional perspective became entwined early in the process with a need to share the experience with others. Reflection is both the creating and the telling of our story, and Clandinin and Connelly (1994) suggest that the telling enables us to reaffirm our versions of events, modify them and create new ones. Sandelowski (1991) recognised that reflection is a complex activity in which both the story and the telling of it are part of the same process, and Watson (1999) also supported the idea that the telling of the story was important in that, by doing so, we might be able to restore our own lives and help others restore theirs.

The idea of telling the story at a professional conference was in a strange way very protective of my feelings. Once the abstract was submitted and had been accepted, I was able to define for myself a place of safety. I had found somewhere to hide the pain until I was strong enough to look at it and transform it into something useful. Remember the Ugly Duckling in his lonely clump of weeds who became a very fine swan indeed? The need to transform the personal pain into something – if not good, at least useful – was strong. There was now a place to which I could go from time to time where the story could be written and changed and where I could describe, explore and account for things. The conference itself would be the chance perhaps to peep out into the world again, maybe even take a step or two and try out a new version of myself that incorporated my sadness, grief and loss and to see if it was acceptable in a professional arena.

The conference presentation.

From my various jottings, I selected four extracts. In chronological order, they do not relate to any particular stage in the grieving process, nor is it possible to identify how long after Luke's death each was written.

> LUKE is dead. Luke IS dead. Luke is DEAD
> Makes no sense at all.
> Pointless. Eight weeks and two days. Now nothing.
> Ha Ha Granny. Got you. Nothing you can do about it.
> There's nothing for you now is there?
> Photos, sympathy cards, order of service, patch of milk on an unwashed cardigan.
> Why did he come if he could not stay?

From the beginning, two stories unfold. One is lived out in public and is validated by my contact with people who know what has happened, who ask and express concern. It has its own reality, constructed by my careful use of words. It follows rules. Neighbours know that grief takes time. Friends and colleagues know that grief follows a model, a trajectory. That even the most uncomfortable emotions are probably 'normal'. This is the story I allow my professional self to live as well as tell. It is true in the sense that there is no such thing as truth, only versions of it, and this is my professional truth. It's a linear story, a check on how I am coping. It should take me through all the stages towards 'acceptance'. In a real sense it is a third-person narrative.

My story, my first-person narrative, is only for me. It takes place behind closed eyelids. It's not linear. I can dip in and out and add to it and revisit or even revise the chapters. A new chapter was being written in our family story. My daughter and I had each entered another generation. I had changed my status to that of grandmother and adopting this new identity had been easy. I had envisaged throughout my daughter's pregnancy the kind of grandmother I would be and I was beginning to try out the new roles.

I had been given a precious gift. When it was snatched away, I found myself having to accept the identity of former grandmother for which I had no preparation nor inclination. Initially this was a public identity created in the interactions with other people. It took much longer to integrate this identity into my personal understanding of myself, and, in that private world, a kind of denial held sway. I did not want to believe that he had gone and I continually imagined a present and a future in which he still lived and we did the things that I, as a grandmother, would want to do with him: things I had done with my own children and the things that I had not been able to do with them. For the first time I understood the tenacity of denial but also its importance in assisting with the process of letting go. I needed to have a story of Luke before I could say goodbye to him and all he meant. What is unacceptable in public can have positive benefit in the personal process of grieving.

> Just a few days with Luke, the night I had him all to myself, a cold little body in a funeral home, a religious service, the grave on a windy hillside.

The order doesn't matter. This to-ing and fro-ing doesn't follow the rules but I would not claim that it has any more truth than the public version. This is where I have to manage not processes and tidy progress, but turmoil. I already have acceptance here, but it comes with strings attached. The guidelines I thought I could use are irrelevant. Acceptance brings with it a burden of pain and devastation. It's not the end of a journey but the start of one.

> Luke's three month check is due. Sits with support, taking notice, smiling, gurgling – still waves his left leg in the air, guzzles his milk.

Thoughts like this must be carefully kept out of the public story. It is not professional. I find that part of the cost of working whilst trying to deal with personal grief is that I respond in approved ways, following the stages of grief so that others can see that I am doing my best: meeting expectations and validating theory.

> The dissonance between the authenticity of my feelings and behaviour widens as time goes on. I am happy to buy into this. I will be an exemplar of good grieving.

But I am hollow inside. I have built a construction of myself that has no foundations. One false move and it will all collapse. Suppressing emotions during the day makes for tearful and exhausting nights: the rebound from colliding worlds.

What have I learned?

The first thing I have learned is the extent to which I compartmentalise my life. As a nurse I have had the rather comforting belief in what is known as the therapeutic use of self: that who I am and the experiences I have had are an integral part of my work with patients and relatives, colleagues and students. The impact of the collision has shown me the dividers that I have put in place over many years between me as a person and me as a professional. They were very strong but now they have been shattered. I now question how much of myself I bring to professional encounters. Maybe I have been naïve in not recognising the editing and filtering that actively creates the professional me.

For many months after Luke's death, I did not have the strength to reconstruct the dividers, and the pain of my personal loss invaded my professional life. Sympathy and kindness overwhelmed me. I have rebuilt some dividers now, but they are less rigid, more flexible, and the division between me as a person and me as a professional is now a negotiable border.

I have learned that many of the tools that professionals rely on to guide their helping may be unreliable. They help us see what we expect to see and we reward ourselves by saying (or writing in the notes) that things are progressing as expected; things are within normal limits. And of course they are within the normal limits of the public story, but what are the normal limits and satisfactory progress in the private, secret narrative?

I have learned that reflection can be both deep and draining, more like counselling than writing. An injunction often given to people coming to terms with life-shattering situations is 'you must not brood'. Reflecting makes brooding a positive force. I have learnt to reflect in short bursts and to set aside time for reflection, to think about Luke and my sense of loss, as a hedge against brooding. 'Human kind cannot bear very much reality' (Eliot 1974, p.190).

I have learned that reflection is an ongoing process. As time has passed reflection has changed. In the beginning, it had the power to engage with the raw pain and overwhelming emotions. To do it at this time means that I had to be prepared to stay within that pain, and not strive for a solution or a quick resolution. I had to accept my own distress, as I would, in my professional role, accept the distress of another. Later I began to think not about Luke's death but about his life, short though it was, and how it has affected and changed me and my family. That brought with it a different, sadder, less fierce pain because there is so little to remember and every memory is precious.

The writing and reflecting I have done so far may be the foundations of a new understanding of myself and my professional life. Equally, they may not. It has been hard work getting this far and the work may stand alone as being all that I can do.

After the conference

After the conference I found myself reflecting on the process of creating and sharing the story. I recognised the significance of moving beyond the narrative itself and taking it out from my personal and into my professional world. As a teacher, an academic rather than a clinician, words are my stock in trade. They are a precious commodity not because of their rarity but because of their power. They make a bargain with us that allows us to use them privately to create a story but our part of the bargain is that we give them their true value by sharing the words we have put together with others.

In return for putting myself at risk by offering my words publically to display my emotions and vulnerability as a person and as a professional I have begun to dismantle the protective barricades that grief required me to build. I recognise that the telling of the story is not about others learning from my experience – though this may happen. It is about me gaining a new perspective on myself and integrating Luke, my love for him and my sense of loss into my own identity.

Words for all their power cannot make sense of the senseless, and Luke's death remains senseless. Writing and telling the story have helped make it more bearable.

Finally, I have been able to do something positive with the experience. Nursing is a doing profession which values activity to make things better. At the beginning, the intrusion of the professional into my personal world was hard to bear but as time goes on I find that my professional self is supporting and caring for my personal self. The boundary between the personal and the professional has become blurred and a sense of wholeness is emerging. Creating the story was only a small part of the reflective process. Telling the story, articulating thoughts and feelings, offering them to others, sharing the experience has provided opportunities I had not expected to make the reflection more meaningful professionally and personally.

The art of paediatric palliative care   *Corine Koppenol*

As a children's community nurse, experienced in paediatric palliative care, I feel very humbled every time to be allowed inside a world of tears and fear and to be allowed to join something very private and difficult.

To start working with families and children at the end of life is like preparing a blank canvas to start an oil painting: the first meeting with the child and the family; the exploration of their sad story…the sketch, the first raw lines…to listen to what they are prepared to share, to get an glance of the their world and what they would like to see happen and what they need…also to feel the almost tangible air between the words, the silences…the hope.

The first meeting starts off an intense thinking process of what I can do to reflect and understand their ideas, the composition, what colours to use to catch the scene. It also seems cruel to touch that serene field, the hard reality to acknowledge that this precious child will not be here for long. There is genuine denial in me especially when they are still so full of life with some belief of a future. To lose a beautiful young person is not supposed to happen; it is unnatural and the last thing you want is to waste this only chance to make it a valuable memory…to spoil the canvas.

Families often feel a very complicated combination of emotions: anger, disbelief, sadness, the pain of pending loss and anxiety as to how the illness will be managed. It will be an emotional rollercoaster for everyone. Each member of the family will be at a different stage of dealing with these emotions: the art is to be aware of this and to anticipate this every day with great sensitivity and respect. To catch reality in a painting with true intensity and honesty is as difficult.

> This journey in life will be a journey that parents have had very little choice about making. On this journey we are 'invited guests' and we will join them for a part of that journey as a guest and accordingly we should behave as a guest. (Brother Francis)

For all these reasons the support during this turbulent journey requires professional skills, experience, empathy and confidence to offer the palette of colours, to know when to catch the right light, and also some indication of how long it will take to create the painting. Working together with the family and the child requires a close relationship, trust and respect which can only be built up in time. However, time is something not many people will be able to predict and it will be an aggravating uncertainty unless accepted.

The pace at which parents learn to adapt and to manage their situation is always highly admirable and fascinating. It is like setting up basic colours and then suddenly seeing the contours of what the picture is going to be like: how they would like it to be managed, how much self-control they can take, how much guidance they need…how much the child wants to be in command and wants to know. You can see the child change rapidly from an innocent playful being to a serious person hit by reality in life startlingly fast.

One intriguing aspect is what children 'know'. They grow spiritually during their illness although they hardly talk about it. The parents and the child often try to protect each other and often are afraid to upset each other.

> 'You know son…when you are with Jesus…you will be able to walk again.'
> 'I know Dad.'
> 'What do you mean?'
> 'Dad, I just know!' (Bertie and his father, two weeks before Bertie died, January 2005)

Sometimes children may have unidentified pain which is extremely difficult to control. My friend describes it as 'soul pain'…it's like that look in eyes you try to catch in a painting and where you fail. The only thing you can do to control that pain is to hold that space and be there. I am sure that siblings, parents and grandparents experience the same pain.

> Don't run away. Wait. All I want to know is that there will be someone to hold my hand when I need it. I'm afraid… I've never died before. (Author unknown)

An important element in the whole process of caring for a very sick person is the whole context in which this happens. Although the world they live in at that moment will be more contained and the future seems far away, the outside world will not hold time, will not wait. There is a reality to live, siblings need support, there is school, and supplies need to come in, a living needs to be made and so on. This is a cruel aspect as the only thing that people want is for the world to stop and to reverse the situation. Therefore there will need to be consideration for other needs, for extra support for the siblings, for schoolmates to understand what will happen, for allowances to be arranged to permit parents to be there. It's the expertise of using different techniques and brushes to catch the elements and to push away anxiety as it has been taken care of.

When, at the last stage of the journey, the finishing touch of the painting is near; there is not much left to be done. When symptoms are controlled, and the caring network has been built up then the art is to wait, to be confident enough to let things happen, for people to come to terms with what life has presented them…to allow the paint to dry.

The memory of this dreadful and tiring journey will last forever and is very much like holding and loving a priceless painting: you can look at it for hours and you will be determined it remains in the family forever.

Case story

When Aidan was diagnosed with a life-limiting condition he was only a few months old. His life expectancy was predicted to be not more than a year or two. This left the parents alone with this shocking news and with a completely different picture of what their family life was going to be.

Aidan managed to surprise many professionals, and he was five years old when I met him for the first time. He couldn't communicate verbally; he could only communicate through emotions and with his sparkling bright eyes. He had a lovely smile and beautiful slim hands with tall fingers his mother loved to hold. At this point my role was to provide respite, medical advice, advocacy, to be a key worker for them and to support the sibling.

By the time he was six years old Aidan's health had started to deteriorate rapidly and became complicated and difficult decisions were likely to be made. Up till this age Aidan had suffered a great deal due to numerous operations and infections and his breathing became more compromised and it was difficult to control his seizures. The parents decided after long and intense conversations with me and the consultant not to interfere any more medically and to focus on the quality of life they could give their son. They wanted to carry and support him safely through this last stage of his journey…to allow nature to take its course. We had many conversations about how to manage this and obviously this could only have happened in a harmonious working relationship where mutual trust and respect were built up and where professional judgement, experience and knowledge were acknowledged. My role now became far more intense and completely different. Every day I would visit or call and see how they all were, to adjust medication, to call for advice and arrange supplies and equipment. The service became 24 hour to help this family manage their dying child at home.

Decisions were extremely important and I can be sure that they must have caused numerous sleepless nights of anticipated grief. It was difficult for the sibling to understand how serious the situation was. Many times before, his brother had been poorly and every time he had told schoolmates that he might lose his brother. But every time Aidan picked up life again. Therefore this time he refused to tell the school his brother was really seriously ill, so as not to look foolish again. How hard it was for this young boy to know his brother was dying at home while he was at school.

The grandparents were there to support the sibling, to take him for a night or a day or to cook the family a meal. Other family members were around, but some found it very hard to be there for the family, causing the parents a lot of sadness.

The parents were adamant that Aidan's room stayed happy. It was filled with love, laughter, music and no sorrow. Of course there were tears, of course there were many times where we doubted the decisions made, especially when we saw Aidan struggle; however, we managed to control his symptoms.

The last night where all things came together was the most difficult night and the longest night ever. I will never forget that one. There was nothing else we could do for that beautiful child, but to be there, to wait and hold him. The journey had turned into a priceless unique picture.

> I will miss you growing and I will miss your laugh... Please, child know that I will always be proud to have known you...love you forever... (*Billy Elliot* the musical)

The art of palliative medicine   *Sinead Donnelly*

Medicine is a healing art. As a doctor I use myself creatively in meeting a patient or family, in listening, interpreting, responding, articulating. The individual interacts creatively, uniquely and individually with me. Recently a man with recurrent head and neck cancer described severe pain from a swollen tongue. During our discussion about what could or could not be done for his progressive cancer I explained that control of pain and swelling was our aim and that unfortunately the cancer was progressing in his mouth. He commented, "It's as if I'm rolling backwards with that news. For other problems I can roll forwards, with this it's rolling back." I can see this movement like a dance or the waves of a receding tide. From that image I feel the ebb and flow of his life out of his control at this time. I appreciate his art.

What is it like for a doctor-in-training to come into this world of dying and more strikingly of death? Perhaps their training rotation has brought them from accident and emergency, psychiatry, perhaps obstetrics and gynaecology. Now they reach a place where each of their patients will die and each family grieves. I consider it necessary to draw on art to help them understand this cycle of life, to make sense of what one registrar described as "this conveyor belt of death."

The aim of medical education is to produce doctors with skill, empathy, compassion and professionalism. In palliative medicine doctors are expected to attend to those who are dying and their families at a time of intense emotion, such as anger, fear, love. They are required to attend holistically. These doctors learn by example in apprenticeship form. Part of the example which I must give as a teacher is in how I treat and teach the student. I will teach the student to be interested in the patient's story.

These are the stories I would like to tell.
1. This afternoon I greeted a man, a shadow of his former self and jaundiced, perched and blanketed in an ambulance waiting to disembark and enter the world of hospice. A few weeks ago, late at night, as I worked in the palliative medicine office, he was a jovial rotund security man to whom I listened absentmindedly as he locked up doors and I burrowed away at night time desk work. Now I see his jaundiced bewilderment and I feel "pain." This is not a physical pain in a sense of neuropathic pain, somatic pain, bone pain, but a felt visceral response to the change in this man and his proximity to death.
2. I am sitting at the hospice desk on ward 2. Lilies create a powerful scent. Their tubular faces stare at me. So does "the rockin rooster," a toy, a charming musical toy, part of the staff book club. The man I have just visited is 58 and the admitting

doctor has ticked yes for suffering, anguish and fear. These are this man's words. "I have no answers." "Next bout of chemotherapy maybe." "Just need to sleep." "No answers." "I have this glass of milk." He holds the glass, looking at me and again, says "I have no answers. I just have this glass of milk." He coughs a bovine cough of a hoarse man whose cancer has caught the nerve to his larynx. I can hear his coughing now from this desk a million miles from where he struggles in his room 30 feet from here. I will remember the scent of proud lilies, the rockin rooster's yellow feet and the whiteness of ice cold milk. I will remember the eyes of a man who cannot sleep.

The next morning:

There is a boisterous breeze blowing through the office window, rattling the blinds. I want to pick up the phone and tell someone…right now to tell someone… That man died. The man whose tiredness and struggle held me in his room last night. That man asked me for cold milk last night.

Through his wife today I know him even better. How they met, he in uniform just returned from Cyprus, she at 19, up to Dublin from Kilkenny, told her friends "that's who I'll marry." Her friend's response "doesn't he have some say!" Their first dance; she in a tight mini and platform shoes; he could twirl and dance on a pin. Every anniversary celebrated in Paris. The energy of their relationship explodes now as she stands remembering in her numbness and dizzy in her loss an hour after her husband's death. I cannot tell you how delightfully she told of their relationship; how he enjoyed her nice jokes, not nice, bawdy and blue jokes; he a hopeless romantic; not ready, not wanting to die.

3. John Mortimer squirts whiskey through the gastrostomy tube, carefully syringing 20mls at a time from the glass. I felt the tension between the frustrated nurse and the psychologist at the multidisciplinary meeting. The social worker speaks in measured tones of the importance of this opportunity for abstinence for John while he is an inpatient. Why should we offer him alcohol when he could use this opportunity to reconnect with Alcoholics Anonymous? The nurse disagrees.

He breathes through a hole in his windpipe where green spit gurgles continuously. He is fed through a plastic tube ballooned behind his stomach wall. His finger mixes with the bubbling phlegm to cover the tracheostomy and give him a voice. Abstinence? He could abstain from breathing. He could abstain from feeding. He wants alcohol. This desire is in fact progress because last week he did not want to live. I am pleased today that his eyes are more alive and that he cunningly explores how to procure, imbibe, ingest and enjoy alcohol.

The occupational therapist was eager to help him by providing 50 laminated cue cards: "I need…" "I want…" So, as he emerged post tracheostomy into the awful reality of a dual tubed existence, Mr Mortimer systematically reviews each cue card, holding us there as his audience, 1 to 50 each morning. On a round I struggle to be as patient as he.

What does a doctor-in-training learn from observing this man's art of living: his feistiness "I want to drink," his directness "I want to die." These phrases were not options on the occupational therapist's cue cards! What does a doctor-in-training learn subsequently in a multidisciplinary meeting where the social worker advocates setting limits on the alcohol-loaded syringes, that he re-learn the benefits of abstinence? Yet he probably will die within a month.

The volunteer-directed drinks trolley swings by his room at night. Volunteering at night they are blissfully unaware of our elegant plans for abstinence. Kindly volunteers unwittingly offer him sherry or brandy or whatever you like. John eagerly welcomes them in.

The art of healing is a creative encounter between people. It involves the art of creating a space and holding a space between. At this time of reflective writing I am learning that in that space everything is important and nothing matters.

20. Reflections Towards the Future

Nigel Hartley

> *... all art aspires to the condition of wordlessness...*
> *Okri (1996, p.5)*

I have witnessed a range of dramatic and successful artistic interventions with patients and families living with death and dying. Patients are normally surprised to come across an artist when they visit a specialist palliative care unit. A doctor with a stethoscope, a nurse administrating medication and a physiotherapist advising on physical movement are all expected but, for patients and their families, it is both unexpected and somewhat strange when a person turns up with an artist's palette or a tambourine. Artists need sensitivity, kindness and understanding; timing can be pivotal in nurturing the beginning of what might become a useful relationship. First and foremost, a relationship is made between human beings, not with the art form itself. The future of arts services depends on our immediate actions to develop the role of artists in healthcare, through detailed examination of educational and supportive needs of artists, patients and professionals.

Working in this setting involves taking risks. Recently, a musician approached a hospice bedside; noticing the guitar, the patient told them in no uncertain terms 'to **** off'. The musician felt like running away, crumbling, backing off, but came back at the patient, 'I do many things, but "****ing off" is not one of them'. The patient laughed and reached out to the musician. They worked together for a number of hours which culminated in planning funeral music. The musician's reaction could have been disastrous, but something was understood between musician and patient and the risk paid off. Sometimes backing off might be right; finding artists with both sensitivity and courage is paramount.

Not all artists have the required interpersonal skills and experience. Candidates in a hospice interview process ran cancer patient groups, observed by the interview panel. A writer began by asking the patients to describe what it felt like when they had first been diagnosed with a terminal illness. Patients got very upset and tears flowed. It became clear that the interviewee did not know what to do with the response that had ensued from the question. One of the interview panel had to step in to support the patients.

Making groups work

Group work as well as individual work with patients, family members and staff are important elements in healthcare settings. Artists have widely varying aims when working with groups. Some want to 'teach' artistic skills. A painter may teach patients techniques such as watercolours or pastels and ask the patients to copy works of well-known artists. Some artists may have more 'therapeutic' aims, allowing patients to explore materials themselves and paint more freely. It can be too easy to impose expectations onto vulnerable sick patients. Moving from 'this is what you are going to do today' to 'what is it you'd all like to work on together?' can be an essential step in making groups work.

A creative writer asked a group of patients to come up with one word which they would use to describe themselves. She wrote the words on a flip chart, and with a little rearranging created a piece of prose. The patients were surprised and delighted. A strength was that the patients began working on something together. Sometimes it is too easy to set up a group where patients work on individual pieces of work, losing the sense of *group* achievement. Some of the most powerful artistic group work I have seen is when they work on bigger works together, supporting and helping towards a shared artistic vision.

Another artist told me of a group of patients she had worked with on a mosaic collage; she was moved by the depth at which the group members spoke to each other during the three sessions. They talked of their lives and their illnesses, their friends and their loved ones. My question around this was 'could they not have had this discussion doing a hundred and one other things? – What was unique about this conversation during this particular activity?' The uniqueness was what they were physically doing – the stages of placing mosaic pieces on a collage that came together in front of their eyes. Once the mosaic collage was finished, the surprise of the patients took over the content of their discussions. They were surprised by the quality of what they had produced – a beautiful sunset – 'Have we really done that?' The mosaic still adorns the reception area of a GP practice within that hospice community. The product as well as the process was clearly of value.

Many artists in healthcare settings ignore an artistic vision in the work in favour of a more 'therapeutic' description. I feel these are based on their fear in being accepted for their work. Perhaps they feel a more therapeutic description will give more credibility amongst other professional staff. The danger is, of course, that artistic integrity is diminished and the quality both of the artistic experience and of the finished product is underacknowledged.

Working with physically ill people

Many artists I have worked with have been surprised and sometimes repulsed by the physicality of patients' illnesses. A hospice artist visited a patient on a ward to continue individually some work begun in a group. He was shocked to see the patient vomiting and, although unsure of what to do, pressed the call button and held the patient to comfort her. The artist felt helpless until the nurse arrived, and then disappeared feeling he had been no use whatsoever. The following day the artist was extremely surprised to be thanked by the patient. In order to work in an environment with physically ill people, we need artists who have the knowledge, skill and conviction to deal with difficult situations. They need to understand and be educated to enter a palliative care environment and deal confidently with whatever it brings.

How do we talk about the work we do?

One of the difficulties of the arts is finding a language that adequately describes them. Should artists understand the doctors' language: names and effects of drug combinations, the working of the physical body? Should a doctor understand the language of the artist – of colour and flow, melody and rhythm? Art often defies explanations and descriptions using words. An artist once told me she felt no one really understood her contribution to multi-professional discussions, as if she struggled to explain what patients were engaging and experimenting with. One day she decided to take some patient artwork along to the multidisciplinary meeting. She showed them the work saying that she had no idea what was happening but here it was. The team became enlivened by seeing it first hand, and, even though none felt they could fully describe what they saw, there was a new and vital understanding of how her work fitted within the multi-professional approach.

It seems to me that the majority of the time, the art does really speak for itself.

Future challenges

Excellent work is done by artists working with those facing the end of life. However, there has been no central organisation of artists, and arts services have been developed in different ways. If the work is to develop as effectively as possible, there are inevitable future challenges.

Training for these artists is paramount, both an examination of suitable background education and qualifications, and training whilst 'in the job'. We need to offer training and support that will create the healthcare artists of the future, enable them to offer safe and effective practice and understand the breadth and depth of possibility when working with such a vulnerable patient group. We also need artists who are not afraid to explore and examine the efficacy of what they do; new paradigms are needed in order to research and evaluate the arts in healthcare effectively and ethically. These paradigms need to be developed by artists themselves, not by those with little real experience of both the pains and pleasures of using the arts with sick people.

Professional regulation can be a painful and difficult experience, as, on the whole, it involves a process which says that one person is suitable to do a job and another not. However, we have to find a way of developing the credibility of artists working in healthcare for the future, if the work is to be truly acknowledged and accepted as successful and relevant within healthcare systems. The future of arts services depends on our immediate actions to develop the role of artists in healthcare, through detailed examination of the educational and supportive needs of our current and future practitioners.

List of Contributors

Haifa Al Sanousi, Associate Professor in Modern Arabic Literature, Kuwait University, is a Kuwaiti woman with a PhD from Glasgow University. A psycho-literary critic, researcher and creative writer, Haifa is interested in therapeutic writing and storytelling, using literary arts in medicine, the art of speech and conversation, and creative teaching techniques.

Ashley Barnes is the Artistic Director and Founder of Sheffield-based Dead Earnest Theatre (www.deadearnest.co.uk). He is a writer, facilitator, actor and director, mainly for the stage, but also with experience in writing and performing for radio and film. He lives in Sheffield with his wife and two children.

Sandra Bertman, Professor of Medical Humanities and Palliative Care, Newton, Massachusetts, lectures and conducts workshops worldwide on the healing power of hope and grief, and fosters clinician renewal and reflective practice through the exercise of practitioners' therapeutic imaginations (www.sandrabertman.com).

Mitzi Blennerhassett, user involvement pioneer, artist and writer, writes and campaigns on healthcare issues, with a particular interest in cancer services and medical education, and has extensive experience of UK national patient partnership work. She runs art classes and therapeutic writing workshops and believes saturating medical education with arts and user involvement would counter medical de-humanisation.

Gillie Bolton (www.gilliebolton.com) was founder member of the Association for Medical Humanities (UK); Literature and Medicine editor of the *Journal of Medical Ethics: Medical Humanities*; author and editor of *The Therapeutic Potential of Creative Writing: Writing Myself* and *Writing Works: A Resource Handbook for Therapeutic Writing Workshops*, as well as series editor of the Writing for Therapy or Personal Development Series, all published by Jessica Kingsley Publishers; author of *Reflective Writing and Professional Development* (2nd edition; 2005, Sage); and co-editor of *Writing Cures: An Introductory Handbook of Writing in Counselling and Psychotherapy* (2004, Routledge); and of two Jessica Kingsley titles.

Ted Bowman, an educator, author and trainer specialising in grief and loss, has taught Family Education classes at the University of Minnesota since 1981. Ted is a member of the board of directors of the National Association for Poetry Therapy (USA) and an active participant in Lapidus (UK and Ireland).

Judy Clinton, Writing the Spirit facilitator, writes because she feels compelled to. Writing allows her to explore and express her inner and outer worlds. Many of these ponderings have inspired others, particularly through Quaker publications. She facilitates writing workshops for personal and spiritual development, knowing that such writing and sharing can be wonderfully healing.

Mark Cobb, Senior Chaplain and Clinical Director of Sheffield Teaching Hospitals, specializes in palliative care, has academic interests in practical theology, bereavement and ethics. He plays the piano and organ, writes poetry and music, sings and sketches, enjoys galleries, concerts and theatres. His latest book is *The Hospital Chaplain's Handbook* (2005, Canterbury Press).

Kate D'Lima is Lecturer in Performing Arts, Writing and Literature in the Department of Adult Continuing Education, Swansea University. She has an MA in the Teaching and Practice of Creative Writing and is researching Creative Writing in Health Settings for her PhD. She is also an award-winning writer of fiction.

Sinead Donnelly MD is a consultant in Palliative Medicine, in Limerick, Ireland, having worked in Cleveland, the US, Glasgow and Wellington, New Zealand. She continues to publish qualitative research, produce documentaries for national broadcast, develop medical humanities and train in psychotherapy.

Sue Eckstein studied drama in the US and English Literature at Durham University. Currently Director of Programme Development at the Centre of Medical Law and Ethics, King's College London, she has an MA in Creative Writing. Her play, *Kaffir Lilies*, was broadcast on BBC Radio 4 in July 2006.

Hilary Elfick, With over 100 broadcasts, seven poetry collections and a novel, Hilary has also been Head of English in the largest prep school in the UK. For 20 years she was a Trustee of The Princess Alice Hospice in Esher and from 1992 to 1997 was International Co-ordinator, Voices for Hospices.

Bobbie Farsides, Professor of Clinical and Biomedical Ethics, Brighton and Sussex Medical School, has long-term interests in ethical issues and care of the dying, has served on the National Council for Palliative Care and St Christopher's Hospice, Sydenham, ethics committees, and with Sue Eckstein is co-editor of the Royal Society of Medicine journal *Clinical Ethics*.

Sheelagh Gallagher has run creative writing and literature courses for the last 12 years in libraries, prisons, a psychiatric day hospital, residential homes and Nottingham University School of Education. Her course, Ways of Writing, at Nottinghamshire Hospice ran for three years and she was Writer in Residence there for six months.

John Graham-Pole is a London University graduate, Professor of Pediatrics and Director of Palliative Care at the University of Florida. His research focuses on holistic and palliative medicine, and how the arts and spirituality relate to human health. He has published five books, and several hundred articles, chapters and poems.

Diana Greenman has worked for Music in Hospitals (www.music-in-hospitals.org.uk) for some 20 years and has a wealth of experience in bringing live concerts to adults and children with illnesses and disabilities. Diana was appointed Chief Executive in 1999, prior to which she was Senior Administrator, organising some 1700 concerts each year.

Robert Hamberger, Adult Social Care Team manager and poet, has been awarded a Hawthornden Fellowship and shortlisted for a Forward Prize. He has three poetry collections: *Warpaint Angel* (1997, Blackwater Press), *The Smug Bridegroom* (2002, Five Leaves), *Torso* (2007, Redbeck Press) and a pamphlet, *Heading North* (2007, Flarestack).

Nigel Hartley is Director, Creative Living Centre, St Christopher's Hospice, London, looking at daycare, arts, creativity and complementary therapy across hospice services. An experienced musician and music therapist, he has worked in end-of-life care at London Lighthouse (for those living with HIV/AIDS), and Sir Michael Sobell House Hospice, Oxford.

Tim Jeeves, who had cancer when he was a teenager, is an artist working with performance and text and sometimes paint to make work that's about the world around us and sometimes the world inside us.

Christopher Johns, a palliative care complementary therapist, has kept a journal for six years in which he has reflected on his practice of easing suffering. The first two years of his journal have been published in Johns (2004) and the following two years in Johns (2006).

Corine Koppenol trained in The Netherlands as an adult and children's nurse from 1997. She left to work and live in England in mid 1999. She now manages and develops the Hospice at Home Service for Children called Demelza James in East Sussex, as part of Demelza Hospice Care for Children.

Amy Kuebelbeck MA, a former journalist, is author of *Waiting with Gabriel* (2003), a memoir also published in Italy (2005, Edizioni San Paolo) and South Korea (2006, Hainaim Publishing) (see www.waitingwithgabriel.com). She lives in St Paul, Minnesota, US. She is working on a new book about perinatal hospice, and edits www.perinatalhospice.org.

Giles Legood, a Church of England priest previously in parish ministry, is Chaplain at Royal Free and University College Medical School, London. Having conducted hundreds of funerals and memorial services and worked with people approaching death and in bereavement, he is co-author of *The Funeral Handbook* (2003).

Anna Lidzey has worked as a qualified art therapist in Suffolk since 1995, following a career of community work in South Africa. Specializing in palliative care, she also works with a wide variety of client groups. Her work has been inspired by both Arnold Mindel's Coma Work and Buddhist meditation.

Yvonne Yi-Wood Mak, palliative care consultant, teaches at Hong Kong Chinese University and Cardiff University. She qualified at Guy's Hospital and her University of Wales MSc dissertation won awards. Honorary advisor for Hong Kong Breast Cancer Foundation, she shares her own cancer experience in a newspaper column and book *Dr Hannah: A Mother's Diary* (2006a).

Christina Mason has worked for 11 years in a number of capacities at St Joseph's Hospice, Hackney. Passionate about communication in healthcare, she has developed a number of research and teaching interests in support of this. She is a psychotherapist both at the hospice and in private practice.

Tim Metcalf, poet and rural GP, born in Melbourne in 1961, has been a barman, army reservist, woodcutter, soapmaker, flying doctor and poetry editor. He edited *Verbal Medicine: 21 Contemporary Clinician-Poets of Australia and New Zealand* (2006). His next poetry collection is *The Solution to Us*. He lives near Bega, New South Wales.

Frans Meulenberg is a researcher and science-writer on medical ethics and fiction, Erasmus University Medical Centre, literature and medicine bi-weekly columnist for a Dutch medical journal, author/editor of literature and medicine books and science-communication, with forthcoming: an anthology dementia in fiction, a medical thriller and non-fiction on First Love: Relics and Pilgrimages.

Filipa Pereira-Stubbs co-founded Rosetta Life following a UK NHS dance/movement therapy career. Taking maternity leave 1998–2000 she rejoined Rosetta as artist-in-residence in 2000 at Arthur Rank Hospice, Cambridge UK. Also a dance teacher/artist, she develops creative practice in education, and is a happy mother of three.

Michele Angelo Petrone was a professional artist who has exhibited at London's Royal Academy and South Bank. *The Emotional Cancer Journey*, paintings concerning his experience of Hodgkins Disease, is used in healthcare and medical education. The MAP Foundation (www.mapfoundation.org) promotes expression, education and understanding of the complex issues of illness and dying.

Chris Rawlence, writer, filmmaker and librettist, is a Rosetta Life artist at a London hospice and Director of Moving Image for Rosetta Life. Operas include *The Man who Mistook his Wife for a Hat* (M. Nyman), The Mariners (L. Jarrett/O. Gough/Rosetta Life); films include *The Mind Traveller* (BBC2/O. Sacks).

Oliver Samuel is a retired GP. His professional interests were in Balint Groups and GP education. He was course organiser of the Northwick Park GP Vocational Training Scheme and developed and ran the MSc in the Evaluation of Clinical Practice at the University of Westminster. Nowadays he paints.

Julie Sanders is a psychotherapist with an MA in transpersonal psychotherapy, and a private tutor for children. She has a BEd from Bristol University and taught in schools for 30 years. She writes poetry, rides a motorbike and is currently a practising artist studying Fine Art at Chelsea College.

Steve Seagull, palliative care nurse, has worked as a miner, counsellor and nurse and is currently employed within the arena of physical rehabilitation at a general hospital. Steve is interested in the ways in which creative expression can be used as a tool to develop hope, meaning and healing.

Lesley Schatzberger is a professional clarinet player whose daughter Jessica died in 1994, struck down by a brain tumour aged nine. Jessie's Fund, a UK charity registered in 1995, aims for as many children with special needs as possible to benefit from music therapy and other forms of creative music-making.

Paul Schatzberger is a photographer and doctor based in Sheffield. His photographic study of Michael Willson's terminal illness was presented at The Hague 2003 Congress of the European Association for Palliative Care. It formed the subject of his 2006 exhibition *Doctors and Dying* at the Viewfinder Photography Gallery, London (www.paul.schatzberger.dsl.pipex.com).

Penelope Shuttle is a poet, has lived in Cornwall since 1970, and is the widow of poet Peter Redgrove. Their daughter Zoe Redgrove is an environmentalist. Her eighth collection, *Redgrove's Wife* (Bloodaxe Books, 2006) was shortlisted for the Forward Prize for Best Single Collection and the TS Eliot Award.

Monica Suswin has been writing ever since she was a little girl; now in her late fifties, she has found her metier with therapeutic writing. Her background is in humanistic psychotherapy and journalism (BBC Radio Four), and she has an MA in Creative Writing from the University of Sussex (2002).

Kaichiro Tamba was born in Kobe, Japan, and has been a physician for 22 years, making poems for 20 years. He lived for 2 years in Birmingham, Alabama and for 3 months in Edmonton, Alberta. He began making personalized poems 19 years ago at a friend's wedding. His favourite is 'TAMBA MIO, SAORI, HIROYUKI, KAICHIRO (wife, kids and me)'.

Kieran Walsh, editor of *British Medical Journal Learning*, worked as a clinician before moving to e-learning in medical education. Previously Royal College of Physicians communications skills tutor in inner London and examination setter, he is interested in online learning, methods of assessment, interdisciplinary learning and teaching and learning communication skills.

Mike White, Director of Arts in Health at the Centre for Arts and Humanities in Health and Medicine, University of Durham, holds a NESTA Fellowship to develop research and evaluation in community-based arts in health and its interface with education and regeneration strategies: areas in which he has a particular interest.

Ann Williams is a lecturer in Primary Care and Community Nursing at the University of Cardiff. She is a nurse and health visitor with an MA in Healthcare Ethics. Since this piece was written Ann has become grandmother to Ryan, Luke's brother, and is thoroughly enjoying it!

Rogan Wolf, Director, Poems for the Waiting Room, ran mental health community centres for 20 years. More recently he founded the charity Hyphen-21 (www.hyphen-21.org) and has run the project Poems for the Waiting Room, whose latest collection – 'In Praise of Diversity' – was launched in October 2005 by UK Poet Laureate Andrew Motion.

River Wolton, poet and writing facilitator, trained as a social worker, practised psychotherapy for ten years and now facilitates creative and reflective writing in schools, community projects and further education. Her poetry has appeared in journals and anthologies; she won first prize in the Red Pepper Poetry Competition 2004.

References

Aldridge, D. (ed.) (2000) *Music Therapy in Dementia Care.* London: Jessica Kingsley Publishers.

Aristotle (1996) *Poetics,* transl. M. Heath. London: Penguin.

Astley, N. (ed.) (2002) *Staying Alive: Real Poems for Unreal Times.* Tarset, Northumberland: Bloodaxe.

Astley, N. (ed.) (2003) *Do Not Go Gentle: Poems for Funerals.* Tarset, Northumberland: Bloodaxe.

Astley, N. (ed.) (2004) *Being Alive: The Sequel to Staying Alive.* Tarset, Northumberland: Bloodaxe.

Austin, D. (2006) 'Songs of the self: vocal psychotherapy for adults traumatised as children.' In L. Carey (ed.) *Expressive and Creative Arts Methods for Trauma Survivors.* London: Jessica Kingsley Publishers.

Bakewell, J. (2005) *Belief.* London: Duckworth.

Barrineau, P. (1991) 'Memo to Cancer: Recent Attempts on My Life.' In *Memo to Cancer: Poems.* Charlotte, NC: Heritage Printers (no publisher).

Barthes, R. (1981) *Camera Lucida.* New York: Hill & Wang.

Batchelor, S. (2004) *Living With The Devil: A Meditation on Good and Evil.* New York: Riverhead.

Benson, J, and Falk, A. (eds) (1996) *The Long Pale Corridor: Contemporary Poems of Bereavement.* Tarset, Northumberland: Bloodaxe.

Bertman, S. (1991) *Facing Death: Images, Insights and Interventions.* New York: Taylor & Francis, Inc.

Bertman, S. (1999) (ed.) *Grief and the Healing Arts: Creativity as Therapy.* New York: Baywood Publishing Company.

Boal, A. (1992) *Games for Actors and Non-Actors.* London: Routledge.

Boal, A. (2000) *Theatre of the Oppressed.* London: Pluto Press.

Bolton, G. (1999) *The Therapeutic Potential of Creative Writing: Writing Myself.* London: Jessica Kingsley Publishers.

Bolton G. (2005) *Reflective Practice: Writing and Professional Development,* 2nd edn. London: Sage.

Bolton, G., Field, V. and Thompson, K. (2006) *Writing Works: A Resume Handbook for Therapeutic Writing Workshops and Activities.* London: Jessica Kingsley Publishers.

Brody, H. (2003) *Story of Sickness,* 2nd edition. Oxford University Press.

Brower, D.R. (ed.) (undated) *Of All Things Most Yielding.* London: Friends of the Earth (Library of Congress cat. 73-8379).

Brown, E. (2007) *Supporting the Child and the Family in Paediatric Palliative Care.* London: Jessica Kingsley Publishers.

Buber, M. (1973(1947)) *Between Man and Man,* trans. R.G. Smith. London: Kegan Paul.

Bush, K., Sladen, M. and Harrison, M. (2006) *In the Face of History: European Photographers in the 20th Century.* London: Blackdog.

Calman, K. (2000) *A Study of Story Telling, Humour and Learning in Medicine.* London: The Nuffield Trust.

Carey, J. (2005) *What Good Are the Arts?* London: Faber and Faber.

Carey, L. (ed.) (2006) *Expressive and Creative Arts Methods for Trauma Survivors.* London: Jessica Kingsley Publishers.

Carroll, L. (1954) *Alice's Adventures in Wonderland, and Through the Looking Glass.* First published 1865. London: JM Dent & Sons.

Cassell, E. (1982) 'The nature of suffering and the goals of medicine.' *New England Journal of Medicine 306,* 639–645.

Causley, C. (1988) 'Eden Rock.' in *A Field of Vision.* London: Papermac.

Charon, R. (2000a) 'Informed Consent: The Imperative and the Therapeutic Dividend of Showing Patients What We Write about Them.' Paper presented at Narrative Matters: Personal Stories and the Making of Health Policy Conference, Airlie, Virginia, March.

Charon, R. (2000b) 'Literature and medicine: origins and destinies.' *Academic Medicine 75,* 23–27.

Charon, R. (2001) 'Narrative medicine.' *Journal of American Medical Association 286*, 1897–1902.

Chodron, P. (2000) *When Things Fall Apart.* Boston, MA: Shambala Press.

Clandinin, D. and Connelly F. (1994) 'Personal Experience Methods' in N.K. Denzin and Y.S. Lincoln (eds) *Handbook of Qualitative Research.* London: Sage.

Cobb, M. (2001) *The Dying Soul: Spiritual Care at the End of Life.* Buckingham: Open University Press.

Cobb, M. (2005) *The Hospital Chaplain's Handbook: A Guide for Good Practice.* Norwich: Canterbury Press.

Collins, Billy (2001) *Sailing Alone Around the Room: New and Selected Poems.* New York: Random House.

Cook, S., Ledger, K. and Scott, N. (2003) *Dancing for Living: Women's Experience of 5 Rhythms Dance and the Effects on their Emotional Well-being.* Sheffield: UK Advocacy Network.

Cottingham, J. (2005) *The Spiritual Dimension.* Cambridge: Cambridge University Press.

D'Lima, K. (2004) *A Study of The Benefits and Best Methods for Integration of Creative Writing into Health Settings.* Swansea: University of Wales, Swansea.

Darling, J. (2003) *Sudden Collapses in Public Places.* Todmorden, Lancashire: Arc Publications.

Darling, J. and Fuller, C. (2005) *The Poetry Cure.* Tarset, Northumberland: Bloodaxe.

Davis, C. (2006) Working with psychological pain and suffering and the importance of taking care of ourselves. St Joseph's Newsletter. Spring, p.6.

Department of Health (1999) *National Service Framework for Mental Health.* London: HMSO.

Diamond, J. (1998) *C, Because Cowards Get Cancer Too.* London: Vermilion.

Duncan, J. (2003) 'The effect of colour and design in hydrotherapy: designing for care.' In D. Kirklin and R. Richardson (eds) *The Healing Environment Without and Within.* London: Royal College of Physicians.

Elfick, H. and Head, D. (2004) *Attending to the Fact – Staying with Dying.* London: Jessica Kingsley Publishers.

Eliot, G. (2003) *Middlemarch.* First published 1872–3. London: Penguin Books.

Eliot, T.S. (1974) *The Four Quartets.* In *Collected Poems 1909–1962.* London: Faber and Faber.

Epstein, M. (2001) *Going On Being.* New York: Broadway Books.

Evans, M. (2003) 'Roles for literature in medical education.' *Advances in Psychiatric Treatment 9*, 5, 380–386.

Everitt, A. and Hamilton, R. (2003) *Arts Health and Community: A Study of Five Arts in Community Health Projects.* Durham: CAHHM. Accessed 8 April 2005 at www.durham.ac.uk/cahhm.

Fox, J. (2003) 'Poetry and Caring: Healing the Within.' In D. Kirklin and R. Richardson (eds) (2003) *The Healing Environment Without and Within.* London: Royal College of Physicians.

Fox, J. (1997) *Poetic Medicine: The Healing Art of Poem-Making.* New York: Jeremy Tarcher/Putnam.

Fox, M. (2002) *Creativity: Where the Divine and the Human Meet.* New York: Jeremy Tarcher.

Frank, A. (1995) *The Wounded Storyteller: Body, Illness, and Ethics.* Chicago: University of Chicago Press.

Freud, S. (1913) *Totem and Taboo*, transl. A. Brill. New York: Courier Dover.

Giblin, M. (2002) 'Beyond principles: virtue ethics in hospice and palliative care.' *American Journal of Hospice and Palliative Care 19*, 235–239.

Gibran, K. (1974) *The Prophet.* London: Heinemann.

Giddens, A. (1990) *The Consequences of Modernity.* Stanford: Stanford University Press.

Glass, J. (2006) 'Working Towards Aesthetic Distance: Drama Therapy for Adult Victims of Abuse.' In: L. Carey (ed.) *Expressive and Creative Arts Methods for Trauma Survivors.* London: Jessica Kingsley Publishers.

Goldberg, N. (1986) *Writing Down The Bones.* Boston, MA: Shambhala.

Goldberg, N. (1991) *Wild Mind.* New York: Random House.

Gormley, A. (2006) 'Souls of Stone.' *Guardian Review* 16 September, p.12.

Graham-Pole, J. (1994) 'Venipuncture.' *Annals of Internal Medicine 120*, 691, reproduced by permission.

Graham-Pole, J. (2000) *Illness and the Art of Creative Self-expression.* Oakland CA: Harbinger Press.

Graham-Pole, J. (2001) 'Cartoons.' In *Physical.* Johnstown, OH: Pudding House Publications.

Graham-Pole, J. (2002) 'Cell Shed.' In *Quick: A Pediatrician's Illustrated Poetry.* New York: Writer's Club Press.

Graham-Pole, J. (2005). 'The "S" in SOAP: Exploring the connection.' *Journal of Poetry Therapy 18*, 165–170.

Greig, A. (2006) *This Life, This Life: New and Selected Poems 1970–2006.* Tarset, Northumberland: Bloodaxe.

Haldane, D. and Loppert, S. (1999) *The Arts in Health Care: Learning from Experience.* London: King's Fund.

Hamberger, R. (1977) *Warpaint Angel.* Leicester: Blackwater Press.

Hamberger, R. (2002) *The Smug Bridegroom.* Nottingham: Five Leaves Press.

Hamberger, R. (2007) *Torso.* Bradford: Redbeck Press.

Harris, J. (2003) *Signifying Pain: Constructing and Healing the Self Through Writing.* New York: State University of New York Press.

Heitsch, D.B. (2000) 'Aproaching death by writing: Montaigne's essays and the literature of consolation.' *Literature and Medicine 19*, 1, 96–106.

Helman, C. (2006) *Suburban Shaman: Tales from Medicine's Front Line.* London: Hammersmith.

Help the Hospices (2005) *Guidelines for Arts Therapies and the Arts in Palliative Care Settings.* London: Hospice Information.

Heyse-Moore, L. (1996) 'On spiritual pain in the dying.' *Mortality 1*, 297,196315.

Higgs, R. (2003) 'The Medical Paradigm: Changing Landscapes.' In D. Kirklin and R. Richardson (eds) *The Healing Environment Without and Within.* London: Royal College of Physicians.

Hirst, D. (2006) 'Death becomes him.' *London Time Out,* 22 November, pp. 46–47. Accessed 22 November 2006 at www.shands.org/AIM.

Hughes, T. (1995) *Paris Review.* Art of Poetry Interview 71 (Interviewer Drue Heinz) Spring, 54–94. Accessed 8 September 2004 at www.informatik.uni-leipzig.de/~beckmann/plath/thint.html.

Jacobs, M. (1998) 'Faith as the "space between".' In M. Cobb and V. Robshaw, *The Spiritual Challenge of Health Care.* Edinburgh: Churchill Livingstone.

Johns, C. (2004) *Being Mindful, Easing Suffering: Reflections on Palliative Care.* London: Jessica Kingsley Publishers.

Johns, C. (2006) *Engaging Reflections in Practice.* London: Blackwell.

Jung, C. (1954) *The Development of Personality.* London: Routledge

Kaplan, B. and Duchon, D. (1988) 'Combining qualitative and quantitative methods in information systems research: A case study.' *Management Information Systems Quarterly 12*, 4, 571–586.

Katz, G.A. (1983) 'The noninterpretation of metaphors in psychiatric hospital groups.' *International Journal of Group Psychotherapy 33*, 53–67.

Kavanagh, A. (1982) *Elements of Rite.* New York: Pueblo.

Kearney, M. (1996) *Mortally Wounded: Stories of Soul Pain, Death and Healing.* Dublin: Marino Books.

Kearney, M. (2000) *A Place of Healing: Working with Suffering in Living and Dying.* Oxford: Oxford University Press.

Kelley, A. (2005) *The Burying Beetle.* Edinburgh: Luath Press.

Kenyon, G. (2003) '"Take art": opening the doors of the National Gallery.' In D. Kirklin and R. Richardson (eds) *The Healing Environment Without and Within.* London: Royal College of Physicians.

Kermode, M. (2006) 'Pain should never be avoided.' *Observer Review,* 5 November, p.11.

Killick, J. and Allan, K. (2000) 'Undiminished possibility: The arts in dementia care.' *Journal of Dementia Care 7*, 1, 22–24.

Kinnell, G. (1994) *Imperfect Thirst: Poems.* Boston: Houghton Mifflin Company.

Kirklin, D. and Richardson, R. (eds) (2003) *The Healing Environment Without and Within.* London: Royal College of Physicians.

Kübler-Ross, E. (1970) *On Death and Dying.* London: Tavistock Publications.

Kübler-Ross, E. (1986) *Some Babies Die: An Exploration of Stillbirth and Neonatal Death,* video. Australia: Langdon Films; University of California Extension Media (distributor), Berkeley CA.

Kuebelbeck A. (2003) *Waiting with Gabriel: A Story of Cherishing a Baby's Brief Life.* Chicago: Loyola Press.

Lander, D. A, Napier, S. D., Fry, B. F., Brander, H. and Acton, J. (2006) 'Memoirs of loss as popular education: Five palliative caregivers re-member the healing art of hope and love.' *Convergence 38*, 121–139.

Lao Tsu (1973) *Tao Te Ching,* trans. G.F. Feng and J. English. London: Wildwood House.

Legood, G. and Markham, I. (2003) *The Funeral Handbook.* London: SPCK.

Lewin, M. (2005) *Buddhist Reflections on Death, Dying and Bereavement.* Isle of Wight: Buddhist Hospice Trust.

Leibovitz, A. (2006) 'My time with Susan.' (Interview: Emma Brockes.) *Guardian Weekend,* 7 October, pp. 18–33.

Loder, T. (2000) *My Heart in My Mouth: Prayers for Our Lives.* Philadelphia: Innisfree Press Inc.

Lynch, T. (1998) *The Undertaking: Life Studies from the Dismal Trade.* London: Vintage.

Lyotard, J. P. (1992) *The Postmodern Explained to Children.* London: Turnaround.

Macduff, C. (2002) 'Developing the use of poetry within healthcare culture.' *British Journal of Nursing 11*, 5, 335–341.

Mackay Brown, G. (1989) 'Interrogation.' In *The Wreck of the Archangel.* London: John Murray.

Maclagan, D. (1989) 'The aesthetic dimension of art therapy: luxury or necessity?' *Inscape,* Spring, 10–13.

MacLeod, A. (2002) *The Dark Ship.* Edinburgh: Luath Press.

MacLeod, A. (2004) *The Blue Moon Book.* Edinburgh: Luath Press.

MacMillan, J. (2003) 'God, Theology and Music.' In S. Darlington and A. Kreider (eds) *Composing Music for Worship.* Norwich: Canterbury Press.

Mak, Y. (2001) 'Meaning of desire for euthanasia in Chinese advanced cancer patients: a hermeneutic study.' MSc dissertation, University of Wales College of Medicine.

Mak, Y.Y.W. (2006a) *Dr. Hannah. A Mother's Diary – Chronicle of Life and Faith through Cancer.* Self-Published, available from Swindon Book Co. Ltd., Hong Kong.

Mak, Y. (2006b) 'A Personal Journey: The Physician, the Researcher, the Relative, and the Patient.' In C. Chan and A. Chow (eds) *Death, Dying and Bereavement: a Hong Kong Chinese Experience.* Hong Kong: HK University Press.

Manley Hopkins, G. (1956) 'Spring and Fall.' In *Poems and Prose of Gerard Manley Hopkins, The Penguin Poets,* selected by W.H. Gardner. London: Penguin.

Marshall, H., Hyde, S. and Barnett, C. (2003) City within a City (A Sense of Space). London: Rosetta Life. Accessed on 10 September 2007 at www.rosettalife.org/content/gallery/projects/2.html

Martin, R. (1995) 'Memento mori manifest.' In J. Spence and J. Soloman (eds) *What Can a Woman Do with a Camera.* London: Scarlet Press.

Martin, R. (1999) 'Too close to home.' *Paradoxa: International Feminist Art Journal 3,* 73–80.

Martin, R. (2006) 'Curating the Museum of Sources: Stilled Lives, Memory, Mortality and Domestic Space.' In K. Newton and C. Rold (eds) *Stilled: Contemporary Still Life Photography by Women.* Penarth, Wales: Ffotogallery Publications.

Matarasso, F. (1997) *Use or Ornament: The Social Impact of Participation in the Arts.* Stroud: Comedia.

Mazza, N. (2003) *Poetry Therapy: Theory and Practice.* Brunner-Routledge: London.

McNiff, S. (1994) *Arts as Medicine: Creating a Therapy of the Imagination.* London: Piatkus.

McWilliams, A.E. (2004) 'Stress in palliative care.' *Progress in Palliative Care 12,* 6, 293–301.

Merwin, W.S. (1993) *The Second Four Books of Poems.* Port Townsend, WA: Cooper Canyon Press.

Metcalf, T. (2001) 'Stages of Dying.' In *Corvus.* Canberra: Ginninderra Press.

Metcalf, T. (2002) *Cut to the Word.* Canberra: Ginninderra Press.

Metcalf, T. (2006) (ed.) *Verbal Medicine: 21 Contemporary Clinician-Poets of Australia and New Zealand.* Canberra: Ginninderra Press.

Meynell, A. (2007) Maternity. Accessed on 2 January 2007 at www.roguery.com/gurrier/verse/maternity.html.

Mindell, Arnold (1989) *COMA: The Dreambody Near Death.* Boston, MA: Shambhala.

Morrison, B. (2006) 'Different Views.' *Guardian Review,* 21 October, pp.12–13.

Mount, B. (1995) 'Whole person care: beyond psychosocial and physical needs.' *American Journal of Hospice and Palliative Care,* Jan/Feb, 28–37.

Newman, J.H. (1986) *The Dream of Gerontius.* London: Mowbray.

NHS Estates (2002) *The Art of Good Health: Using Visual Arts in Healthcare.* London: NHS Estates.

O'Connor, S., Schatzberger, P. and Payne S. (2003) 'A death photographed: One patient's story.' *British Medical Journal 327,* 233.

Okri, B. (1996) *Birds of Heaven.* London: Phoenix House.

Okri, B. (1997) *A Way of Being Free.* London: Phoenix House.

Olds, S. (1992) *The Father.* London: Jonathan Cape.

Othen N. (2006) 'Doctors and Dying' exhibition narrative. Accessed on 1 November 2006 at www.viewfinder.org.uk/exhibitions/paul_schatzberger.htm.

Padfield, D. (2003) *Perceptions of Pain.* Stockport: Dewi Lewis Publishing.

Pavlicevic, M. (ed.) (2005) *Music Therapy in Children's Hospices: Jessie's Fund in Action.* London: Jessica Kingsley Publishers.

Petrone, M. A. (1999) *Touching the Rainbow: Pictures and Words by People Affected by Cancer.* Eastbourne: East Sussex Health Promotion Service.

Petrone, M. A. (2003) *The Emotional Cancer Journey.* London: MAP Foundation.

Philipp, R. (2002) *Arts, Health and Well-being.* London: The Nuffield Trust.

Price, L. (2004) 'Music: Windows onto God'. Accessed on 27 August 2007 at www.sherborneabbey.com/sermons/MusicwindowsuntoGod.shtml .

Price, Reynolds (1994) *A Whole New Life: An Illness and a Healing.* New York: Atheneum.

Pugh, S. (1997) 'What If This Road.' In *Id's Hospit.* Wales: Seren.

Pullman, P. (2000) *The Amber Spyglass.* London: Scholastic.

Remen, R. (1996) *Kitchen Table Wisdom.* New York: Riverhead Books.

Rinpoche, S. (1992) *The Tibetan Book of Living and Dying.* San Francisco: Harper Collins.

Robertson, R. (1996) *Music and the Mind.* London: Channel 4 Television.

Robinson, A. (2004) 'A personal exploration of the power of poetry in palliative care, loss and bereavement.' *International Journal of Palliative Nursing 10,* 1, 32–38.

Rogers, C.R. (1961) *On Becoming a Person.* Boston: Houghton Mifflin.

Rosen, M. and Blake, Q. (2004) *Michael Rosen's Sad Book.* London: Walker Books.

Sacks, O. (1985) *The Man who Mistook his Wife for a Hat.* London: Picador.

Salinsky, J. (2002) (ed.) *Medicine and Literature: The Doctors' Companion to the Classics Vol 2*. Abingdon: Radcliffe Press.

Sampson, F. (2004) *Creative Writing in Health and Social Care*. London: Jessica Kingsley Publishers.

Sandelowski, M. (1991) 'Telling stories: narrative approaches to qualitative research' *IMAGE Journal of Nursing Scholarship 23*, 3, Fall, 161–166.

Sands, J. (2002) 'Performing Miracles? How Performance Arts can Contribute to Healing and to Healthcare Settings.' Talk to The London Forum for Arts in Health, 3 December, St Thomas' Hospital, London.

Sartre, J.P. (1950) *What is Literature?* London: Methuen.

Saunders, C. (1964) 'Care of patients suffering from terminal illness at St Joseph's Hospice Hackney.' *Nursing Mirror*, 14 February, vii–x.

Saunders, C. (1978) 'The Philosophy of Terminal Care.' In: C. Saunders (ed.) *The Management of Terminal Malignant Disease*, 2nd edition. London: Edward Arnold.

Saunders, Dame C., Wald, F., Kübler-Ross. E. and Mount, B. (2004) *Pioneers of Hospice: Changing the Face of Dying*. (DVD) Vermont: Madison-Deane Initiative see www.fanlight.com/catalog/films/415_poh.php.

Schaper, E. (1968) 'Aristotle's catharsis and aesthetic pleasure.' *The Philosophical Quarterly 18*, 71, 131–143.

Schatzberger, L. (2001) 'Music-making in Children's Hospices.' *Hospice Bulletin 9*, 1, 2–3.

Schneider, M. (2003) *Writing my Way Thorough Cancer*. London: Jessica Kingsley Publishers.

Schneider, M. and Killick, J. (1997) *Writing for Self-discovery*. Dorset: Element Books.

Seftel, L. (2006) *Grief Unseen: Healing Pregnancy Loss through the Arts*. London: Jessica Kingsley Publishers.

Seligman, M.E.P. (2002) *Authentic Happiness: Using the New Positive Psychology to Realize your Potential for Lasting Fulfillment*. New York: Free Press.

Shapiro, A. (1997) *Vigil*. Chicago: University of Chicago Press.

Shuttle, P. (2006) Redgrove's wife. Tarset, Northumberland: Bloodaxe.

Smith, R. (2002) 'Spend (slightly) less on health and more on the arts.' *British Medical Journal 325*, 1432–1433.

Snow, S., Damico, M. and Tanguay, D. (2003) 'Therapeutic theatre and well-being.' *Arts in Psychotherapy 30*, 2, 73–82.

Sontag, S. (1978) *Illness as Metaphor*. London: Penguin.

Sontag, S. (1979) *On Photography*. London: Penguin.

Sontag, S. (2003) *Regarding the Pain of Others*. London: Penguin.

Staricoff, R.L. (2004) *Arts in Health: A Review of the Medical Literature*. London: The Arts Council of England.

Staricoff, R. and Loppert, S. (2003), 'Integrating the Arts into Health Care: Can We Affect Clinical Outcomes?' In Kirklin, D. and Richardson, R. (eds), *The Healing Environment Without and Within*. London: Royal College of Physicians.

Steiner, G. (2001) *Grammars of Creation*. London: Faber and Faber.

Stevens, W. (2001) 'Sunday Morning.' In *Harmonium*. London: Faber and Faber.

Storey, P. and Knight, C.F. (1997) *Unipac Two: Alleviating Psychological and Spiritual Pain in the Terminally Ill*. Gainesville, Florida: American Academy of Hospice and Palliative Medicine.

Suswin, M. (2002) 'Apples and Pears.' Autobiographical memoir for MA in Creative Writing, Sussex University, Unpublished.

Tasker, M. (2005) 'Something inside so strong… .' *Hospice Information Bulletin 4*, 3, 1–2.

Transtromer, T. (2002) 'From March 1979.' In N. Astley (ed.) *Staying Alive: Unreal Poems for Unreal Times*. Tarset, Northumberland: Bloodaxe.

Tufnell, M. and Crickmay, C. (2004) *A Widening Field: Journeys in Body and Imagination*. Alton, Hampshire: Dance Books Ltd.

Watson, J. (1999) *Postmodern Nursing and Beyond*. New York: Churchill Livingstone.

Wertheim, M. (1999) *The Pearly Gates to Cyberspace: A History of Space from Dante to the Internet*. London: Virago.

White, M (2002) *Determined to Dialogue: A Survey of Arts in Health in the North and Yorkshire*. Durham: Centre for Arts and Humanities in Healthcare and Medicine.

White, M. (2004) 'Arts in Mental Health for Social Inclusion: Towards a Framework for Programme Evaluation.' In J. Cowling (ed.) *For Art's Sake – Society and the Arts in the 21st Century*. London: Institute of Public Policy Research.

Williams, W. C. (1955) 'Asphodel, that Greeny Flower, Book III.' In *The Collected Poems of William Carlos Williams, Volume II, 1939–1962*. New York: New Directions.

Winnicott, D. W. (1962) 'Ego Integration in Child Development.' In *The Maturation Processes and the Facilitating Environment*. New York: International Universities Press.

Wolton, R. (2002) *Our Lives Our Group: The Thursday Club Book*. Sheffield: Sheffield Women's Cultural Club.

Zabel, S. (2003) Poem published in *Lombardi Magazine*. Washington, DC: Lombardi Cancer Center, Spring 2003 (quoted with permission).

Subject Index

Author Index